Mastering Xcode

SECOND EDITION

DEVELOP AND DESIGN

Maurice Kelly and
Joshua Nozzi

PEACHPIT PRESS
WWW.PEACHPIT.COM

Mastering Xcode: Develop and Design, Second Edition
Maurice Kelly and Joshua Nozzi

Peachpit Press
www.peachpit.com

To report errors, please send a note to errata@peachpit.com
Peachpit Press is a division of Pearson Education.

Editor: Robyn G. Thomas
Production editor: David Van Ness
Copyeditor: Scout Festa
Technical editor: Mark Goody
Compositor: David Van Ness
Indexer: Valerie Haynes Perry
Cover design: Aren Straiger
Interior design: Mimi Heft

ISBN-13: 978-0-321-86162-7
ISBN-10:   0-321-86162-0

9 8 7 6 5 4 3 2 1

Printed and bound in the United States of America

To my wife, Fiona, and our beautiful daughters, Aoibhínn and Caoimhe—
I thank you for your support and patience while I've been distracted by this book.

To my parents—thank you for buying our first family computer and
setting me on the course that led me to do what I love.

— Maurice Kelly

Thanks to my peers, my friends, my family, and my partner
for their enthusiastic support. Special thanks to my coauthor:
May our Caoimhes live long, happy lives.

— Joshua Nozzi

MAURICE KELLY

ABOUT THE AUTHOR

Maurice Kelly has been a software engineer since leaving university in 2001. After spending a decade working on carrier-grade server software in C, C++, and Java, he decided to take a career departure and switched to developing Mac and iOS software. As well as being an eager consumer of all things tech, he has a passion for consuming and creating music. He lives with his wife and children just outside Dromara, a small village in the small country of Northern Ireland.

ACKNOWLEDGMENTS

I would like to thank Josh for giving me the opportunity to work on this project in ever-increasing capacities. The first edition of this book gave me inspiration to change my career, and it has been an honor to work with him in producing the second edition. I would also like to thank my employers, Andrew Gough and Andrew Cuthbert at GCD Technologies (www.gcdtech.com), for allowing me to take on this side-project and for introducing me to Mark Goody—a newfound friend, an amazing developer, and an excellent technical editor. I would like to extend many thanks to Robyn Thomas for her encouragement and for guiding this ship through patches of both stormy water and dead calm!

While Xcode is the day-to-day tool of my trade, there were a number of tools without which this book could not have been completed:

- Sublime Text 2 (www.sublimetext.com/2). Combined with Brett Terpstra's Markdown-Editing package, this makes a much better writing environment than Xcode's editor!
- Marked (http://markedapp.com). For previewing Markdown output, there is no better application than Marked.
- ScreenFloat (www.screenfloatapp.com). Capturing and managing the quantity of screenshots required for this book needed an app like ScreenFloat.

JOSHUA NOZZI

ABOUT THE AUTHOR

Joshua Nozzi is a self-taught technologist who has been developing software for the Mac platform since Mac OS X 10.0 debuted. He's been using Xcode since version 1 for publishing, increasing productivity, and building scientific research applications. He's haunted several developer communities over the years, offering help and snark in equal measures. He loves to teach technology to others. Josh lives with his partner in Southern Virginia, where he toils in obscurity, usually in sweatpants and little else.

ACKNOWLEDGMENTS

I wish to thank the following people, whose work I used while writing this book.

Cyril Godefroy: Cyril's masterfully broken code examples demonstrated some nice highlights of the Clang static analyzer. You can find them at http://xcodebook.com/cgodefroy.

Colin Wheeler: Colin's Xcode shortcut cheat sheet has saved me loads of tedium on many projects. You can find the original, downloadable version that Colin maintains at http://xcodebook.com/cwheeler.

CONTENTS

PART I   Getting Started

PART II Building Applications

PART III Further Exploration

INTRODUCTION

This book is an intermediate-level introduction to Xcode 4, Apple's integrated development environment. It assumes you have some development experience and are familiar with Objective-C and the Cocoa and Cocoa Touch APIs. It won't teach you how to write code or much at all about the frameworks needed to develop OS X and iOS applications. There are other books for that. This one is strictly focused on how to use Xcode itself, whatever your development endeavors.

Of course, since Xcode is most often used with the Cocoa and Cocoa Touch APIs and Objective-C, there are basic introductions to concepts and a few code samples sprinkled here and there to illustrate various points. In these cases, you will be pointed to the documentation that Apple provides (to save you some trouble looking it up), but remember that the focus of this book is really on getting the most out of the tools and not necessarily on what you'll be building with them.

A MOVING TARGET

When the first edition of this book was released, Xcode 4.0 had just become Xcode 4.1. It was hard for anyone to predict how rapidly Apple would iterate, but in a short space of time there have been five major versions of Xcode 4 released. Each version brings enhancements, fixes, and new tools—and headaches to the authors of this book.

So just as in the introduction to the first edition, we will once again make our excuses up front and say that this book was current when we wrote it, and may or may not be by the time you read it. We hope that, however Apple chooses to change Xcode, our guidance is still relevant for the foreseeable future and that this book will be a trusty companion for up-and-coming developers for some time to come.

WHAT YOU WILL LEARN

This book is divided into three major parts and includes appendixes.

PART I: GETTING STARTED

In very short order, you'll install Xcode and take a tour around its interface's major points of interest, and you'll learn where to look for answers when you need help.

PART II: BUILDING APPLICATIONS

Next, you'll dive into the process of building OS X and iOS applications. Through the development of a pair of basic apps, you will learn how to create projects and workspaces; manage resources and code; build and edit user interfaces; and debug and deploy your work.

PART III: FURTHER EXPLORATION

Then you'll dive a little deeper and find out how to bring older Xcode projects into the modern era, tackle advanced editing and refactoring, and unravel the complexity of Xcode's build system. You'll work with libraries and frameworks, and you'll improve the quality of your work using a combination of profiling, analysis, advanced debugging, and unit testing. You will investigate the extension possibilities offered by Xcode scripting support and command-line interfaces, and you'll wrap up with an overview of Xcode's integrated source code management support.

APPENDIXES

Appendix A helps you manage your iOS devices. Appendix B shows you how to manage Xcode documentation updates. Appendix C provides you with Apple and third-party resources for additional information.

WELCOME TO XCODE

Whether you are a complete newcomer or a seasoned programmer, Xcode can be an intimidating environment for a developer getting involved in Apple development for the first time. Under its shiny, easy-to-use interface, a lot of power lurks. Xcode 4 lets you write and manage your code, design and build user interfaces, analyze and debug your apps, and more.

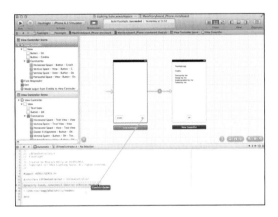

INTERFACE BUILDER

Build and edit rich user interfaces with Interface Builder. Drag and drop outlets and actions directly into your code using the Assistant editor.

CLANG STATIC ANALYZER

Find subtle errors in your programs with the Clang static analyzer. Follow the blue arrows through your code as the problem is broken down step by step.

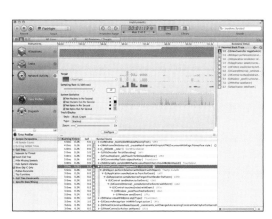

INSTRUMENTS

Trace and profile your code with Instruments. Follow your application's activity through time to find and analyze performance problems and more.

SOURCE CODE MANAGEMENT

Manage your source code with the integrated source code management features. Branch, merge, pull, push, and resolve conflicts—all from within Xcode.

PART I

Getting Started

CHAPTER 1

Installing Xcode

Xcode is Apple's suite of developer tools. Version 4 is a near-complete departure from earlier versions, and worlds apart from its ancestor, ProjectBuilder. It is aimed squarely at developing, testing, and packaging OS X and iOS applications, utilities, and plug-ins written with the Cocoa frameworks in Objective-C. It's worth noting, however, that Xcode is well suited for C and C++ development on the Mac as well.

Note the mentions of OS X and iOS: This is an Apple development package. To follow most of the examples in this book (which are based on the latest features in Xcode 4.6), you'll need an Intel Macintosh computer running OS X version 10.8 or above.

In this chapter, you'll learn how to download Xcode and install it on your Mac.

DOWNLOADING

You can download the latest stable release of Xcode 4 from the Mac App Store. You do not need to join Apple's developer program to obtain and use Xcode 4; simply launch the App Store application from your Applications folder and search the store for Xcode. Click the Install button in the store and provide your (required) Apple ID to authorize the installation.

Now grab some coffee while the very large download streams its way to your Mac. This will take a while.

Just like any application purchased through the App Store, Xcode will appear in the OS X Mission Control screen and display a progress bar on its icon. When it's finished downloading, you'll have a fully self-contained application that houses several other, related applications, some of which you'll be using later in this book. The application can be found in your Applications folder as well as in Mission Control.

The first time you run Xcode, you may be asked to install related items. The first time you build a project, you're likely to be asked to "enable Developer Mode" on your Mac, which requires an administrator-level account password.

NOTE: The download contains Xcode, some tools, and relevant SDKs. It does not contain the documentation for those SDKs, however. When you launch Xcode, it will check for the latest version of this documentation and download it in the background. These files are large as well. The processor, disk, and network activity this causes can be alarming, given that Xcode seems to be peacefully awaiting orders. You can turn off this automatic updating in the Documentation panel of Xcode's preferences, but it's best to leave it on, because Apple tends to be proactive in documentation maintenance.

GETTING WITH THE PROGRAM

In the previous section, I mentioned you don't need to join Apple's developer program in order to download and use Xcode. This gives anyone—those new to the platform or to software development in general—a chance to kick the tires and write some working code without commitment.

It's when you want to test iOS apps on an actual device (as opposed to the included iOS Simulator) or deploy your applications through the Mac or iOS App Stores that you'll need to "get with the program." A paid membership to the Mac or iOS programs—or both—will get you access to prerelease content and the ability to deploy and sell your applications through Apple's App Store ecosystem. If you want to play in their sandbox, you'll need to pay your dues.

An important aspect to keep in mind has to do with a choice you'll be asked to make when you join: Will you be distributing your apps as an individual or as a business (a protective LLC, for example)? If the latter, you'll need proper business documentation before you can complete the process.

None of this is necessary to follow most of the concepts and examples in this book.

EVEN MORE STUFF

If you think you got it all with that massive download, think again. Users of earlier versions of Xcode may notice that some of their favorite tools are conspicuously absent. They can now be found as downloads at http://developer.apple.com/downloads. You must be logged in to view the list of available goodies, which include the command-line tools (installable from within Xcode—more on that later in this book), Auxiliary Tools for Xcode, Graphics Tools (including Quartz Composer), and more. If your favorite tool is missing, you can likely find it there.

WRAPPING UP

That's all there is to it. You're ready to rock. Welcome to Xcode! In the next chapter, you'll take a whirlwind tour of Xcode's UI by creating a throwaway example project.

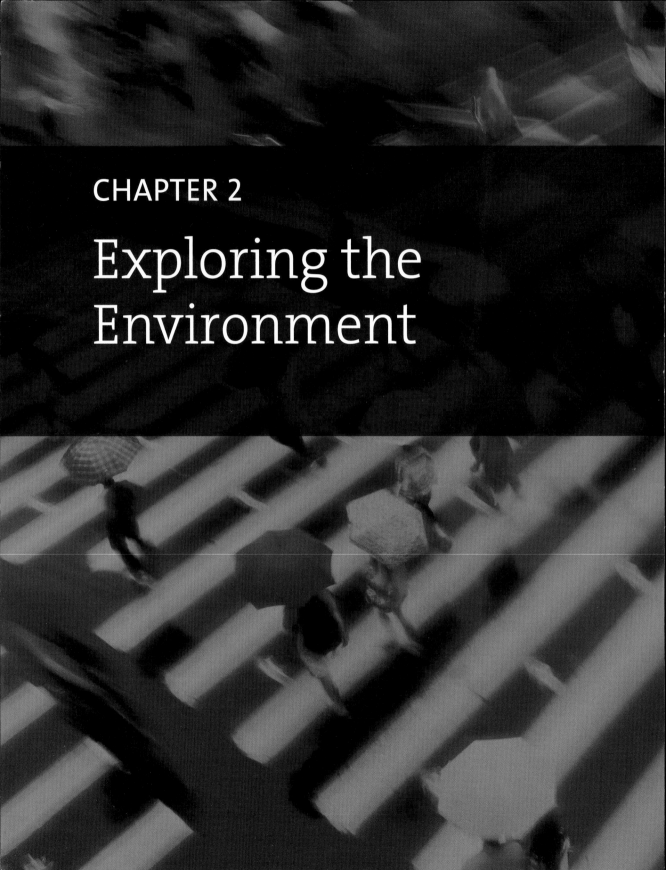

CHAPTER 2
Exploring the Environment

In this chapter, you'll create a throwaway application called Tour.app. You'll explore the anatomy of this project and familiarize yourself with Xcode's user interface. Then you'll throw the project away. If you're not accustomed to throwing stuff away, get over it—making throwaway projects for testing things is a common and useful practice. Tour.app will never see the light of day in the App Store, but its short life will be meaningful.

YOU GET ONE WINDOW

Earlier versions of Xcode allowed users to select a multiple-window interface, but the default was a single window that contained most views related to the open project. Single-window mode wasn't quite single-window mode, however; a number of auxiliary windows could appear. In Xcode 4, Apple has taken the all-in-one-window design approach much further.

You get one window, and Xcode avoids opening more unless you direct it to (double-clicking a file will cause it to open in a separate window). You'll probably find it awkward, however, to work with multiple windows rather than one window with various Assistant panels or tabs.

Let's create our sacrificial lamb, called Tour.app, and dig in.

CREATING A PROJECT

FIGURE 2.1 The Welcome to Xcode window

The Tour project will serve as meat on the bones of the Xcode UI, giving you a chance to explore. To create a new project, follow these steps:

1. Launch Xcode if it's not already running. You'll see the Welcome to Xcode window (**Figure 2.1**).

2. Click the button labeled Create a New Xcode Project. A fresh project window, presenting the template chooser, appears (**Figure 2.2**).

3. Choose the OS X > Application category, select Cocoa Application, and click Next.

4. In the next panel (**Figure 2.3**), enter **Tour** in the Product Name field.

5. Enter **WhistleStop** as the organization name—you can change this but it helps to set it from the beginning as it is inserted into the comments at the head of every source file Xcode creates for you.

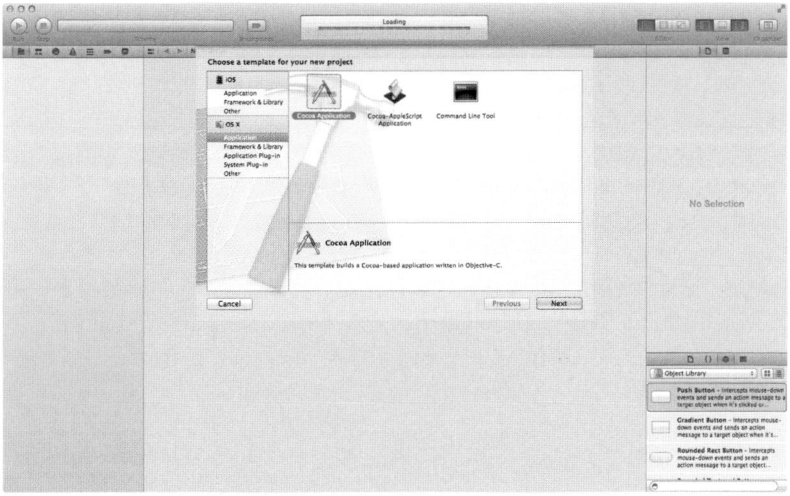

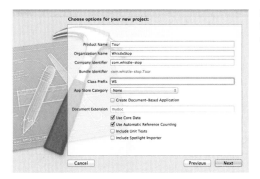

FIGURE 2.2 Choose a template for your new project.

FIGURE 2.3 Setting the initial project options

6. The Company Identifier field takes a reverse-canonical DNS string—for our example we would use "com.whistle-stop".

7. For completeness, enter **WS** in the Class Prefix field so all created classes will get this prefix (this keeps your objects distinct from Cocoa or third-party objects; for example, your buttons will be WSButton rather than NSButton).

8. Select the Use Core Data and Use Automatic Reference Counting check boxes (more on these topics later); leave the rest unselected.

9. Click Next. This screen asks whether you want to create a Git repository. We'll explore Git later, so deselect this option for now.

10. On the same screen, choose a location to save the project to. I suggest the desktop, the default location for tons of stuff.

11. Click Create. The new Tour project appears in its single-window glory.

> **NOTE:** You can build and run Tour.app as soon as it's created. Press Command+R to trigger the build and run the application. An empty, useless window will appear, complete with a generic application icon in the dock and a main menu bar that performs similarly useless functions.

THE WORKSPACE WINDOW

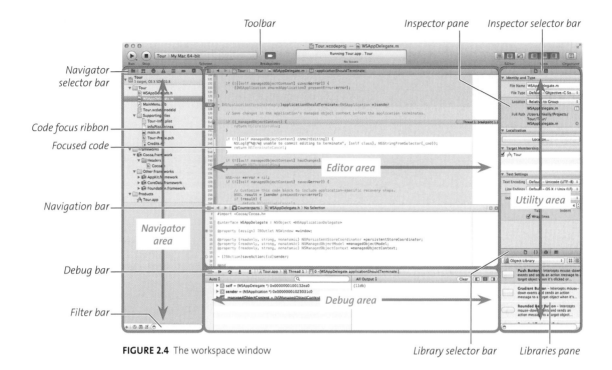

FIGURE 2.4 The workspace window

An Xcode project consists of source files (such as Objective-C files, Interface Builder nibs, and Core Data managed object models), resources (such as images and rich text files), and the Xcode project file (in which the various settings and build rules are maintained). It's helpful to think of an Xcode project as a collection of sources and resources, with a project file to bind them together. For such a basic app, Tour has plenty of files (**Figure 2.4**).

Xcode 4 allows you to combine multiple related projects into a single *workspace* (see Chapter 4). The main window for a given project or workspace is called the *workspace window*.

The workspace window is divided into multiple areas, which you'll examine in detail in this chapter. Almost everything related to your workspace is contained within these areas, whose responsibilities include organization, navigation, editing, inspection, and debugging.

THE NAVIGATOR AREA

The Navigator area consists of a complex set of panes. Found along the left edge of the workspace window, it is the primary interface for organizing and exploring the files, symbols, build issues, run logs, breakpoints, threads and stacks, and search results for the project.

The navigator selector bar along the top edge of the Navigator area allows you to switch between the various navigation panes. You can toggle the Navigator area on and off using the View buttons in the upper-right corner of the workspace window.

PROJECT NAVIGATOR

FIGURE 2.5 The Project navigator

You can use the Project navigator (**Figure 2.5**) to find your way around the source and resource files of your project (or projects, in the case of a multi-project workspace). Clicking any of the resources (except groups, which are merely logical containers within the project) causes Xcode to navigate to that resource and open it in an appropriate editor in the Editor area (immediately to the right of the Navigator area). Double-clicking an item opens the item in another window; Option-Shift-clicking an item causes Xcode to ask where you'd like to see the item. We'll explore this later, but it's a handy thing to know right now.

The Project navigator allows you to organize your project using groups (represented by yellow folders). You can create nested groups and move resources around just as you would with a file system. Groups can also represent real subfolders in your project folder. To create a group, choose File > New > New Group.

The Project navigator works much the same way as the OS X Finder in List view mode. You can add to, delete from, and reorganize resources in your project. In Chapter 5, you'll explore adding files and resources to, and removing them from, a project. In Chapter 6, you'll explore Xcode's source code management capabilities.

The filter bar along the bottom of the pane (at the very bottom of the window) lets you further filter the project list. Starting from the left, the + button lets you add new files and resources to your project (more on this later). The clock button will show only recently modified files. The drawer button shows only files with source control status updates (see Chapter 6). The pen and paper button (beside the search field) shows only files with unsaved changes. The search field itself filters the list, using the supplied term.

SYMBOL NAVIGATOR

FIGURE 2.6 The Symbol navigator

The Symbol navigator (**Figure 2.6**) gives you a somewhat different look at your project. Depending upon the filters you select in the filter bar (the button bar at the bottom of the list), you can jump to symbols defined within your project or within the Cocoa frameworks. A *symbol* is a class you created or one of its members (such as a property or method).

For example, rather than selecting a file from the Project navigator and then looking for your method or instance variable in the editor, you can type the symbol name in the search bar at the bottom of the Symbol navigator and then click the symbol in the list to jump directly to that symbol in your source.

The filter bar at the bottom offers several list-filtering options. The first filter button (starting from the left) lets you choose whether to show only class symbols or symbols of any type (such as protocols, structs, enums, and so on). The second button, when active, filters the list to show only those symbols that are defined in your project, rather than all symbols from your project, the Cocoa frameworks, and any other linked frameworks and libraries. The third button specifies whether members of a given symbol are shown (for example, the methods of a class). The search field further filters the list by a given search term.

SEARCH NAVIGATOR

The Search navigator (**Figure 2.7**) allows you to search your entire project in any way you can imagine. The search field at the top of the pane searches the project, while the one at the bottom further filters the search results themselves. The results are arranged first by filename and then by matches within the file. Searching and replacing is covered in more detail in Chapter 12.

ISSUE NAVIGATOR

Upon building your project, the Issue navigator (**Figure 2.8**) lists any issues it finds in your workspace (including coding errors and incorrect settings). In Xcode, an *issue* can be an error or a warning. Like the Search navigator, the Issue navigator can organize the issues by the file in which the issues appear. Additionally, Xcode can show you issues organized by type. Clicking to select an issue will cause Xcode to navigate to the issue in the Editor area.

Figure 2.8 shows Xcode reporting that the WSAppDelegate.m file has, like most people, some issues (added for demonstration purposes—your fresh Tour project will not have these). You can click the disclosure triangle next to each issue to get a more detailed explanation of Xcode's grievance.

At the top of the Issue navigator are buttons that let you choose to show issues by the file in which they exist or by their type. The controls at the bottom of the navigator let you filter the list. The first button (starting from the left) lets you choose to show issues only from the latest build (only "new" issues). The second button lets you choose to show only errors (as opposed to warnings or static analyzer results). The search field lets you further filter the list by a given search term.

NOTE: You can also jump from issue to issue using the arrows just above the upper-right corner of the Editor area.

DEBUG NAVIGATOR

FIGURE 2.9 The Debug navigator

While execution is paused in an active debugging session (because of encountering a breakpoint or a crashed thread), the Debug navigator (**Figure 2.9**) allows you to navigate the threads and stacks of your application. You can organize the information by thread or by queue using the icon to the right of the application name at the top of the list.

The controls along the bottom of the navigator adjust how much information the navigator displays. When activated, the button (which is at the far left) control area causes the navigator to show only crashed threads or threads for which there are debugging symbols available (typically your own code). The rest of the control area contains a slider that controls the amount of stack information that is displayed. Sliding all the way to the right shows the full stack, and sliding to the left shows only the top frame; the middle slider position (the default) shows only the stack information that Xcode feels is "useful" to you. Clicking the icons to either side of the slider moves the slider all the way to that side.

The icons to the left of each stack frame indicate to whose code the frame belongs. For example, frames with a blue-and-white icon depicting a person's head belong to your code, whereas frames with a purple-and-white icon depicting a mug belong to the Cocoa frameworks.

BREAKPOINT NAVIGATOR

FIGURE 2.10 The Breakpoint navigator

All the breakpoints associated with your project are collected in the Breakpoint navigator (**Figure 2.10**). When you set breakpoints in the Source editor (see Chapter 9), they appear in the Breakpoint navigator list, grouped by file.

Clicking a breakpoint's name navigates to its location in the editor. Clicking the blue breakpoint marker toggles the breakpoint on and off. Right-clicking a breakpoint and selecting Edit Breakpoint from the context menu pops up a detailed view that lets you set additional breakpoint properties (also covered in Chapter 15).

The controls along the bottom of the navigator allow you to add and remove breakpoints, as well as further filter the list. The Add (+) button pops up a menu when clicked, offering to add one of two non-workspace-specific breakpoints (to break on exceptions or at a named symbol you supply manually). The Remove (–) button removes any selected breakpoints. The next button, to the right of the Remove button, can filter the list to show only enabled breakpoints, and the search field can filter the breakpoints by a given search term.

LOG NAVIGATOR

FIGURE 2.11 The Log navigator

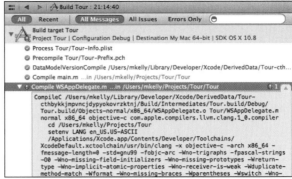

FIGURE 2.12 The run log output in the Editor area

The Log navigator (**Figure 2.11**) collects the various logs (including build, analyze, test, and debug). Clicking a log in the navigator displays it in the Editor area.

When you select a debug log (also known as a *run* log), the contents of the Debug area's console are displayed as plain text for you to browse. When you select a build log, the Editor area displays a set of controls along the top edge, which let you filter the types of messages you want to see (including all messages, issues only, or errors only). Clicking the list icon at the right edge of a message will expand it to display its associated command and output (**Figure 2.12**).

The controls along the bottom of the navigator let you filter the list. The button lets you choose to show only the most recent logs of a given type. The search field lets you filter the list with a given search term.

THE JUMP BAR

FIGURE 2.13 The jump bar, `WSAppDelegate.m` selected

FIGURE 2.14 The jump bar pop-up menu showing folders in the project

FIGURE 2.15 The jump bar showing document items with a filter applied

The jump bar, found above the Editor area, shows you where you are in the organizational structure of your project (**Figure 2.13**). It additionally serves as a more compact version of the Project navigator. It is accessible even when the Navigator area is hidden and can be used to navigate your project by clicking any one of the segments and choosing a different path from the pop-up menu (**Figure 2.14**).

The jump bar goes beyond the group and file level—it allows you to drill further down into the contents of the file. In the case of a source file, you can jump around the file's contents by clicking any segment after the file's segment. You can begin typing a symbol name to filter this list at any time while it's open (**Figure 2.15**). With Interface Builder files, you can navigate the window and view the hierarchy of your user interface. When Xcode finds issues in your workspace, issue navigation buttons appear on the right edge of the jump bar.

The jump bar also appears in Assistant windows (covered later in this chapter) and can be used to select various behaviors in addition to individual files.

THE EDITOR AREA

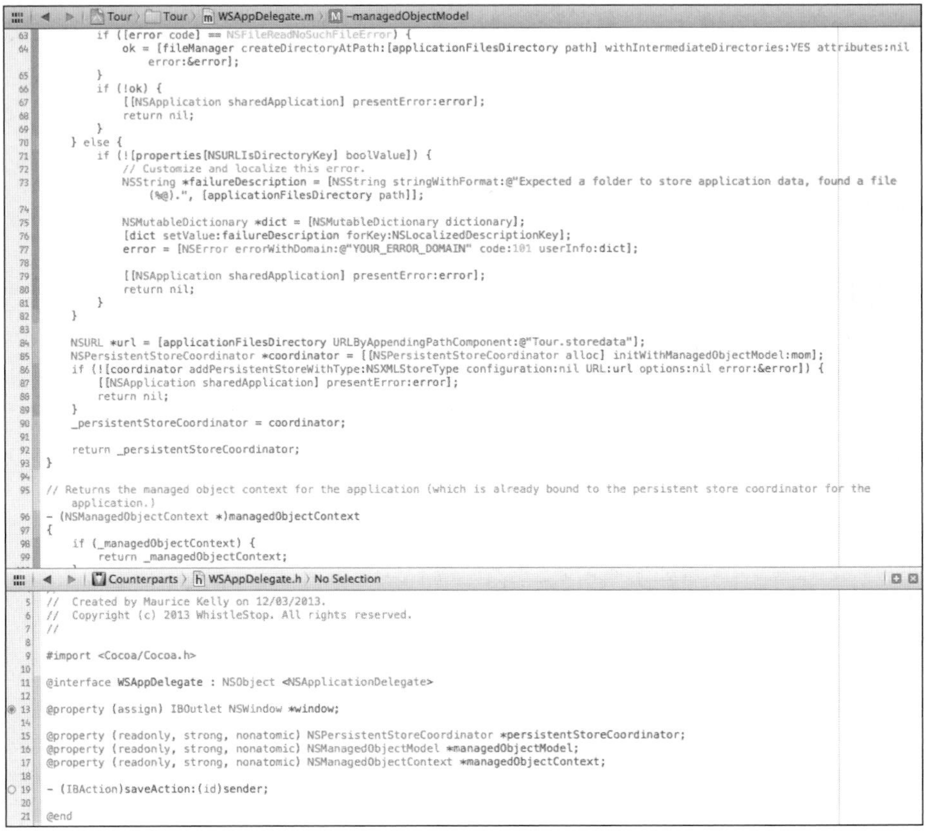

FIGURE 2.16 The
Editor area showing
the Source editor

The Editor area (**Figure 2.16**) dynamically switches between editors appropriate to the currently selected file (either through the Project navigator or through the jump bar). This means that for source code files, you'll see the Source editor, for Interface Builder files, you'll see the Interface editor, and so on. Among the other available editor types are the Data Model editor, the Project editor, the Version editor, and the Rich Text editor.

Although it is called the "Editor" area, this is something of a misnomer where some items are concerned. Some items are not editable, which means the Editor area serves more as a "Viewer" area. For example, the area might display an image resource (such as the application icon) when selected; however, there is currently no image-editing facility in Xcode 4, so you can only view the image.

The other major editors are covered in related chapters throughout this book.

INTRODUCING THE ASSISTANT

FIGURE 2.17

The Assistant

The Editor area conceals a deceptively powerful feature called the Assistant (**Figure 2.17**). The Assistant acts as a "split pane" editor with some added intelligence, depending on the behavioral mode you use. You can toggle the Assistant using the middle button of the Editor button bar that sits toward the right side of the toolbar area.

The Assistant is a very flexible contextual tool that helps you perform common tasks ancillary to the current editing context. For example, in the Data Model editor, if you select a Core Data entity with a corresponding managed object subclass, the Assistant can display that subclass for reference or editing. If you select a xib or storyboard to edit in Interface Builder, the Assistant can show the source file corresponding to the class of the selected object (see Chapter 7) to facilitate establishing action and outlet connections via drag and drop.

OPENING FILES IN THE ASSISTANT

When you turn on the Assistant using the toolbar, it displays the selected source file's counterpart in a single pane in Manual behavior mode (where you choose what is displayed in the Assistant pane yourself using its jump bar). You can use the Assistant's jump bar to view or edit any file in your workspace. There will always be at least one Assistant pane visible while the Assistant is active.

ADDING AND REMOVING ASSISTANT PANES

You can add or remove additional Assistant windows using the Add (+) and Remove (x) buttons in the upper-right corner of the existing Assistant pane (at the right edge of the panel's jump bar).

To add a new pane, click the Add button on any pane. The new pane will have its own jump bar and will be added after the pane whose Add (+) button you clicked. That is, if you click the Add (+) button of the last pane, the new pane will appear after the last one; if you click Add (+) on the first of several panes, the new pane will appear after the first one. To remove a pane, click its Remove (x) button.

FIGURE 2.18 The destination chooser

You can also open Assistant panes using keyboard shortcuts. By default, holding down the Option key and clicking an item in the Project navigator will open the item in the Assistant when only one pane is present. If more than one Assistant pane is present or you press Option-Shift-click (as mentioned earlier in this chapter), Xcode asks you where you'd like to view the file with an intuitive destination chooser (**Figure 2.18**).

TIP: You can customize keyboard shortcuts in the General tab of Xcode's preferences (choose Xcode > Preferences from the main menu).

CHANGING LAYOUT BEHAVIOR

In the previous section, the phrase "after the pane whose Add (+) button you clicked" is intentionally vague. This is because you can customize the Assistant's layout behavior. To do so, choose View > Assistant Editor to see and select the available layout modes (**Figure 2.19**).

FIGURE 2.19 The Assistant layout options

CHANGING ASSISTANT BEHAVIOR MODES

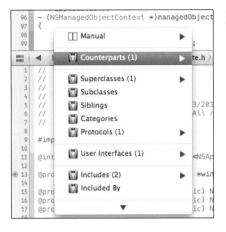

FIGURE 2.20 The Assistant's behavior modes in the jump bar

You can change the Assistant's behavior by clicking the segment of the jump bar immediately to the right of the navigation buttons. A menu appears (**Figure 2.20**) listing the available behaviors.

When in Manual mode, the Assistant behaves like a glorified—if neatly arranged—split pane editor. Its real power is in its automatic behavioral modes. When you choose any behavior other than Manual, the Assistant becomes contextually aware—it will show files related to the file (or a sub-selection within it) currently displayed in the main editor (the selection in the Project navigator). The term *selection* in this context means "the project member that is currently selected in the Project navigator and shown in the main editor."

The power of this feature becomes evident when you're faced with a scenario where it's necessary to edit a class's implementation, header, and associated protocol, or when you select an object in Interface Builder's dock and need to add a new outlet or action while connecting it to the interface at the same time.

When there is more than one related file that the Assistant can display, additional controls appear to the left of the Add (+) and Remove (x) buttons. The controls include standard back and forward navigation buttons, with the count of available associated files between them. These controls are not visible if there are fewer than two available associated files. The count is shown in the jump bar when selecting the behavior mode.

The available modes are explored in their related chapters.

THE UTILITY AREA

FIGURE 2.21 The Utility area

The Utility area (**Figure 2.21**) provides supplementary information and controls for the current editor. Essentially, anything you would expect to be in a floating palette for the editor can be found in the Utility area. To toggle the Utility area, click the rightmost View button in the toolbar.

Like the Editor area and its Assistant, the Utility area is highly contextual. Additional buttons representing various inspectors appear along the top, depending on what you're editing. For example, when you're editing a storyboard, buttons will appear for the Attributes inspector, Size inspector, Connections inspector, and more. With a data model selected, the Data Model inspector button appears. In most situations, two inspectors remain omnipresent: the File inspector and the Quick Help inspector.

The bottom panel contains the File Template library, the Code Snippet library (Chapter 12), the Object library, and the Media library, which contains your project's media resources as well as any media included in your workspace.

THE DEBUG AREA

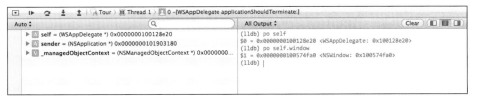

FIGURE 2.22 The Debug area

The Debug area (**Figure 2.22**) appears by default when you run your application. You can also toggle to it by clicking the middle View button in the toolbar.

The Debug area is the primary interface for the debugger. It includes a control bar, a console, and a view for inspecting in-scope variables when program execution has been paused. The Debug area and its controls are covered in more detail in Chapters 9 and 15.

CUSTOMIZING DEBUGGER BEHAVIOR

You can customize the Debug area's behavior in Xcode's preferences, on the Behaviors tab. There you can choose what actions the debugger takes when certain events occur (including run, pause, unexpected quits, successful quits, and so on).

For example, you could choose to show the Debug navigator when debugging starts or pauses. You could also choose to show the Project navigator and close the Debug area when the application quits normally. If the application quits unexpectedly, you could choose to show the Log navigator, navigate to the most recent run log, and play an alert sound to draw attention to the problem. Custom behaviors are covered in more detail in Chapter 15.

THE ACTIVITY VIEWER

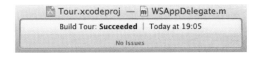

FIGURE 2.23 The Activity viewer

The Activity viewer (**Figure 2.23**) isn't overly complicated and offers little interaction, but its prominent (and immutable) placement in the center of the toolbar makes it worth mentioning. It provides you with visual feedback of all the activities Xcode is performing on the workspace.

When more than one activity is underway, the Activity viewer alternates between them (like an ad banner) and displays the number of concurrent tasks on its left side. You can click the number to display a pop-up that lists all the current activities and their progress individually.

In previous versions of Xcode, the right side of each window's bottom edge had its own status field showing the same information (mostly related to build and debug status). Xcode 4's all-in-one approach makes it easier to have a single place to see the current status of any actions Xcode is performing.

If there are any issues (errors, warnings, and so on), the number of issues will be displayed in the Activity viewer as well. Clicking the issue counter will switch to the Issue navigator so you can find and review the issues.

TABBED CODING

FIGURE 2.24 Two tabs, showing WSAppDelegate.m and a named tab (called Debugger)

Another new feature in Xcode 4 is tabs. Just as in the Safari browser, you can create tabs within the same workspace window for various project members in the workspace. For example, **Figure 2.24** shows a source file open in one tab and a user interface file open (in the Interface editor) in another.

To create a new tab, choose File > New > New Tab from the main menu. Click any tab to switch to it and navigate to the project member the tab represents. You can reorder tabs by dragging them. To rename a tab, double-click the title, type a new name, and then press Return. To close a tab, click the X icon that appears when you mouse over the tab, or choose File > Close Tab from the main menu.

TIP: Keyboard shortcuts are handy ways to speed up tab use. Pressing Command+T creates a new tab, and Command+W closes the currently selected tab. Press Command+} and Command+{ to switch between the next and previous tabs, respectively.

THE ORGANIZER WINDOW

FIGURE 2.25 The Organizer window

The Organizer window (**Figure 2.25**) stands apart from workspace windows as a collection point for project and device management, including repositories, archives, snapshots, and more. The various aspects of the Organizer will be explored throughout the book. To open the Organizer, choose Window > Organizer from the main menu.

WRAPPING UP

This chapter gave you a taste of the most obvious user interface elements in the workspace window. You'll explore more of the user interface in later chapters, but there's far more to Xcode than can fit in a book this size. In the next chapter, you'll learn how to use Xcode's built-in documentation browser and help facilities to get help with your coding and with using Xcode itself.

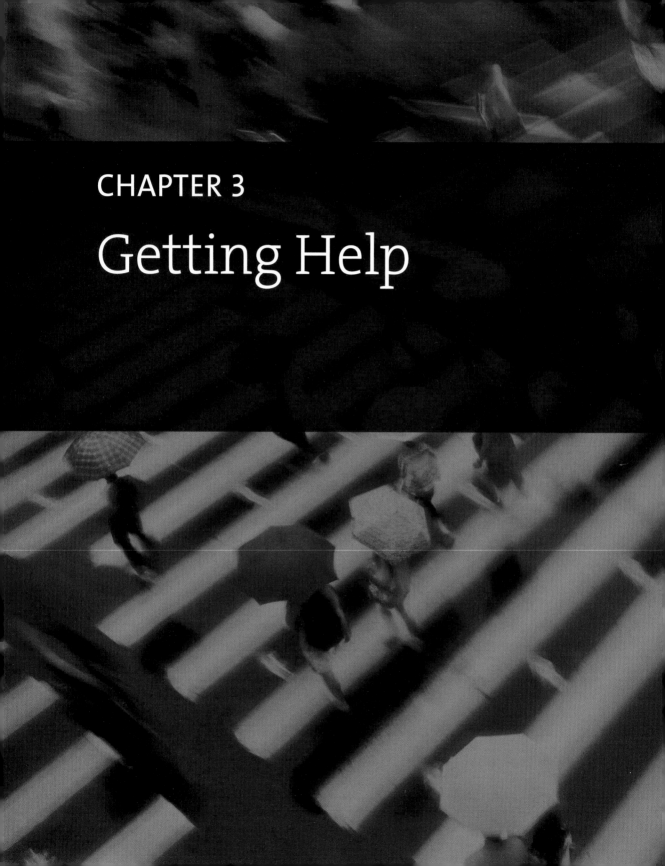

CHAPTER 3

Getting Help

You can get help in Xcode 4 for the Integrated Development Environment (IDE) as well as the Cocoa frameworks in a number of ways. In this chapter, you'll learn how to find the answers you need.

THE HELP MENU

FIGURE 3.1 The Xcode Help menu

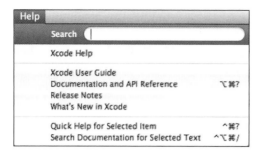

You'll start with the most obvious place. If you're familiar with OS X, you should be familiar with the Help menu. The Help menu (**Figure 3.1**) features a standard Search field, which shows you not only help topics but main menu items that match your search term.

Beneath the Search field are menu choices that open the help libraries you should familiarize yourself with. A link to Xcode's release notes is also listed there. Most of these will open the Organizer window, which you saw in Chapter 2.

XCODE HELP

The Xcode Help menu item opens the user manual for Xcode. Inside you'll find in-depth explanations and how-to instructions for all Xcode features.

XCODE USER GUIDE

The Xcode User Guide menu item opens a splash page containing video and links about how to find help in Xcode.

DOCUMENTATION AND API REFERENCE

The Documentation and API Reference menu item simply opens the Organizer window in Documentation mode so you can browse or search the installed documentation libraries. It will remain on the currently selected page without navigating away and simply show the window.

THE REST

The two remaining menu items trigger quick help for the currently selected code in the active workspace window, and open the Organizer window in Documentation mode with the text input cursor in the search bar.

THE ORGANIZER'S DOCUMENTATION TAB

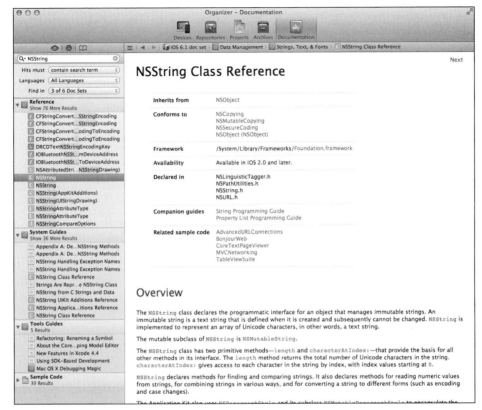

FIGURE 3.2
The Organizer's
Documentation tab

The Documentation section of the Organizer is Xcode's main viewer for all SDK and developer tools documentation. Open the Organizer by choosing Window > Organizer from the main menu, and then click the Documentation tab in the toolbar (**Figure 3.2**).

The Organizer responds by showing you a pane on the left (similar to Xcode's Navigator area) and a main viewing area. Along the top of the main viewing area, you'll see a jump bar similar to the one you explored in Chapter 2. This jump bar, however, allows you to navigate the documentation as opposed to your project. The button bar at the top of the Organizer's navigation area (above the search bar) switches between three modes: Explore, Search, and Bookmarks.

EXPLORE

In Explore mode, an outline of each of the documentation sets and their sections displays. You can drill down by topic through the guides and API reference documents.

SEARCH

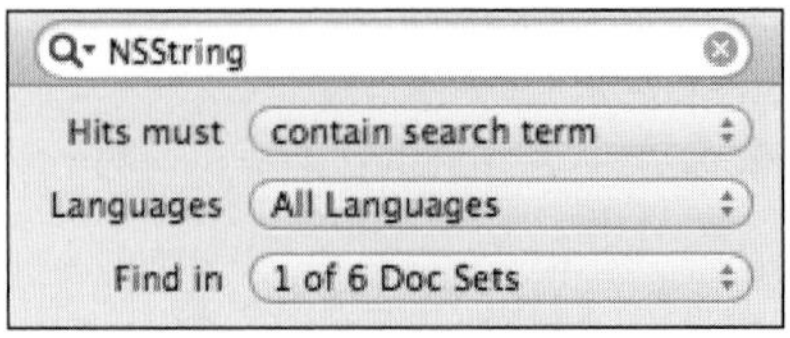

FIGURE 3.3 The Organizer's search options panel

In Search mode, a search field appears, allowing you to search all installed documentation sets. Clicking the magnifying glass icon and choosing Show Find Options from the context menu reveals a set of filtering options (**Figure 3.3**) that let you ignore unwanted document sets and more. The results are grouped by type (such as Reference, System Guides, Sample Code, and so on).

> **TIP:** The fewer document sets you have selected, the faster the search. If you work primarily in iOS, for example, you may wish to select only the iOS set for your daily searches.

BOOKMARKS

In Bookmarks mode, you can jump directly to documentation pages you've bookmarked. You can set bookmarks by choosing Editor > Bookmarks from the main menu or by right-clicking anywhere in the page and choosing Add Bookmark for Current Page from the context menu. To delete a bookmark, select it and press the Delete key.

THE SOURCE EDITOR

Although you'll explore the depths of the Source Editor in Part II, there are a couple of useful ways to find contextual help from within your code.

QUICK HELP IN THE UTILITY AREA

As you saw in Chapter 2, Xcode's Utility area gives you access to properties, code snippets, user interface elements for Interface Builder, and Quick Help. The Quick Help utility continuously updates its content, depending on what you've selected in the Source Editor.

To get a feel for this utility, make sure your Tour project is open and then select the WSAppDelegate.m source file from the Tour group in the Project navigator. Open the Utility area, and select the Quick Help utility. In the Source Editor, click persistentStoreCoordinator in the @synthesize persistentStoreCoordinator; statement. Quick Help responds by showing you the name of the header file in which the symbol is declared (the Tour project's WSAppDelegate.h file).

For a more interesting example, scroll down to - (NSURL *)applicationFilesDirectory
and click the NSURL symbol. Quick Help responds by showing a much more detailed description of the NSURL class (**Figure 3.4**), which is part of the Cocoa frameworks and is documented by the built-in document libraries. Any text highlighted in blue is a hyperlink to the corresponding documentation. Clicking a Quick Help hyperlink opens the linked information in the Documentation section of the Organizer.

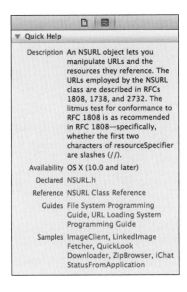

FIGURE 3.4 The Quick Help utility

SEARCH DOCUMENTATION FOR SELECTED TEXT

Another handy way to find the documentation for symbols such as NSURL is to select the symbol in the Source editor and then choose Help > Search Documentation for Selected Text from the main menu. As with hyperlinks in the Quick Help pane, choosing this option will open any corresponding documentation it finds in the Documentation section of the Organizer.

TIP: It's not necessary to open the Utility pane to see Quick Help content. The same information will appear in a pop-up bubble by Option-clicking the symbol you want to locate.

COMMUNITY HELP AND FEEDBACK

There are a number of community websites for finding more help than is available in the documentation, including Apple's own developer forums. See Appendix D for more information.

APPLE'S DEVELOPER FORUMS

Apple's developer forums are accessible to Apple developer program members (http://devforums.apple.com). There you can receive help and advice from the Cocoa developer community as well as the occasional Apple engineer. Because this is a public forum, it's important to keep in mind that most people there are developers like you and are volunteering their time. Take extra care to search for similar questions before posting, ask detailed and clearly written questions, and be civil. As with any community, anything less than civility and courtesy will make the community less likely to help you in the future.

DOCUMENTATION ERRORS

If there is anything about Apple's documentation that is unclear, incorrect, or lacking in any way in Xcode, you are encouraged to submit feedback to Apple. At the bottom of every page of the documentation are hyperlinks that allow you to submit feedback—good, sort-of-good, and bad—to the Apple documentation team. Constructive, detailed feedback helps Apple provide better documentation, and improvements are released often.

WRAPPING UP

Xcode offers many ways to find help. Most of those ways point to the same documentation set, but even the documentation pages help you submit suggestions for improvement. In addition, you will find that a quick Internet search will turn up a number of community websites (one of which is Apple-hosted) and blogs. Even if the built-in documentation doesn't help, the chances are quite good you'll find your answer on the World Wide Web.

You should now have your bearings in the Xcode IDE. In Part II, you'll use Xcode to set up an "application suite" workspace. It's safe to close and throw away Tour.app. We hardly knew ye.

PART II

Building
Applications

CHAPTER 4

Setting Up Your Workspace

In Part I, the Tour.app project was just that—an Xcode project. The collection of files and folders in an Xcode project are bound by an `.xcodeproj` file that contains all the project-wide settings (such as a description of your schemes and targets). So far, the word "workspace" has been used as a general description of the project and the window that contains it all. A true workspace in Xcode, however, is a container that encompasses multiple projects that share common resources.

From this point forward, we're going to need something a bit more complex than a single project to demonstrate Xcode's organizational capabilities. We're going to create an *application suite* consisting of an OS X application, an iOS application, and a shared framework that encapsulates all the common components.

For this book's demonstration, we'll create our own version of one of the most innovative and popular uses of a bright white screen—the comical "flashlight" app. The suite will be composed of Flashlight.app (for iOS devices) and Lamp.app (for OS X). We'll call the workspace "Lighting Suite."

WORKSPACES DEFINED

Xcode 4 introduced the idea of a *workspace* as a kind of project binder—a container for multiple projects. A project groups its related files and settings; a workspace binds multiple related projects. A workspace merely contains pointers to Xcode projects. Projects remain distinct in that you can remove them from a workspace without affecting the project's content or settings. In other words, the project can still be opened and edited outside its workspace. Workspaces give you several advantages over projects that reference files and built products from other projects.

Projects contained within the same workspace share a common build location. This makes it possible for one project to use another's built products. This one feature makes a world of difference for managing complex applications and application suites. It makes it far easier, for example, to include the built product of a common framework project into one or more of your application projects.

The automatic dependency detection that you'll learn about in Chapter 13 extends to the workspace level as well. This means that including a product's framework in the target of an application project within the same workspace usually requires no additional work for Xcode to recognize the dependency. As with dependent targets within the same project, Xcode will see this dependency and build the framework before building the application. In other words, you don't have to copy shared libraries into each project folder in which you intend to use the library.

NOTE: Xcode may not be able to detect complex dependencies automatically. In such cases, you'll need to disable the Find Implicit Dependencies setting of the affected scheme and add and sort the interdependent targets manually.

Another benefit of a workspace is shared indexing. A project index is used primarily for features such as code completion (sometimes referred to as "code sense"). Xcode's automatic code completion and refactoring facilities will take the symbols of *all* projects included in the workspace into account. This means code completion will automatically find your framework project's symbols and make them available to you when you're editing source files in the application project that uses the framework.

Still another benefit of workspaces pertains to schemes (Chapter 13). A standalone project might contain a primary scheme for building, testing, and profiling a primary product in addition to schemes for smaller, dependent targets (such as a Spotlight plug-in). In a workspace, you may only want to see the scheme for each project's primary product. Using the Manage Schemes panel that you'll explore in Chapter 13 you can specify whether the schemes for those smaller "sub-targets" are visible at the workspace level or only when the project is opened individually. This can help keep the list of schemes short and manageable, hiding unnecessary detail within the workspace.

WHEN TO USE A WORKSPACE

It's hopefully obvious that a workspace is useless without two or more projects. Less obvious but just as important is that a workspace doesn't help with multiple *unrelated* projects. A workspace is only helpful for two or more projects that share each other's code and resources. Let's look at two real-world examples.

DISTINCT APPLICATIONS

Imagine Acme Corporation has a host of unrelated desktop (and even mobile) applications. Here, *unrelated* means a calculator application, a calendar application, and an address book application. Each of these applications has only one thing in common: They're products of Acme Corporation.

Being the property of the same business entity, the applications presumably use the same software registration system, company logo, contact information, and so on. They may even be able to share user data among them. This means each application would use the same code, the same resources, or both.

A change to the Person and Event classes, for example, might need to be updated in both the address book and calendar applications. While these classes may or may not be wrapped in a library or framework, it makes little sense to maintain two copies of Person and Event (one in each project). Here, a separate project that at least contains the common model-layer classes (and corresponding unit tests) makes sense. A separate framework project makes even better sense.

Since the applications are otherwise unrelated, each application might have its own workspace that includes the application project and the shared framework project. The benefit of such a setup is that changes made to a project that belongs to a workspace are available to that workspace. For example, if you have two applications (each in its own workspace) that share a common framework, changes to the framework from one app are automatically available to the other by virtue of including the framework in their respective workspaces.

APPLICATION SUITES

Imagine Acme Corporation's desktop calendar application has gone where no calendar application has gone before. Against all odds, it has become a best seller, and users are clamoring for mobile versions for their various devices. Acme Corporation, in addition to its other products that share company-wide resources, now has a product that supports *two* platforms, shares company-wide resources, *and* has a device synchronization library to let users share calendar information between their devices and their desktop computers.

In this case it would make sense to have a workspace containing the two application projects (OS X and iOS), their sync library project, and the company-wide resource project.

CREATING THE LIGHTING SUITE WORKSPACE

FIGURE 4.1 Saving a workspace

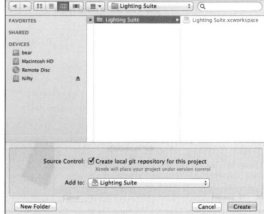

FIGURE 4.2 Adding the project to a workspace using the Add To menu

Creating a workspace is easy. Choose File > New > Workspace from the main menu. A new workspace window will appear, with a Save As sheet prompting you for a location in which to save it (**Figure 4.1**). Again, I recommend the desktop for convenience. Create a folder called **Lighting Suite** to hold everything, and select it. Name the workspace **Lighting Suite** and click Save.

You'll be presented with an eerily empty workspace window, whose workspace file lives inside the Lighting Suite folder you created. Now on to the projects. As mentioned, we'll need two projects: the Mac app and the iOS app. The projects will live inside the Lighting Suite folder, along with the workspace, for good organization.

ADDING PROJECTS TO THE WORKSPACE

Now we'll create the individual projects.

Let's do iOS first. This project will contain a universal app that will work on iPhones, iPod touches, and iPads. Choose File > New > Project. Pick the iOS Application category, and select the Single View Application template. Click Next. We'll call this product **Flashlight**.

Accept the rest of the defaults (Use Storyboards, Use Automatic Reference Counting, Include Unit Tests), but choose Universal from the Devices menu. Click Next. You can choose whether or not you want to create a Git repository for the project, but make sure that you choose Lighting Suite from the Add To menu (**Figure 4.2**). Also make sure the main Lighting Suite folder is selected, and click Create.

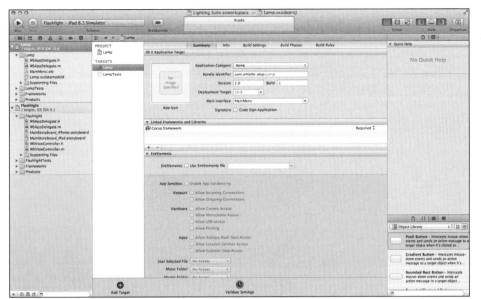

FIGURE 4.3 A freshly minted workspace containing two projects

Now for the desktop version of Flashlight, Lamp.app. Choose File > New > Project, and select the OS X Application category. Pick Cocoa Application, and click Next. We'll call this product **Lamp**. This time we want to select Use Core Data, Use Automatic Reference Counting, and Include Unit Tests (we don't want a Spotlight importer). Click Next. Choose Lighting Suite from the Add To menu, and make sure the main Lighting Suite folder is selected to ensure the projects are kept together. This time, an extra Group option appears when you're asked to save. Make sure the group is set to the Lighting Suite workspace. Again, you can select "Create local git repository for this project" if you wish. You should end up with a workspace that looks like **Figure 4.3**, all contained within the Lighting Suite folder in Finder.

WRAPPING UP

The idea of Xcode's new workspaces feature can seem intimidating at first. You've seen that it's really quite straightforward. A workspace provides a way of tying related projects together to take advantage of Xcode's (usually) intelligent dependency discovery. In the next chapter, you'll add some code and resources to Lighting Suite's projects.

CHAPTER 5

Adding Resources and Code

All but the simplest applications will likely need additional source code files, multiple nibs, artwork, HTML-based help files, and frameworks or libraries. There are two basic categories of files you might add to a project: source code and resources. In this chapter, you will learn how to add new or existing source and resource files to your project as well as how to remove them. You will also look at how to use the Source editor and its built-in tools to make writing source code more efficient.

WORKING WITH FILES

There are a number of ways to add files and resources to an Xcode project. To add existing files, you can use the Add Files sheet, or you can use drag and drop. To create new files, you can use the New Files template sheet or the File Template library.

USING THE ADD FILES SHEET

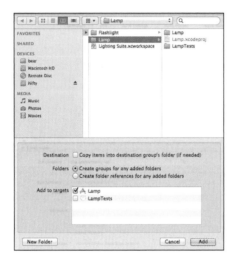

FIGURE 5.1 The Add Files sheet

You can add files to a project or to a workspace. When dealing with projects in a workspace, you have to make sure nothing is selected (Command-click any selected files) in the navigator to add the files to the shared workspace; to add files to individual projects, select the project (or a member of the project) before you add the content. You access the Add Files sheet by choosing File > Add Files To "[*Project Name*]" from the main menu. Depending on whether you have a project selected or nothing at all, you'll see the project name or the workspace name (Add Files to "Lamp" or Add Files to "Lighting Suite").

The sheet in **Figure 5.1** is a standard Open File sheet with additional options at the bottom. These options tell Xcode what do with the files when you click Add.

> **TIP:** Files that already belong to the selected project or workspace are grayed out when adding files.

DESTINATION

The Destination check box instructs Xcode to copy the selected files into the physical disk folder represented by the group currently selected in the Project navigator, if one exists. If the currently selected group does not have a physical disk folder, then Xcode will place the files in a disk folder belonging to the first parent group that actually has one. Leaving this option unselected will cause Xcode to add a reference to the file without actually copying the file into the project.

> **NOTE:** In most cases, it's best to allow files to be copied into the project folder. This ensures that all the parts of your project are kept together. However, referencing files outside the project folder has its advantages. One reason to do so would be when using resources stored on a shared network volume for team development.

FOLDERS

The Folders option lets you choose what Xcode will do when adding file system folders to the project. The first option creates groups of the same name as the folder and then adds the folder's contents under that group. The second option creates folder references. These are similar to groups but represent the physical folder itself, preserving its file system hierarchy.

ADD TO TARGETS

The Add to Targets option instructs Xcode to add the files to the appropriate build phases for the selected targets within your project, depending on the file type. Xcode automatically adds source files to the Compile Sources build phase of the selected targets. Most other file types are added to the Copy Bundle Resources build phase. Targets and build phases are discussed in more detail in Part III.

USING DRAG AND DROP

In addition to using the Add Files sheet, you can add files to your project by dropping them into the Project navigator. A sheet similar to **Figure 5.2** will appear, offering the same options shown in the Add Files sheet. Choose your options, and click Finish to add the files to the project. If you drag and drop into the workspace rather than into a specific project, there will be no Add to Targets section.

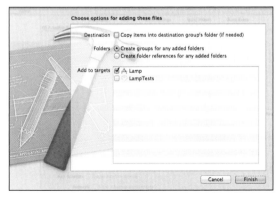

FIGURE 5.2 The Add Files drag and drop options sheet

> **NOTE:** It is common to add additional libraries and frameworks to a project. Adding libraries and frameworks, as well as packaging frameworks for distribution with the application, is discussed in depth in Part III.

CREATING NEW FILES

FIGURE 5.3 The New File sheet

Xcode includes templates and options for creating a variety of common file types and adding them to your project. To begin adding a new file, choose File > New > File from the main menu. A sheet similar to **Figure 5.3** will appear.

The sheet contains a sidebar on the left that categorizes the available templates first by SDK and then by file type. The top area to the right of the sidebar contains the specific templates that are available for the selected category. Select your desired template there. The area immediately below the templates shows a description of the selected template.

Some templates have additional options that allow you to specify things such as a superclass. Such options are displayed when you click Next (**Figure 5.4**). When choosing a subclass, make your choice carefully—Xcode provides detailed templates for some sub-classes (for example, UITableViewController), which can be a real time-saver. Keep clicking Next and you'll eventually see a standard Save As sheet offering two additional options (**Figure 5.5**): the group in which to place the new file and the targets in which to include it. Click Create to create the file.

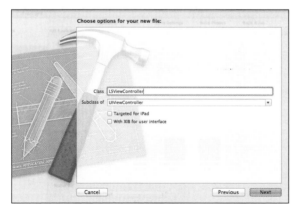

FIGURE 5.4 Choosing options for a new file

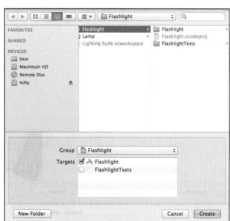

FIGURE 5.5 The Save As sheet

USING THE FILE TEMPLATE LIBRARY

FIGURE 5.6 The File
Template library

You can also use the Utility area's File Template library (**Figure 5.6**) to create new files in your project. Just drag the desired template straight into the Project navigator and drop it in the desired folder. A Save As sheet similar to Figure 5.5 will appear, with which you can name the file and specify its group and targets. Although this is a good way to create resources quickly, you lose the flexibility provided when you select File > New > File. For example, you do not get an opportunity to select a superclass. For a class like `UITableViewController`, you will miss out on a lot of boilerplate code using the File Template library method.

REMOVING FILES FROM THE PROJECT

To remove a file from a project, select it in the Project navigator and press Delete. Xcode will prompt you to make a decision (**Figure 5.7**) to remove only the reference to the file within the project or to remove the reference and delete the file from disk. The operation cannot be undone, so if you discover you need the file after you've deleted it, you'll need to restore it and then add it to the project as shown earlier in this chapter.

FIGURE 5.7 Deleting
a file

ADDING FILES TO LAMP

We only need one set of files for our Lamp project: a Cocoa class to serve as our lamp view. This custom subclass of NSView will draw itself black when the lamp is off and white when it's on. We don't need an equivalent for the Flashlight project due to the increased flexibility of the UIView class.

Select the Lamp project in the navigator. Choose File > New > File from the main menu. Choose the OS X category, select the Objective-C Class template, and click Next. In the Class field, enter **LSView** (replacing "LS" with whatever prefix you chose). In the Subclass Of field, enter **NSView**. Click Next. Click Create when asked to save. You can organize the project members however you like, or you can leave the files wherever Xcode puts them.

WORKING WITH THE SOURCE EDITOR

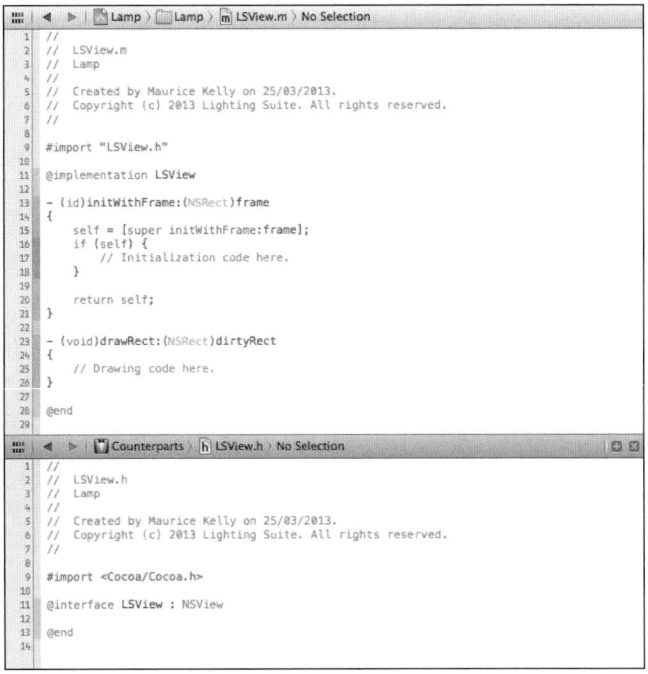

FIGURE 5.8 The Source editor

The Source editor (**Figure 5.8**) appears when you select source code files, when you view issues within source code files, and when you stop at a breakpoint in your own source in the debugger. This is the editor in which you will spend most of your time.

Note the gutter that runs along the left edge of the Source editor. The gutter can display breakpoints, line numbers, connection indicators, and the code-folding and focus ribbon. Breakpoints are discussed in more depth in Chapter 9. You can toggle line numbers and the code-folding ribbon via Xcode's preferences.

When you're editing source code, the Assistant window—seen at the bottom of Figure 5.8—can be used to open one or more files (or even separate parts of the same file) alongside the file displayed in the main editor. The Assistant in this case serves as a split-pane editor. In the Assistant pane's jump bar, you can select various automatic modes—such as Counterparts, Includes, Categories, and so on—to cause the Assistant to display context-sensitive files depending on the main selection in the Project navigator.

FOCUSING AND FOLDING CODE

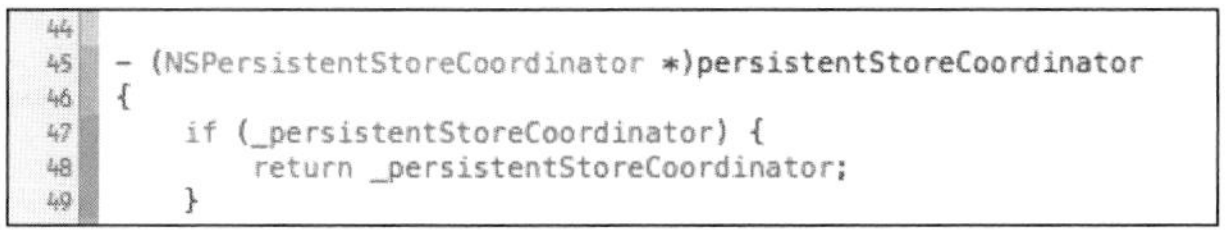

```
44
45    - (NSPersistentStoreCoordinator *)persistentStoreCoordinator
46    {
47        if (_persistentStoreCoordinator) {
48            return _persistentStoreCoordinator;
49        }
```

FIGURE 5.9 The code-folding ribbon showing nested scopes

The code-folding ribbon is enabled by default. It is the narrow strip in the gutter directly to the left of the text area of the Source editor. The ribbon lets you concentrate on a particular scope within your code (anything within a matching pair of brackets) through folding or focusing. Nested scopes are depicted by darker shading within the ribbon (**Figure 5.9**). The boundaries of each scope are marked with arrows when you hover your mouse over them.

FOCUSING ON CODE

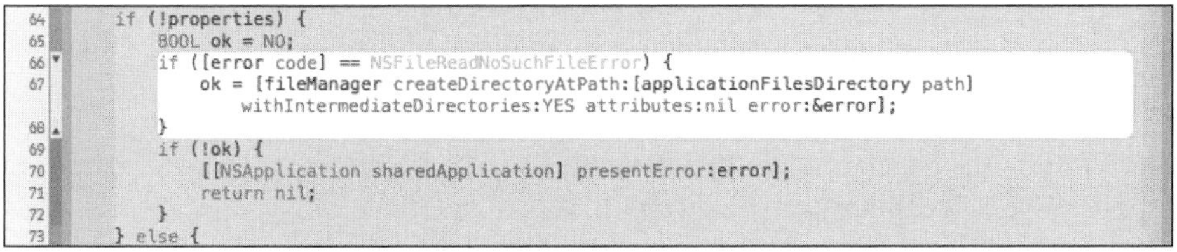

```
64    if (!properties) {
65        BOOL ok = NO;
66        if ([error code] == NSFileReadNoSuchFileError) {
67            ok = [fileManager createDirectoryAtPath:[applicationFilesDirectory path]
                    withIntermediateDirectories:YES attributes:nil error:&error];
68        }
69        if (!ok) {
70            [[NSApplication sharedApplication] presentError:error];
71            return nil;
72        }
73    } else {
```

FIGURE 5.10 Focused code, using the code-folding ribbon

Focusing refers to darkening out all but the desired scope. Focusing does not obscure text; it only shades out anything outside the focused scope. **Figure 5.10** shows the focused body of a simple if block.

To focus on a scope, hover the mouse over the desired scope in the ribbon. Xcode will leave only the code within that scope unshaded.

FOLDING CODE

```
16
17    - (void)applicationDidFinishLaunching:(NSNotification *)aNotification
18  ▸ {(…)}
21
```

FIGURE 5.11 Folded code, using the code-folding feature

Folding refers to collapsing and hiding the text within the desired scope. This does not change the text within the file but rather obscures it, making the file effectively shorter and easier to navigate. **Figure 5.11** depicts the LSAppDelegate.m file with the -applicationDidFinishLaunching: method folded; the "folded" code is depicted as a yellow marker containing an ellipsis.

To fold code, click the desired scope in the folding ribbon. In cases where there are nested scopes, it's easiest to click one of the arrows at either end of the desired scope. A code block can be unfolded again by clicking the right-facing arrow in the gutter or by double-clicking the yellow ellipsis.

ADDING CODE AUTOMATICALLY

Developing software is a text-intensive process, and you will spend a large portion of your time in the Source editor creating text. Fortunately, Xcode provides some ways to speed up this process—code completion and the Code Snippet library. We'll explore both of these methods as we flesh out the NSView subclass that we created earlier.

CODE COMPLETION

When you begin to type a symbol that Xcode recognizes from your project or from linked libraries and frameworks, an inline suggestion as well as a list of other possible suggestions appears. You can choose to accept the inline suggestion by pressing Tab. To select an alternative suggestion, use the arrow keys to choose, and then press Return to use the selection. When there is more than one suggestion for a given prefix (such as NSSet or NSSetFocusRingStyle()), the common prefix will be underlined, and pressing Tab will complete only up to the underlined portion; subsequent Tabs will complete to the next whole or part of the inline suggestion.

Code completion can be canceled by pressing Escape or Control+spacebar. Completion can also be requested by placing the text insertion point at the end of an incomplete symbol and pressing Control+spacebar.

Although by default Xcode will automatically suggest code completion while you type, you can turn this feature off in the Text Editing panel of Xcode's preferences by toggling the check box named "Suggest completions while typing." When this feature is disabled, you may still request suggestions by pressing Control+spacebar while the text insertion point is at the end of an incomplete symbol.

To see code completion in action, open the `LSView.h` file you created earlier and add the following lines to the interface section of the file:

```
@property (nonatomic, strong) NSColor *color;
- (void)switchLamp:(BOOL)on;
```

You'll now use these definitions in the implementation file. Open `LSView.m` and place the cursor inside the implementation section.

To draw the white and black backgrounds for the on and off states of the lamp, you need to provide a custom implementation of the `NSView` method `-drawRect:`. There should already be an empty implementation of `-drawRect:` that was generated from the template, but for the sake of example, delete that empty implementation and start typing the following:

```
- draw
```

The code completion tool should spring to life and offer a number of potential completions (**Figure 5.12**). Use the arrow keys to select the `-drawRect:` completion, and press Return to accept it. Complete the method body by pressing Return, typing a curly brace ({), and then pressing Return again. Xcode will sense that you are creating a method and add the closing brace for you (helpfully flashing it yellow so that you know it intervened), and then Xcode will place your cursor between the two braces.

FIGURE 5.12 Code completion suggestions

To flesh out the method, type `self.` (including the period). When you type the period, Xcode will present you with any properties available to your class, which should include the `color` property you defined in the header file moments ago. Select the `color` property using the arrow keys if necessary, then press Return.

Next you need to call the `-setFill` method on the `color` property, so type a space and then `setF` and press Return to accept the remaining completion. To complete the method, type a closing bracket (]), and observe as Xcode inserts the opening bracket at the start of the method call (again, flashing it yellow for attention).

FIGURE 5.13 The Fix-it
dialog offering to insert
a missing semicolon

```
13    - (void)drawRect:(NSRect)dirtyRect
14    {
15        [self.color setFill];                    ● Expected ';' after expression
16    }
17
18    @end        Issue  ● Expected ';' after expression
19              Fix-it  Insert ";"
```

At this point your method call is complete but is missing the semicolon at the end of the line. Unfortunately, Xcode doesn't seem capable of entering the semicolon automatically, but it is capable of detecting that you've missed it. Build the project by pressing Command+B, and you should notice a small red circle appear in the gutter beside the line you just entered. Click the circle to activate the Fix-it pop-up (**Figure 5.13**). You can fix many common coding problems this way—just double-click the blue line containing the proposed change.

You should begin to see that code completion can be a real time-saver, but it is important to learn when to use it to your greatest advantage. It is best to type enough characters to really narrow down the number of options.

Complete the –drawRect: method as shown:

```
- (void)drawRect:(NSRect)dirtyRect
{
    [self.color setFill];
    NSRectFill(dirtyRect);
}
```

THE CODE SNIPPET LIBRARY

FIGURE 5.14 The Code
Snippet library

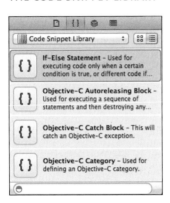

Xcode provides a fairly comprehensive collection of predefined snippets and has helpfully grouped them together in the Code Snippet library. Better still, it is a library that you can edit and add to, so you can cultivate your own collection of useful boilerplate code.

The Code Snippet library is located at the bottom of the Utility area (**Figure 5.14**). You can filter the snippets using the pop-up button at the top; you can choose to show all snippets, OS X snippets, iOS snippets, or your own custom snippets. You can also filter by keyword using the search bar at the bottom of the library panel.

The `LSView` class is almost complete but needs an implementation for the `-switchLamp:` method. Enter the following code to define the basic method body:

```
- (void)switchLamp:(BOOL)on
{

}
```

The method takes a `BOOL` that indicates if the lamp is being switched on or off, so you need some conditional logic. Rather than type it all out by hand, take advantage of a predefined code snippet. Place the cursor in the method body and type `ifelse`. This time Xcode will display a new type of completion—a code snippet from the library (**Figure 5.15**). Press Return to accept the snippet, and Xcode will helpfully insert a traditional if-else block with three placeholders to fill in (**Figure 5.16**)—the first placeholder will be selected and is ready for you to start typing.

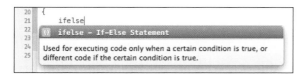

FIGURE 5.15 The ifelse code snippet displayed via code completion

FIGURE 5.16 The ifelse snippet with placeholders

Type the condition on and press the Tab key to move to the next placeholder. Type `self.color = [NSColor whiteColor];` then press Tab again to move to the next placeholder, and type `self.color = [NSColor blackColor];` (don't forget the semicolon). Just one more statement is necessary, so move the cursor outside the `else` block and add the following line of code:

```
[self setNeedsDisplay:YES];
```

To examine the contents of a snippet, click to select it in the library. A pop-up (**Figure 5.17**) window will appear containing a description and the code snippet. It also shows the shortcut that can be used via code completion, if one has been defined.

FIGURE 5.17 The snippet details pop-up

FIGURE 5.18 The
snippet details pop-up
in edit mode

To create a snippet, select the desired "template" code, then drag it into the Code Snippet library. The snippet will be added to the list of available snippets. To edit the snippet, select it in the library. When the pop-up window appears, click the Edit button in the lower-left corner. The pop-up will reveal editing controls (**Figure 5.18**).

You can set the title and description that appear in the library list, as well as the platform and language the snippet targets. You can also set a completion shortcut to use when editing code. Finally, you can edit the snippet itself. When you're finished editing, click Edit or Done. If in the future you decide you no longer need a custom snippet, click its entry in the Code Snippet library to select it, then press Delete. Xcode will prompt for confirmation; click the Delete button to make the snippet disappear forever.

An example of a useful snippet is a set of the three primary NSTableViewDataSource protocol methods. When using this protocol to populate an NSTableView programmatically, the quickest way to get up and running used to be to copy the method signatures from the documentation and then insert the brackets, the if conditionals for determining the table being operated on, and so on. Now you need to define this only once, format it as you want, and then save it as a snippet for reuse in any future projects and workspaces.

You can also insert placeholder tokens that are parts of the snippet (such as arguments) that must be filled in to complete the code. For example, to add a placeholder for an NSNumber argument, you would type <#NSNumber#> where the argument belongs. When the snippet is used, the text that appears between the hash marks is what will appear in the snippet. The token's text should serve as a helpful prompt regarding what should be filled in when using the snippet.

Finally, if you want to insert the snippet using code completion, add a unique identifier to the Completion Shortcut field.

WRAPPING UP

A typical project will require adding many new source and resource files. You should also expect to remove files while maintaining and improving the application. You've seen how straightforward both of these actions are.

Editing code is the primary task of software developers. Becoming proficient at using the source-editing tools available to you increases your productivity as a developer. Allowing Xcode to intelligently generate code is an excellent way to improve it further.

In the next chapter, you'll learn how to use Xcode's snapshots feature to keep track of the changes you make to your code.

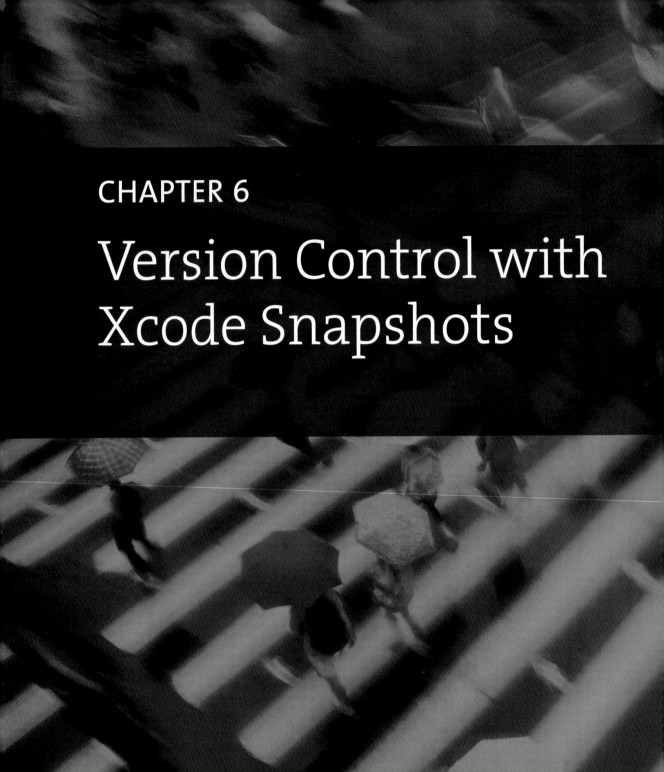

CHAPTER 6

Version Control with Xcode Snapshots

Source code management, also known as *revision control* or *version control*, is a form of change control that is vital to any medium to large development project. In team environments, a full source code management system is often used for managing work that is done by multiple people on the same resources.

Xcode offers two primary ways to manage your source code: by using snapshots and through its integration with two full source code management (SCM) systems. In this chapter, we will explore Xcode's snapshots feature, and in Chapter 18 we will look in depth at its SCM integration.

XCODE SNAPSHOTS

The simplest way to place your code under version control is to use Xcode's snapshots feature. A snapshot is merely an archived copy of your entire workspace. Xcode lets you restore a snapshot, which is the equivalent of extracting a copy of the workspace folder from the time of the snapshot.

It's the most basic form of version control there is, and if you don't use a full SCM system, you owe it to yourself to at least use snapshots. If you ever make complicated experimental changes that don't work out, you'll be thankful you took that snapshot before you started really messing things up. It's so important that Xcode attempts to coerce you into enabling automatic snapshots the first time you use the Refactor features.

CONFIGURING SNAPSHOTS

FIGURE 6.1 The project's Snapshots settings

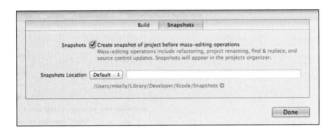

Snapshots can be configured by choosing File > Workspace Settings (or Project Settings, if you're working with individual projects) from the main menu. The Workspace Settings sheet will appear. Click the Snapshots tab to reveal the Snapshots settings (**Figure 6.1**).

The check box controls whether snapshots are taken automatically before mass-editing operations (such as refactoring or workspace-wide find and replace). Since Xcode asks you if you want to enable automatic snapshots prior to your first use of a mass-editing feature, it's unnecessary to enable this feature through this panel, but it can be useful if you want to disable it later in favor of a full SCM system.

The Snapshots Location control lets you specify where you'd like to store snapshots for the current workspace or project. The default is a location in your home folder, which lives alongside Xcode's derived data and archive folders.

Snapshot settings belong to individual projects or workspaces. That is, any settings you change here affect only the current workspace or project.

TAKING A SNAPSHOT

You can create a snapshot of your project at any time by choosing File > Create Snapshot from the main menu (or by pressing Command+Control+S). You'll be prompted for a name and description. Leaving all your snapshots named "New snapshot" and without a description will be useless to you later. You should choose a good name and description so you can identify exactly at what point the snapshot was taken if you need to find it later (**Figure 6.2**).

FIGURE 6.2 The Create Snapshot sheet

Choose whatever naming and description system works best for you, but you should definitely *have* a system. Click Create Snapshot to take the snapshot. A complete copy of your workspace—exactly as it is now—will be archived and stored in the snapshots location that you specified.

MANAGING SNAPSHOTS

Snapshots are managed in the Organizer window. Choose Window > Organizer from the main menu, and select the Projects tab. Select the project or workspace for which you want to manage snapshots (**Figure 6.3**).

In Figure 6.3, you can see that a filter bar is positioned directly above the list of snapshots. The search field filters by keyword (in the title as well as the description). You can also choose to show all snapshots for the workspace or only those you took yourself (that is, you can exclude automatic snapshots).

The list shows the snapshots sorted by date. Selecting a snapshot enables the Export Snapshot and Delete Snapshot buttons along the bottom edge. The Export Snapshot button will place an extracted copy of the snapshot into the location of your choosing, while the Delete Snapshot button will remove the snapshot permanently.

FIGURE 6.3 A project's snapshots

RESTORING FROM A SNAPSHOT

You can restore a snapshot by choosing File > Restore Snapshot from the main menu. Select the snapshot from the list (**Figure 6.4**), and click Restore.

A snapshot review sheet will appear (**Figure 6.5**). The sidebar on the left lists the files that will be affected by restoring the snapshot. You can view the changes that will be made to a file by selecting the file. When you're looking at a file, the content in the left editor pane is the file content in the snapshot, and the right editor pane is the current state of the file. When you are satisfied that this is indeed the snapshot that you wish to apply, click Restore. The project will be restored to the state it was in when you took the snapshot. As a bonus, Xcode will automatically create a snapshot just before restoring a snapshot so you can undo your undo. This will happen only if you selected the "Create snapshot of project before mass-editing operations" check box (Figure 6.1).

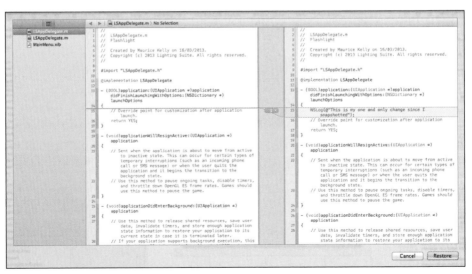

WRAPPING UP

Version control is a feature of software development that used to be prohibitive unless you had the time and experience to devote to setting up a full SCM system. Xcode's snapshots feature is a very basic form of version control, but if your needs are likewise basic, they can be a very effective safety net should your experimentation go awry.

In the next chapter, we will examine the Interface Builder component of Xcode—the toolset used to transform your ugly code into beautiful GUI applications.

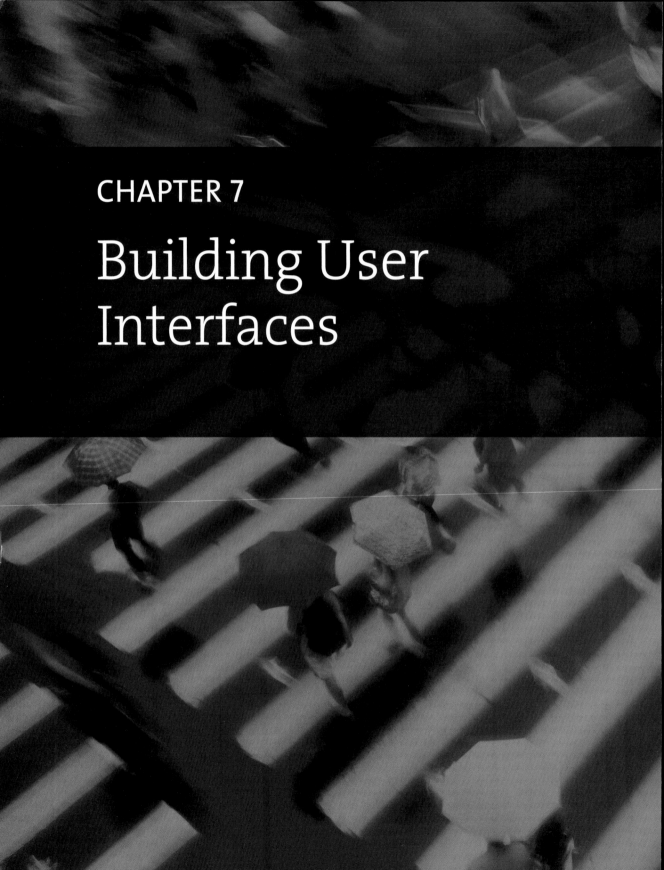

CHAPTER 7

Building User Interfaces

In this chapter, you'll learn how to use Xcode's integrated user interface tools. You'll need some familiarity with Cocoa development, which is beyond the scope of this book. Basic background is given where necessary, but you are encouraged to read Apple's Cocoa Fundamentals Guide (http://developer.apple.com/library/mac/#documentation/Cocoa/Conceptual/CocoaFundamentals/Introduction/Introduction.html) to understand the design concepts behind user interfaces in Cocoa applications.

UNDERSTANDING NIBS

Cocoa and Cocoa Touch applications load their graphic user interfaces from Interface Builder files (called *nibs* or *xibs*). The files are essentially "freeze-dried" object graphs representing the user interface you've constructed and the connections between the UI elements and one or more controller objects. Several key concepts are important to grasp when designing and working with an OS X or iOS application.

NOTE: The name nib stands for NeXTSTEP Interface Builder, which is a holdover from the original creators of these tools, Next, Inc. Interface Builder files are now stored in an XML format called XML Interface Builder files, and their extension is `.xib`.

FILE'S OWNER AND CONTROLLER OBJECTS

A nib and its contents always have an owner. Whether it's an instance of `NSWindowController`, `UIViewController`, `NSDocument`, or any other object, the owner is the top-level object that serves as the primary point to which to wire the user interface elements found in the nib.

Generally speaking, File's Owner is intended to be a controller object (or, in the case of `NSDocument`, a model-controller). There can be and often are multiple controller objects within a single nib, any of which can provide outlets or actions.

ACTIONS AND OUTLETS

Two types of connections exist between your code and a nib's contents: actions and outlets. Both types of connection are established by drag and drop.

An *action* is a method that is called by a control in response to some form of user input; for example, a mouse click in OS X or a tap on the screen in iOS. Any given control's action requires two elements: the action itself and a target. Actions are defined in source code as follows:

```
- (IBAction)performSomeAction:(id)sender;
- (IBAction)performSomeOtherAction:(id)sender;
```

An *outlet* is an instance variable of an object (typically a controller or view object) that serves as a pointer to an element in a nib. Outlets are used to communicate with these objects. An example would be an outlet named `tableView` that points to an `NSTableView` instance that exists within a nib. The outlet could be used to ask the table view to refresh after some change to its underlying contents. Outlets are defined in source code as instance variables of a controller as follows:

```
IBOutlet NSTextField *titleField;
IBOutlet NSTableView *userListTable;
```

COMPARTMENTALIZATION

It's common for an application to have multiple xib files that contain portions of the UI. In all but the simplest applications, there are usually some parts of the application that the user won't access in every session, so it's not necessary to load every part of the UI every time the application is executed.

The first advantage of this approach is performance. Your application will save memory by loading only the parts of the interface that the user needs when they need it, which is a necessity on an iOS device. Since your application is creating controllers and their associated UI on demand, it takes less time to launch the application and reach a ready state for the user.

The second advantage is maintainability for the developer. By separating the user interface into distinct areas of responsibility, your application's architecture is clearer and more easily managed and navigable.

Seemingly flying in the face of compartmentalization is the concept of storyboards, which Apple introduced in Xcode 4.2, for working with iOS apps. A storyboard is a single document that allows you to define your iOS application views and the actions that connect them. Storyboards are covered in more detail later in this chapter.

GETTING FAMILIAR WITH INTERFACE BUILDER

FIGURE 7.1 Interface
Builder showing a nib

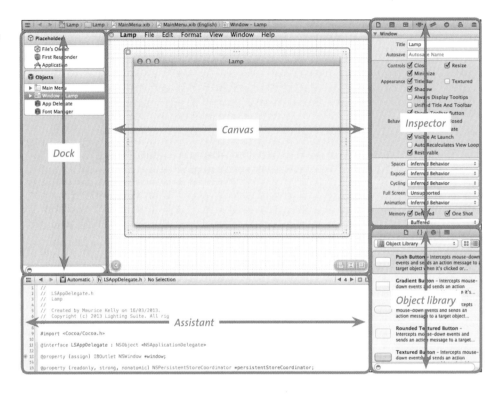

The Interface Builder tools in Xcode 4 consist of the editor, the Utility area (which includes a library of user interface elements and inspectors with which to configure them), the dock, and the Assistant for defining actions and outlets. **Figure 7.1** shows a project nib ready to edit in the Interface Builder editor. The Assistant and Utility area are also shown in Figure 7.1.

THE EDITOR AREA

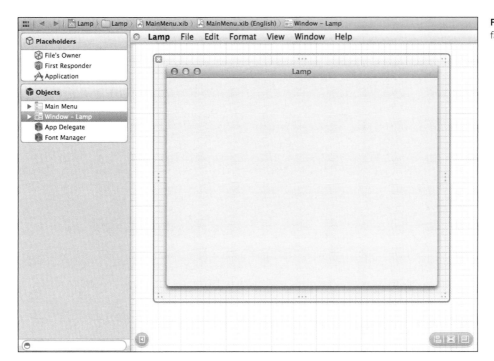

FIGURE 7.2 The Interface Builder editor area

The editor area (**Figure 7.2**) is where you construct the interface. This involves dragging interface elements from the Utility area's Object library into the canvas (the grid area) of the editor and sizing and positioning them as needed. You can also create interface elements and controller objects by dragging them into the dock, immediately to the left of the canvas.

The dock along the left side of the editor in Figure 7.2 is expanded to show more detail about the objects contained in the xib. The button at the bottom left of the editor is used to expand or collapse the dock. Only user interface elements (such as buttons and windows) can be dragged into the canvas. Instances of controllers or other classes that aren't part of the user interface can be created in the nib to serve as a connection point between the UI and your code; therefore, they exist only in the dock. To create these elements, you must drag them from the Object library and drop them directly into the dock area.

The jump bar follows the same hierarchy as the windows and views in the nib and represents the currently selected object.

OUTLET CONNECTIONS

Outlets are the means by which your code can send messages to items in the user interface. For those messages to be sent properly, you first need to establish a connection between your code—represented in Interface Builder by controller or other classes in the dock—and the interface elements.

FIGURE 7.3 The con-
nections window

You can make connections to outlets by holding down the Control key and dragging from the controller in which the outlet is defined to the desired interface element. The controller could be File's Owner (the controller to which the contents of the nib belong) or some other controller object instantiated in your nib. When you release the mouse on an interface element, Interface Builder will present a small pop-up menu containing a filtered list of valid outlets that you can connect to the interface element.

Alternatively, you can right-click the controller or object in the dock, causing Xcode to present a complete list of the object's outlets, the outlets of other objects that reference it, and actions the object can receive (**Figure 7.3**). Connections can be formed from this window by dragging a connection from the circle at the right of a given outlet to the target. To disconnect an outlet, click the X in the middle of the connection. Moving the mouse pointer over an established connection will highlight the connected item in the dock or in the editor area as appropriate.

ACTION CONNECTIONS

The other side of the communication between code and user interface is sending action messages from the user interface to the controller classes. You can make connections to actions by holding down the Control key and dragging from the interface element to the controller that defines the desired action. Alternatively, you can Control-drag from a user interface element in the dock to a controller object in the dock to achieve the same effect.

Right-clicking a user interface element in the dock will present a pop-up menu listing all the possible (and currently established) connections to and from the element.

More than one user interface element (such as a menu item) can be connected to a given action. The sender of the action is always passed along to the action, allowing you to respond differently depending on the sender or to query the sender for its state, such as whether a check box is selected or deselected.

THE UTILITY AREA

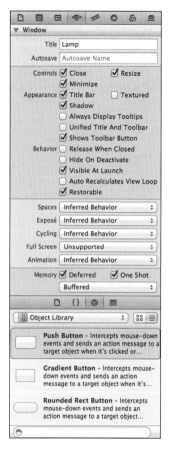

FIGURE 7.4 The Utility area showing available Interface Builder inspectors

When a nib is selected in the navigator, the Utility area (**Figure 7.4**) adds additional inspectors to the File and Quick Help panes, such as the control's style, auto-sizing settings, and animation settings. Select any element or controller object in the canvas or the dock to view or adjust its properties using the inspectors.

IDENTITY

The Identity inspector is most commonly used when assigning a custom class to a user interface element or a controller. Accessibility information can be added to UI elements here.

ATTRIBUTES

The Attributes inspector is frequently used when fine-tuning the behavior of user interface elements. Figure 7.4 shows available configurable attributes for the main window of the Lamp app. The range of options displayed here varies according to the element selected in the editor or dock. Note that not all attributes of a UI element can be configured here—some may be exposed only through code.

SIZE

The Size inspector (**Figure 7.5**) is an alternative means to control the position and dimensions of a user interface element. While the editor is suitable for most interface layouts, it may sometimes be necessary to delve into the Size inspector to fine-tune the pixels.

The appearance of the Size inspector will vary according to whether you are using traditional autosizing (using springs and struts) or the newfangled Auto Layout to control the positioning of your UI elements. We'll look at these in more detail later in the chapter.

> **TIP:** If you find yourself dipping into the Size inspector regularly just to check the positioning of your interface elements, then try this: click the element in the editor, hold the Option key, and move the mouse around the rest of the interface. Interface Builder will pop up guidelines showing distances between relative elements.

CONNECTIONS

The Connections inspector (**Figure 7.6**) shows the same information as the pop-up window that appears when you right-click an element in the editor or in the dock. While it may seem redundant, it can be useful to have this information presented in an inspector that does not disappear from the screen when you want to perform other actions (for example, adjusting the source file in the assistant before making a connection).

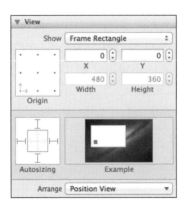

FIGURE 7.5 The Size inspector

FIGURE 7.6 The Connections inspector

BINDINGS

The Bindings inspector is present only for OS X nib files. Cocoa Bindings is a Cocoa Frameworks feature that allows user interface elements to be bound to controllers or other observable objects. When changes occur, the user interface elements can be updated automatically. For example, an `NSTableView` could be bound to an `NSArrayController`—when the underlying array is changed, the `NSTableView` can be automatically updated.

VIEW EFFECTS

The View Effects inspector is also present only for OS X nib files. It allows you to work with the selected user interface element's Core Animation properties and sub-elements. This inspector allows for quickly creating visual effects, but the details are beyond the scope of this book.

LIBRARIES

Below the inspectors is the Libraries pane. The Object library (**Figure 7.7**) contains a list of standard Cocoa objects as well as objects belonging to other frameworks and code libraries.

The pop-up at the top filters the list by SDK; the search field at the bottom filters by search term. Clicking once on an object provides a description of the object if one exists. Drag an object from the library to the canvas or the dock to add it to the nib (or to a specific view or window).

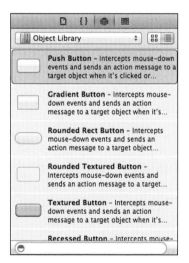

FIGURE 7.7 The Interface Builder Object library

THE ASSISTANT

```
13    @property (assign) IBOutlet NSWindow *window;
14
15    - (IBAction)saveAction:(id)sender;
```

As you learned in Chapter 2, the Assistant acts as a secondary editor that can display "counterparts" to the selected project member. In the case of a nib, the counterpart is the interface of the class represented by the File's Owner placeholder or that of a selected controller object.

In the past, adding actions and outlets required that you type them yourself. Using the Assistant with Interface Builder allows you to add actions and outlets by dragging a connection from a control directly into class interface source code. Xcode responds by inserting the appropriate source code for the action or outlet.

One handy behavior to note when using the assistant with Interface builder is the small circle in the gutter beside actions and outlets (**Figure 7.8**). This circle indicates the connection status of the action or outlet—an empty circle indicates that the item has not been connected, and a circle within the circle indicates that the item is connected. Hovering your mouse pointer over the connection indicator for a connected action or outlet will highlight the connected user interface element in the editor. Additionally, you can drag from a connection indicator to establish a new connection.

AVAILABLE ASSISTANT BEHAVIORS

Automatic behavior shows the files that Xcode considers to be the best choice for the selected item or view in the xib.

- *Top Level Objects* behavior shows the objects at the "top" of the nib's object hierarchy. This can include the windows and views as well as any instantiated objects (such as custom classes and ready-made object controllers).

- *Sent Actions* behavior shows any files containing actions called by the selected item.

- *Outlets and Referencing Outlets* behaviors show any files that contain outlets for the selected item or any files that are referenced by the selected item's outlets, respectively.

- *Class* behavior shows any file containing the class of the selected item.

ADDING USER INTERFACE ELEMENTS

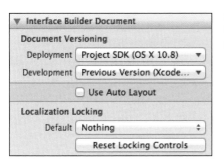

FIGURE 7.9 The Interface Builder Document file settings

Now that you're familiar with Interface Builder, you're ready to add some user interface elements to the apps of Lighting Suite. Since the OS X market for lighting apps is far from saturated, you'll start there.

To prepare, locate and select the `MainMenu.xib` file in the Project navigator. Click the window icon in the dock to open the application's main window in the canvas. Click the Assistant button so the Assistant area is visible, and make sure the Assistant is showing the `LSAppDelegate.h` file for the Lamp app. The project window should look similar to Figure 7.1.

For the sake of proving a point, select the File inspector in the Utility area, look for the section called Interface Builder Document, and deselect the Use Auto Layout check box (**Figure 7.9**).

ADDING AN ON-OFF SWITCH

Since your app is a lamp, you need to be able to switch it on and off. In the Object library in the Utility area, locate the Push Button control and drag it onto the window in the editor area. As you drag, you'll notice that Interface Builder displays blue guidelines when the button approaches the edges of a window, the center of a window, or other UI elements. These guidelines are not just visual—they are also Apple's guidelines for how user interfaces should be laid out. For now, drag the button to the lower-right corner of the window, and release it when it aligns with the guidelines (**Figure 7.10**).

Click the button to select it—or select it directly in the dock—and open the Attributes inspector in the Utility area. Note the Title attribute for the button—it should be named "Button." Double-click the button text, and change it from "Button" to "On." The Title attribute in the inspector should change to match.

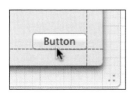

FIGURE 7.10 Positioning the button using guidelines

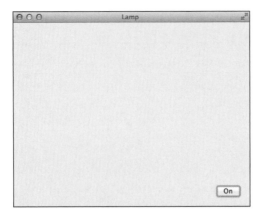

FIGURE 7.11 The bare-bones Lamp app

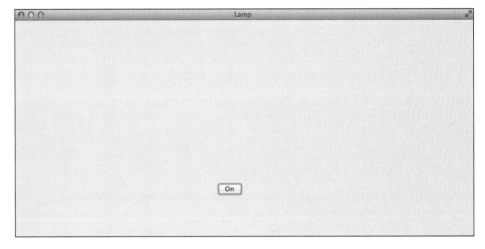

FIGURE 7.12 The On button that refuses to move

You have another requirement for your lamp—you'd like to be able to run it in full-screen mode so that you get that completely immersive, distraction-free lamp environment. From OS X Lion onward, this has become very easy. Select the Window element (Figure 7.4), and in the Attributes inspector use the Full Screen drop-down menu to choose the Primary Window option.

You're now ready to run for the first time. In the scheme selector control on the toolbar, select the Lamp scheme and the My Mac 64-bit run destination. Then click the Run button in the toolbar and watch as your app springs to life (**Figure 7.11**).

If you click the On button, you'll be dismayed to discover that nothing happens. This is because you have added it to the user interface but have not yet connected it to an action. If you click the Full Screen button on the right side of the title bar, the app should move into full-screen mode, but there's a slight problem—the On button stays in exactly the same position relative to the top and left edges of the window. This behavior also manifests when you resize the window in non-full-screen mode (**Figure 7.12**). The answer to this lies in the Size inspector.

USING SPRINGS AND STRUTS

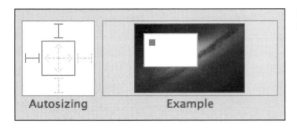

FIGURE 7.13 The Autosizing control

When you turned off Auto Layout, the nib reverted to using the older auto-resizing style of element layout, also known as "springs and struts." The springs and struts concept has been around since the earliest days of Cocoa. It's not without its frustrations, but for pre-iOS 6 and pre-OS X 10.7 applications, it still reigns.

The concept is simple: Views (custom views, tables, buttons, and so on) are contained within a "superview" and may be resized or moved around if the superview is resized. Internal springs dictate whether the view will be stretched or compressed vertically and horizontally relative to its superview. External struts dictate whether the left, right, top, and bottom edges of the view maintain a certain distance from the bounds of the superview or are free to float around.

Figure 7.13 shows the Autosizing control, found in the Size inspector—the On button is selected in this case. The springs are shown in the inner box (the vertical and horizontal red lines with arrows on their ends); the struts are the outer red lines. The selected (active) springs and struts are a solid, brighter red; the inactive ones are lightly shaded. Clicking any spring or strut will toggle it active or inactive. The Example control, on the right, animates and shows how the view (the red rectangle) would behave relative to its superview (the enclosing white rectangle).

Note the settings for the On button. Only the top and left struts are active, indicating that the top and left edges of the button will maintain the same distance from the bounds of its superview (the window's content view) and that the button will not resize vertically or horizontally. This is exactly the case in Figure 7.12; the button will remain stubbornly stationary even when the window becomes larger or smaller.

You can solve this fairly easily. Deselect the top and left struts—the Example control will animate and show that the button will remain in the center of its enclosing view. This is not what you want, so instead select the bottom and right struts and note the effect in the Example control—it should indicate that the button will remain in the lower-right corner of its enclosing view. This is exactly what you want, so save the nib, re-run the application, and try resizing the window. Everything good? Now let's make it even easier.

USING AUTO LAYOUT

Auto Layout was introduced with OS X Lion (10.7) and iOS 6. Xcode now opts to use Auto Layout by default, so if you're working with older target platforms (OS X 10.6 or iOS 5), then you'll need to disable it (as you did earlier in this chapter). So far Auto Layout has received a mixed response—it's fair to say that it doesn't always work exactly the way you might expect—but it is worth trying out if only to determine that it's not for you.

To re-enable Auto Layout for Lamp, open the File inspector for the nib and select the Use Auto Layout check box (Figure 7.9). You'll notice something different immediately. **Figure 7.14** shows the new Constraints entries in Interface Builder's Objects dock. Constraints are real objects, just like buttons and windows. They define the sizing and positioning behavior of the controls they constrain. Because they're real objects, you can select, configure, or remove them in Interface Builder the same as you would a button or a window.

NOTE: Automatically added constraints have a purple icon in the dock, whereas manually added constraints (known as "user constraints") have a blue icon. You can convert an automatic constraint to a manual one by editing it in the Attributes inspector.

Figure 7.15 shows a Vertical Space constraint selected—you can do this by clicking the constraint itself in the editor or by clicking the name of the constraint in the dock (often an easier way in complex interfaces). This constraint manages the vertical space between the On button and its superview's bottom border. With Auto Layout, dragging controls into a window or view and snapping them to the guides will automatically create the constraints that the system determined appropriate for best positioning.

Constraints have properties that you can adjust in the Attributes inspector in the Utility area. For example, if you select the On button's Vertical Space constraint, you'll see the settings in the Attributes inspector (**Figure 7.16**).

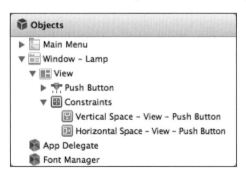

FIGURE 7.14 Constraint objects added to the document

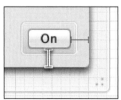

FIGURE 7.15 A Vertical Space constraint selected

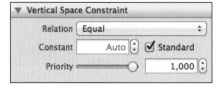

FIGURE 7.16 Constraint settings in the Utility area

FIGURE 7.17 Overlapping buttons

Try running Lamp now that Auto Layout is enabled, and verify that it has the same effects as the springs and struts you used to use.

> **TIP:** For details about the Auto Layout system, including the types of constraints and which ones are best for a given scenario, see the Cocoa Auto Layout Guide at http://xcodebook.com/autolayoutguide.

Constraints are not just used to pin controls to specific areas of your user interface—they can also be used to maintain the spacing between controls. To give yourself proper recognition for your achievements in writing Lamp, it is only fair to add a button to display the credits for the app. Drag and drop a Push Button control from the Object library, and use the guidelines to position it at the bottom left of the window. Rename the button title **Credits**.

Run the app, and try resizing the window to a very narrow width. You should observe an effect like that shown in **Figure 7.17**, where the buttons are able to overlap or even disappear. To overcome this, you need to manually add a constraint that specifies a minimum width between the two buttons.

You can add constraints manually by choosing Editor > Pin from the main menu and selecting the desired type of constraint. We won't explore each of these exhaustively here, but it's important to note the variety of constraint types available: width, height, horizontal and vertical spacing, leading space to superview, top and bottom space to superview, equal widths and heights, and more. You can also create constraints to align interface elements by choosing Editor > Align from the main menu and then choosing the type. For example, you might create a constraint that aligns the left edges of buttons so that they appear uniform onscreen.

FIGURE 7.18 Quick constraint buttons

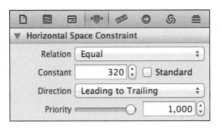

FIGURE 7.19 A Horizontal Space constraint

Constraints can also be added by means of a set of three buttons that will have appeared in the bottom right of the editor when you re-enabled Auto Layout (**Figure 7.18**). The first button presents the equivalent of the Editor > Align menu, the second button presents the equivalent of the Editor > Pin menu, and the third button determines how constraints react to resizing user interface elements in the editor—you can elect to have constraints apply to siblings and ancestors of the selected view, to descendants of the selected view, or to both.

To maintain the spacing between the two buttons in the Lamp interface, select both buttons and then choose Editor > Pin > Horizontal Spacing from the main menu. The resulting Horizontal Space constraint (**Figure 7.19**) will prevent the buttons from getting any closer but will also stop them from moving farther apart, so you will need to edit the new constraint to suit. You want to maintain a minimum distance between the buttons, so choose either Greater Than or Equal from the Relation menu, and enter **100** in the Constant field.

Run the app again, and try narrowing the window now—you should not be able to get the buttons any closer than 100 pixels.

MAKING CONNECTIONS

Your app is now Auto Layout-enabled and can be resized or put into full-screen mode without the UI getting messed up, but it still doesn't really do anything. Pressing the On or Credits button has no effect, because they are sitting in the nib file in isolation—they have no connection to anything.

For a control to do something, you need to give it an action connection. Ensure that the LSAppDelegate.h file is displayed in the Assistant editor. Control-drag a connection from the button over the source code in the Assistant, releasing where you want the code to be dropped. For best results, place the action after the - (IBAction)saveAction:sender; line and before the @end directive, as in **Figure 7.20**.

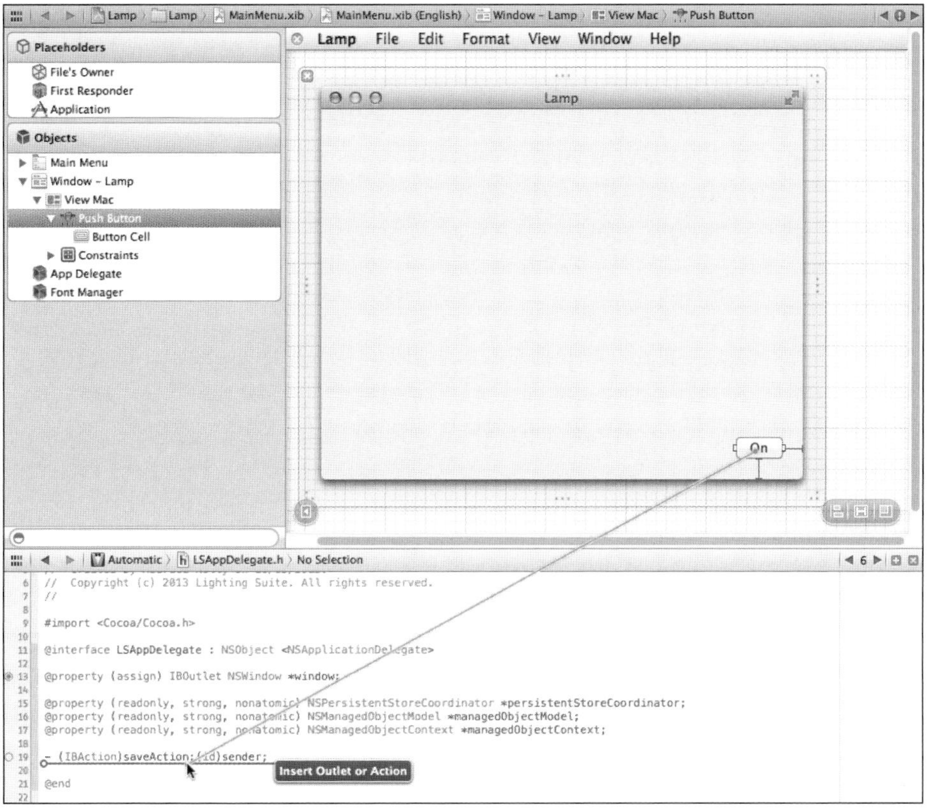

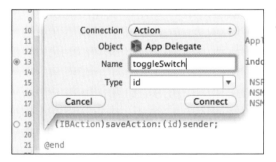

FIGURE 7.20 Dragging a connection into the Assistant

FIGURE 7.21 The connection creator pop-up window

A pop-up will appear (**Figure 7.21**). Make sure the Action connection type is selected, and then type **toggleSwitch** in the Name field. The method name should actually be toggleSwitch: (with a colon), but Xcode will add the colon for you automatically. Press Return or click Connect to add the action. Note that there is a connection indicator circle in the gutter beside your new -toggleSwitch: method; if you hover the mouse pointer over the connection indicator circle, the On button becomes highlighted in the editor.

FIGURE 7.22 Changing the Class attribute to LSView

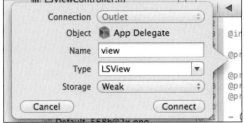

FIGURE 7.23 Creating a connection to the LSView instance

To make your rudimentary Lamp application switch on and off, you need to change the color of the background. Back in Chapter 5 you created a custom NSView subclass named LSView that has the ability to do this, but there is no instance of LSView in your user interface. Fortunately, Interface Builder allows you to use the Identity inspector to set a custom class for user interface elements. Click the view in the editor, and open the Identity inspector. Change the Class attribute under Custom Class to **LSView** (**Figure 7.22**).

There's just one thing missing—a way for the LSAppDelegate class to send a message to the LSView. For that you'll need to create an outlet that connects LSAppDelegate and LSView. Control-drag a connection from the main view to the LSAppDelegate.h file, and name the resulting outlet **view** (**Figure 7.23**).

This will cause a compilation error because the LSAppDelegate class does not yet have visibility of your LSView class. To resolve this, add the following to the top of the file:

```
#import "LSView.h"
```

Now that you have a working connection to the view, you can open the LSAppDelegate.m file and update the -toggleSwitch: method to update the view based on the state of the switch. It also takes advantage of the fact that the action sends a reference to the control that triggered it to check the existing state of the button and change the label.

```
- (IBAction)toggleSwitch:(id)sender
{
    if ([sender isKindOfClass:[NSButton class]]) {
        NSButton *button = (NSButton *)sender;
        if (button.state == NSOffState) {
            [self.view switchLamp:NO];
            button.title = @"On";
        }
        else {
            [self.view switchLamp:YES];
            button.title = @"Off";
        }
    }
}
```

FIGURE 7.24 Template-defined actions for File's Owner (NSApplication)

That just leaves the Credits button to connect. A default Mac app template comes with a lot of predefined actions that you can take advantage of. One of those actions displays the standard About window for an app (usually accessed by selecting Lamp > About Lamp from the main menu). To do the same from your Credits button, Control-drag a connection from the button to File's Owner in the dock. A list of available actions will be displayed in a pop-up menu (**Figure 7.24**)—choose the action named orderFrontStandardAboutPanel.

> **TIP:** If you want to change the credits, they are defined in a file named Credits.rtf, accessible through the Project navigator by opening the Supporting Files group.

All your connections have been made, and the app is now ready to test. Run it, turn it on and off, and have fun with it.

STORYBOARDS

Interface Builder offers an extra feature that makes your life as an iOS apps developer just a little bit easier. Unlike Mac apps, which often consist of a central window in which most of the work is carried out, iOS apps tend to have many smaller, interconnected views. When each view existed in its own nib file, it was hard to visualize the experience the user would have when navigating the app.

Storyboards were introduced to give developers the ability to manage most of the application's views in one Interface Builder file. The advantage to this approach is that it also allows the developer to visually define the relationships between views by using the concept of segues. In this section, you will quickly bring your Flashlight app nearly to feature parity with Lamp, and then add a Credits screen for the app.

FIGURE 7.25 Interface
Builder displaying a
storyboard file

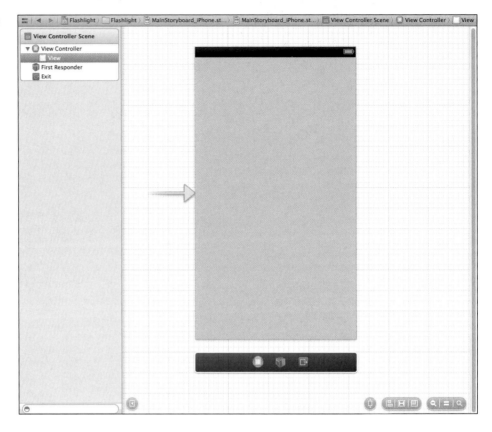

First, you'll need to open the storyboard file, so look in the Flashlight project for the file
named `MainStoryboard_iPhone.storyboard`. Select the file to open it, and you should see a
familiar Interface Builder view (**Figure 7.25**). You are now looking at an iOS project, but with
two things to note.

First, the dock area no longer displays two sections (Placeholders and Objects). Instead,
there is one section (View Controller Scene). In storyboard parlance, an interface screen in
your app is called a *scene*; when you later add an extra scene, there will be another section in
the dock.

The second difference is that there is a large arrow pointing "into" the first (and only)
scene. This is the entry point of this storyboard—if you ever want to change the entry point
of a storyboard, this arrow can be dragged into place.

ADDING THE UI

As with the Lamp app, you want a button to switch Flashlight on and off. Open the Object library, search for a Round Rect Button object, and drag it onto the lower-right corner of the main view, using the guidelines. Double-click the button's title, and change it from Button to **On**.

> **TIP:** By default, the view is set up with the dimensions of a 4" iPhone screen. On iPhone-targeted storyboards, along the bottom edge of the editor window there is a button to the left of the constraint controls that will toggle the view between 4" and 3.5" dimensions. Use it regularly to make sure your interface behaves appropriately on all devices.

Open the Assistant editor to the LSViewController.h file, and Control-drag a connection from the On button into the Assistant editor. In the pop-up window, set the connection type to Action, and set the name to **toggleSwitch**. Additionally, you need to have an outlet connection to the button so that you can set up an initial state for it. Control-drag another connection, and this time set the connection type to Outlet and the name to **button**.

You should now have a method definition in the header file for -toggleSwitch, a property in the header file for button, and an empty method in the LSViewController.m implementation file for -toggleSwitch:. Open the implementation file, and fill out the new method as follows:

```
- (IBAction)toggleSwitch:(id)sender
{
   if (sender == self.button) {
      if (self.button.selected) {
         self.view.backgroundColor = [UIColor blackColor];
         [self.button setTitle:@"On" forState:UIControlStateNormal];
         self.button.selected = NO;
      }
      else {
         self.view.backgroundColor = [UIColor whiteColor];
         [self.button setTitle:@"Off" forState:UIControlStateNormal];
         self.button.selected = YES;
      }
   }
}
```

In the scheme selector, select the Flashlight scheme and the iPhone 6.1 Simulator run destination. Run the application. Unfortunately, it starts with Flashlight on (white screen), and the initial button state does not seem to match. You've got some debugging to do, but we'll conveniently save that for Chapter 9.

WORKING WITH SCENES AND SEGUES

Your Flashlight app has almost the same features as its Mac sibling, but it is currently missing the Credits button. You want that same sense of validation in Flashlight, so you need to create a new scene in your storyboard and then create a segue between the existing scene and the Credits scene.

CREATING A NEW SCENE

Open the Object library, and drag a View Controller object over to the storyboard canvas. As the mouse moves over the canvas, it will expand to show a full view controller that you can place where you see fit. To keep a sense of flow through your app, it would make sense to place the new view controller to the right of the existing controller (**Figure 7.26**).

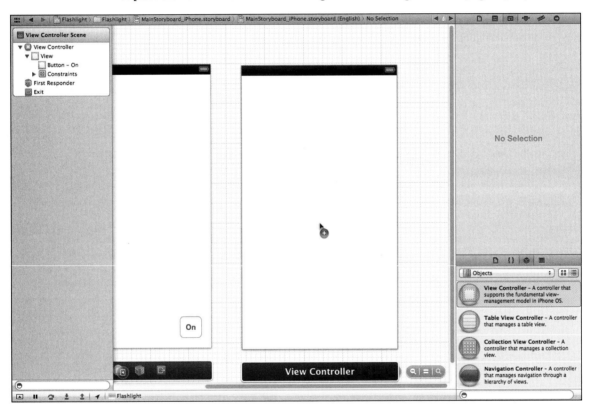

FIGURE 7.26 Adding a new view controller to the storyboard

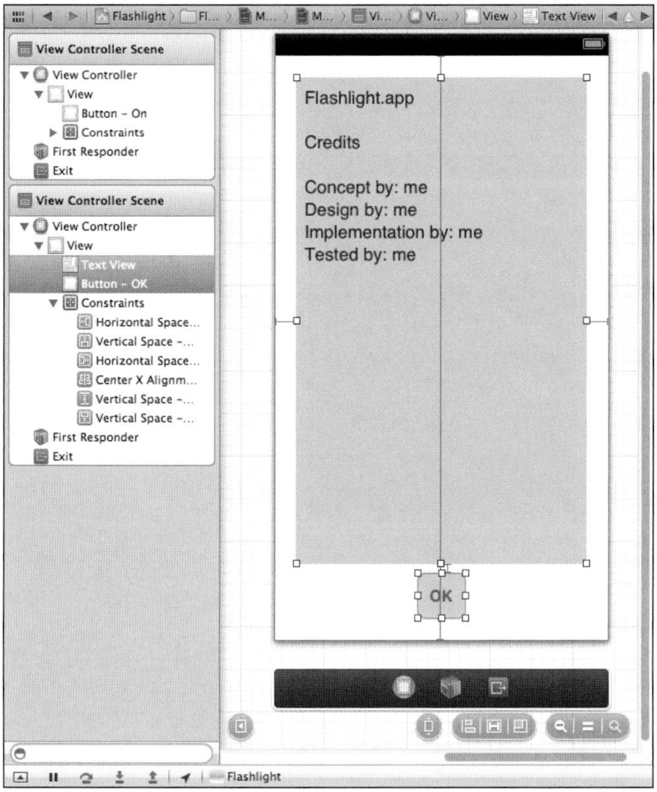

FIGURE 7.27 The fully assembled Credits scene

To add the credits, return to the Object library and drag a Text View object onto the new scene. Position and size it so that it aligns with the guidelines on the top, left, and right, but leave some space at the bottom. To return from this scene, you need another button; drag a Round Rect Button object onto the view, place it at the bottom of the Credits scene (using the bottom guideline), and align it on the center guideline also. Pull the bottom of the text view down until a guideline appears between it and the button. Double-click the text view to enter some text (press Option-Return to insert new lines), and then open the Attributes inspector and deselect the Behavior attribute so that the control is non-editable. Change the button title to **OK**. The result should resemble **Figure 7.27**.

CREATING A SEGUE BETWEEN SCENES

Before creating a segue, you need a UI control to which it can be attached. In this case, drag a Round Rect Button object from the Object library onto the primary scene, and change the name from Button to **Credits**.

FIGURE 7.28
Control-dragging to
create a segue

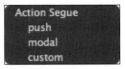

FIGURE 7.29 Segue type
selection

FIGURE 7.30 The Storyboard
Segue attributes

To create a segue, just Control-drag from the Credits button over to the newly created scene; when the scene is highlighted in blue, release (**Figure 7.28**). A small pop-up menu should appear—choose Modal from the available options (**Figure 7.29**). The segue will be created and an arrow will appear between the two scenes, indicating that they are now connected.

Click the arrow between the two scenes, and open the Attributes inspector to see the segue attributes (**Figure 7.30**). You're not required to define a name for a segue, but if you plan to use it programmatically, it's important to name it here. You can also change the style (which you set to Modal) and how it transitions into view. If you select the Push style or the Custom style, the options will be different.

Before you can declare the app complete, you need a way to get back from the Credits scene. You could connect a regular action to the OK button and dismiss the modal view controller, but when you're working with storyboards there is another option. You might have noticed that each scene has a green Exit icon in the dock. If your controller has a special action type defined, you can connect your OK button to it to exit the Credits scene.

Open the `LSViewController.m` file, and add the following code:

```
- (IBAction)returnFromCredits:(UIStoryboardSegue *)segue
{
}
```

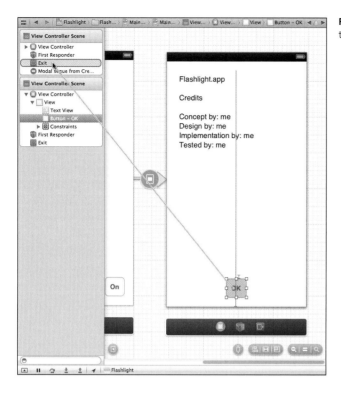

FIGURE 7.31 Unwinding the segue

This is an empty method, but you can add code to it to be executed on return. Return to the storyboard, and Control-drag from the OK button in the Credits scene over to the Exit button in the Flashlight scene (**Figure 7.31**). When you release the mouse, a pop-up menu will list the `returnFromCredits:` method. Click to select it, and note that a new icon appears in the dock of the Credits scene—the icon is labeled "Unwind segue from OK to Exit."

You are ready to try the segue interaction—run the app, press the Credits button, read them, and then click OK to return to your regular Flashlight activities.

WRAPPING UP

Although it is possible to use Xcode to write non-GUI applications, and it's also possible to write GUI applications completely in code, it is rare for developers not to spend a significant portion of their time in Interface Builder. This chapter has been a long but hopefully valuable trip through its features.

It is worth spending some time to experiment thoroughly with Interface Builder before progressing to the next chapter, where you will delve into the world of creating and editing Core Data models.

Creating Core
Data Models

Xcode comes with an integrated data model editor tool. In this chapter, you'll learn how to use the data modeler to give your application the ability to create, manage, manipulate, save, and load its data with a minimal amount of code.

INTRODUCING CORE DATA

A data model gives your application a well-defined structure for managing and persisting its data. The model corresponds with the Model layer of the Model-View-Controller design pattern. There are a number of ways to manage your application's model layer, but Apple has created a solution that works well in many situations: Core Data. This facility is well integrated with Xcode.

Apple is very careful to specify Core Data as an "object graph management and persistence framework." Although the framework shares much in common with a relational database, it is important to note that it is *not* intended to act as one. Core Data is primarily focused on the needs of desktop and mobile applications (though it can be used in server applications as well, provided care is taken to manage it properly).

The framework provides standard persistent store types (binary, SQLite, and XML) and can be extended with custom store types. The minimum requirement the developer must supply is a managed object model, which describes the application's entities (such as Person, Group, Account, or BlogPost) and their relationships to one another, if any. With this model and UI to manipulate it, Core Data is smart enough to handle managing, saving, and loading your application's data without you having to write a single line of code. In practice, however, a moderately complex application will need further customization.

There are a few key concepts you'll need to understand to use this API and its related Xcode features.

NOTE: Throughout the rest of this chapter, the term *model* can be assumed to refer to a Core Data managed object model.

MANAGED OBJECT MODELS

A managed object model (MOM) is Core Data's facility for describing the application's data model. It can be described in code but is most often built with the Data Model editor. When you create a project from a template that uses Core Data, all the necessary code is included, as well as an empty MOM file that shares the application's name. For Lighting Suite, only Lamp.app uses Core Data, so the MOM file is Lamp.xcdatamodeld. The extension, xcdatamodeld, stands for "Xcode Core Data model directory" and designates that a folder holds a versioned set of data models for your application.

PERSISTENT STORES

A persistent store is the on-disk representation of the data created with your managed object model. Core Data supports three store types by default: XML, SQLite, and binary. Each store type has its advantages and disadvantages (see the Core Data documentation for details). Additionally, Core Data supports developer-implemented custom store types. The managed object model does not care about how (or even if) the data is persisted in a store.

Developers new to Core Data sometimes confuse the model with a data store created using the model. Some even look for a way to browse (in Xcode) the data they put into a store with their application. It's important to understand that the data created in your application is not stored in the managed object model but rather in a store.

ENTITIES

Entities represent your model objects. *Entity* in this context means the same as it does in relational databases. It is a description of a type of object and its properties. In Core Data terminology, a *managed object* is an *instance* of an entity.

When an entity is selected in the editor, containers appear that allow you to add attributes, relationships, and fetched properties.

An attribute requires, at minimum, a name (such as `shortDesc` or `dueDate`) and a type (such as a string or a number). A relationship requires a name (such as `categories`) and a destination entity (such as `Category`) and can be a one-to-one or one-to-many relationship. Relationships also need an *inverse*—a corresponding relationship defined in the destination entity.

Xcode is fussy about capitalization—entities must begin with an uppercase letter, and attributes, relationships, and fetched properties must begin with a lowercase letter. Try to break these rules and you will get told off!

MANAGED OBJECT CONTEXTS

A managed object context can be thought of as a "scratch pad," a context in which managed objects are created or pulled from a persistent store, potentially modified, and potentially saved back to the store. To work with Core Data, you must have at least one context.

You may have multiple contexts to keep sets of changes separate. For example, a desktop application might create a separate context for an "import" task that runs in the background while the user continues using the existing data. A server application might have one context for each session (connected user) to isolate their activities until they're ready to "commit" any additions, changes, or deletions they may have made.

Separate contexts are merged using one of several available merge policies that dictate how conflicting changes are to be handled. The merged contexts can then be persisted to the store. In the case of the import example, the contexts can be merged (and persisted) when the import completes successfully, revealing the newly imported data to the user in the main user interface.

USING THE DATA MODEL EDITOR

FIGURE 8.1 A simple MOM in the Data Model editor

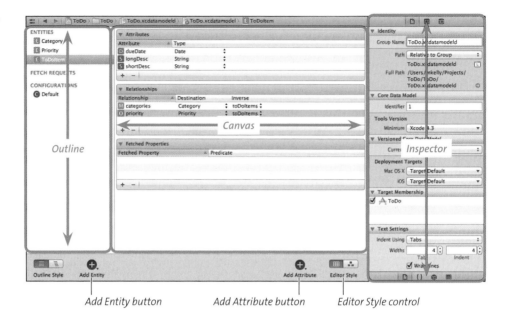

Add Entity button   Add Attribute button   Editor Style control

When you select an `.xcdatamodeld` file in the Project navigator, the file opens in the Data Model editor (**Figure 8.1**). The editor is separated into two main areas: the outline and the editor area. The jump bar reflects the model's hierarchy, and the Utility area, when visible, shows the details of the selected items in the Data Model inspector.

The outline represents the entities, fetch requests, and configurations of the MOM. New entities, fetch requests, and configurations can be added by pressing and holding the Add Entity (+) button in the bottom toolbar or by choosing from the Editor > Add options in the main menu. These items can be deleted by selecting them and pressing Delete.

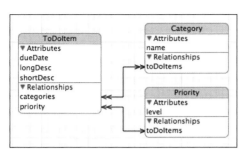

FIGURE 8.2 A MOM in the model graph mode

FIGURE 8.3 The Data Model inspector

The editor has two primary styles: table and graph. You can switch between the styles using the Editor Style control. Table mode is what you see in Figure 8.1. Graph mode is shown in **Figure 8.2** and represents the relationships and inheritance of the model. When using the graph editor style, you will need to use the Utility area to edit entities and their attributes and relationships.

Attributes can be created for an entity by selecting the entity in the outline and then clicking the Add Attribute (+) button in the toolbar below. Press and hold the button to display a pop-up menu that allows the creation of relationships and fetched properties. If you are working in the table editor, the individual Attributes, Relationships, and Fetched Properties sections all feature their own Add (+) and Remove (−) buttons.

When you're creating a new relationship, there are three important factors to consider: the destination entity for the relationship, the inverse relationship, and the type of relationship (shown as an M or an O to the left of the relationship name). The destination entity and the inverse relationship can be selected directly in the table editor, but for fine-grained control of a relationship, you need to visit the Data Model inspector in the Utility area (**Figure 8.3**).

Figure 8.3 shows a relationship named *priority*, whose destination is an entity called Priority—it might seem unoriginal, but it's helpful to keep the relationship names as descriptive as possible. The inverse relationship has been set to a relationship named *toDoItems*, already defined on the destination entity. In this model, a ToDoItem entity can be related to only one Priority entity, so the To-Many Relationship check box is not selected.

CREATING A BASIC DATA MODEL FOR LAMP

Now that you've toured the Data Model editor, you're ready to expand Lamp's capabilities by adding a simple data model. For this example, the goal is simply to keep track of when the lamp is turned on and off—a lamp log, if you will.

PLANNING

We'll need an Event entity with two attributes: a time stamp and the lamp state. Core Data supports native date and Boolean objects, so nothing special needs to be done there. We want the objects to be created anytime we switch the lamp on or off.

BUILDING THE MODEL

To create the Event entity, navigate to the `Lamp.xcdatamodeld` file. Click the Add Entity button. An entity will be added with a default name of Entity, ready to be renamed. Type **Event** and press Return to rename the entity.

Add the `timeStamp` attribute by clicking the Add (+) button in the Attributes table in the editor. Change the attribute name to **timeStamp**, and set its type to Date. Add another attribute, and name it **switchedOn**; set its type to Boolean. The MOM should now look like **Figure 8.4**.

FIGURE 8.4 Lamp's managed object model

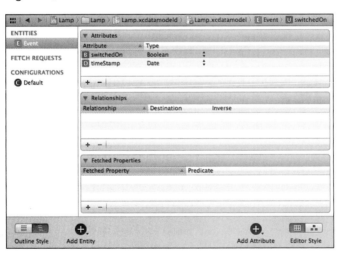

Now that the model is defined, you can use it from your application code. When you created the Lamp project back in Chapter 4, you selected the option Use Core Data. As a result, an empty model was created for you (which you've already used), and some boilerplate code for instantiating and using the model was added to the `LSAppDelegate` class. You can take advantage of that now to make a straightforward change to the action that is executed when the On/Off button is clicked in the user interface.

Open the `LSAppDelegate.m` file and navigate to the `-toggleSwitch:` method you created in Chapter 7. Replace the entire method with the following code:

```
- (IBAction)toggleSwitch:(id)sender
{
   if ([sender isKindOfClass:[NSButton class]]) {
      NSButton *button = (NSButton *)sender;
      NSManagedObject *event =
         [NSEntityDescription
         insertNewObjectForEntityForName:@"Event"
         inManagedObjectContext:self.managedObjectContext];
      [event setValue:[NSDate date] forKey:@"timeStamp"];
      if (button.state == NSOffState) {
         [self.view switchLamp:NO];
         button.title = @"On";
         [event setValue:@(NO) forKey:@"switchedOn"];
      }
      else {
         [self.view switchLamp:YES];
         button.title = @"Off";
         [event setValue:@(YES) forKey:@"switchedOn"];
      }
   }
}
```

The change is simple. Before switching the lamp on or off, an `NSManagedObject` is created using the Event entity as a template, and its `timeStamp` field is updated with the current time. At the point where the lamp state is switched, the `switchedOn` field for the Event entity is filled in.

Run the app, switch the lamp on and off a few times, and then press Command+Q to quit the app (this uses some of the boilerplate code mentioned earlier to save the events to disk). Using the Finder, navigate to the home directory, then to the Library folder, and then to the Application Support directory. Find and open your application-specific directory using the bundle ID you set up when creating the application—in our example, this is named `com.lightingsuite.lamp`.

Within the directory should be a file named `Lamp.storedata`, which you can open in your favorite text editor. The contents of this file is your Core Data store in an XML-based format—it's a tough read, but your event logs are all there.

> **TIP:** Apple decided to hide the Library folder in Mountain Lion. In the Finder, press Command+Shift+G, type `~/Library`, and press Return to get back to it temporarily. To restore it permanently, execute `chflags nohidden ~/Library` at the Terminal prompt.

GENERATING SUBCLASSES

In the previous section, you added some code that created a generic NSManagedObject based on the Event entity type. To access the attributes of the Event entity, you used Key-Value Coding (KVC)—if you're not familiar with KVC, it was the setValue:ForKey: code.

While this was convenient for quick access, using KVC in this way has its disadvantages. In a complex application with many different types of entities, it becomes more difficult to remember the attribute names for all the entities, and typing errors can go unchecked, potentially leading to crashes at runtime. When you start passing large numbers of generic NSManagedObjects around, it becomes more difficult to determine what type of entity you are working with, and you could end up using KVC on properties that simply don't exist.

Fortunately, Xcode provides a quick means to generate a subclass of NSManagedObject from an entity defined in your data model. To create an Event class, select the Event entity in the Data Model editor, and then select Editor > Create NSManagedObject Subclass from the main menu. A Save dialog will appear (**Figure 8.5**), allowing you to choose the group that the class files will appear under in the Project navigator, as well as the targets that the new class will be built with. The "Use scalar properties for primitive data types" check box allows you to use primitives (such as float or double) but requires additional work on your part, so it is better to leave this option unselected unless you know you need it.

FIGURE 8.5 Save options for a generated subclass of NSManagedObject

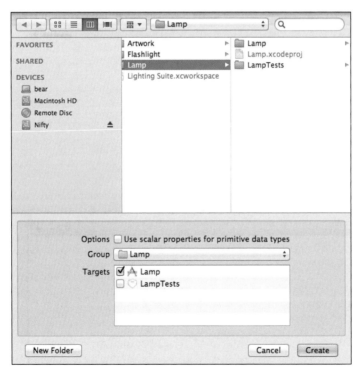

When you click Create, Xcode will produce two new files: `Event.h` and `Event.m`. To simplify the event logging code in `LSAppDelegate.m`, add the following import to the head of the file:

```
#import "Event.h"
```

Change the `-toggleSwitch:` method to read as follows:

```
- (IBAction)toggleSwitch:(id)sender
{
    if ([sender isKindOfClass:[NSButton class]]) {
        NSButton *button = (NSButton *)sender;
        Event *event =
            (Event *)[NSEntityDescription
            insertNewObjectForEntityForName:@"Event"
            inManagedObjectContext:self.managedObjectContext];
        event.timeStamp = [NSDate date];
        if (button.state == NSOffState) {
            [self.view switchLamp:NO];
            button.title = @"On";
            event.switchedOn = @(NO);
        }
        else {
            [self.view switchLamp:YES];
            button.title = @"Off";
            event.switchedOn = @(YES);
        }
    }
}
```

Note that the entity creation code now casts to an Event type, and where the event instance is used, properties are set directly rather than using KVC. This gives you the safety of type checking and the convenience of code-completion.

ENCAPSULATION

One of the key principles of object-oriented programming is encapsulation, or "information hiding." There are some aspects of the event logging process that could be safely abstracted away from the `-toggleSwitch:` method; namely, the creation of the event (with that ugly cast) and the addition of the timestamp.

The Event class that Xcode generated from the Event entity is completely customizable, so it makes sense to start hiding some of your Event-specific code in there. Open `Event.h`, and create a method declaration as follows:

```
+ (Event *)eventInManagedObjectContext:(NSManagedObjectContext *)moc;
```

Now open Event.m, and add the method implementation as follows:

```
+ (Event *)eventInManagedObjectContext:(NSManagedObjectContext *)moc
{
    Event *event = (Event *)[NSEntityDescription
        insertNewObjectForEntityForName:@"Event"
        inManagedObjectContext:moc];
    event.timeStamp = [NSDate date];
    return event;
}
```

With the extra functionality in the Event class, you can open LSAppDelegate.m and modify -toggleSwitch: to read as follows:

```
- (IBAction)toggleSwitch:(id)sender
{
    if ([sender isKindOfClass:[NSButton class]]) {
        NSButton *button = (NSButton *)sender;
        Event *event =
            [Event eventInManagedObjectContext:self.managedObjectContext];
        if (button.state == NSOffState) {
            [self.view switchLamp:NO];
            button.title = @"On";
            event.switchedOn = @(NO);
        }
        else {
            [self.view switchLamp:YES];
            button.title = @"Off";
            event.switchedOn = @(YES);
        }
    }
}
```

There is one thing to be aware of when you put custom code in a generated subclass: If you were to add a new attribute to the Event entity and try to regenerate the subclass, it will overwrite the existing files, wiping out your custom code.

You can avoid this by planning your entities well, minimizing the need for changes later. When you inevitably do need to add an attribute (or even multiple attributes), you can select one or more and then choose Edit > Copy from the main menu. Open the implementation for the generated subclass, place the cursor at the point in the source file where you want the accessor to be inserted, and then choose Edit > Paste Attribute Implementation. Xcode will generate and insert valid accessor code in the desired location. You can repeat the process for the header file (the menu item will be Paste Attribute Interface in that case). This can also work for relationships and fetched properties.

> **TIP:** If you find yourself doing this a lot, you may want to investigate the integration of a tool like mogenerator (http://rentzsch.github.io/mogenerator/) to help with the generation and management of NSManagedObject subclasses.

WRAPPING UP

Core Data is a complex Cocoa topic, and you've only scratched the surface of creating a very simple data model with Xcode. For more information, refer to Apple's online guide Getting Started with Core Data, at http://developer.apple.com/library/mac/#referencelibrary/ GettingStarted/GettingStartedWithCoreData/index.html.

In the next chapter, you'll learn how to debug and analyze your work.

CHAPTER 9

Debugging Your Applications

Xcode provides a comprehensive set of well-integrated tools to approach the tasks of debugging and analyzing your applications. In this chapter, you'll learn how to use Xcode's built-in debugger and static analyzer. In Chapter 15, you'll learn more advanced debugging techniques.

INTERACTIVE DEBUGGING

For runtime debugging, Xcode now integrates the LLDB debugger by default. This replaces the Gnu Debugger (GDB), which will be deprecated in future versions of the tool chain, though it is still available for die-hard fans and is configured through the build system (see Chapter 13). Xcode provides a UI for managing breakpoints, controlling program execution, exploring the threads and stacks of the running application, accessing the debugger console, and more.

By default, all newly created Xcode projects run in the debugger. The application will pause at the point of failure if it crashes, or at any breakpoints you set if they're encountered. The Debug area (**Figure 9.1**) appears when you're running an application with a debugger attached. The current line of code is highlighted with a green arrow in the Source editor gutter.

NOTE: Whether or not a debugger is attached to the running application is controlled by the active scheme. Schemes are covered in Chapter 13.

USING THE DEBUG BAR

The basic program execution controls—including Step Into, Step Over, and Continue—and the Threads and Stacks navigator are located in the Debug bar (**Figure 9.2**) at the top of the Debug area. You can pause a program (or trigger other actions in Xcode) by setting breakpoints. You can navigate threads and stacks using the navigation pop-up.

FIGURE 9.2
The Debug bar

USING THE BASIC CONTROLS

- ▲ / ▼ The Show/Hide button shows or hides the Debug area.

- ‖ / ▶ The Pause/Continue button pauses and resumes program execution. The keyboard shortcut for this action is Control+Command+Y.

- ↻ The Step Over button executes the currently highlighted instruction while execution is paused. If the instruction is a routine, the routine is executed and the debugger stops at the next instruction in the current file. The keyboard shortcut is F6.

- ↓ The Step Into button executes the currently highlighted instruction while execution is paused. If the instruction is a routine, the debugger moves on to the first line of that routine and pauses. The keyboard shortcut is F7.

- ↑ The Step Out button finishes the current routine and jumps back to the calling routine or next instruction after the routine was called. The keyboard shortcut is F8.

You can find additional debugger actions under the Product > Debug submenu of the main menu.

> **TIP:** Holding Control or Control+Shift while clicking the step buttons will vary the functionality of the buttons. You can step through assembly instructions or through only the instructions in the current thread. See the Xcode documentation for details.

NAVIGATING THREADS AND STACKS

The Threads and Stacks navigator, which occupies the rest of the Debug bar, is used to switch between applications, threads, and items in the call stack. It works in the same way as the jump bar. **Figure 9.3** shows the selection of Lamp, Thread 1, and the current call stack while paused at a breakpoint in the -applicationDidFinishLaunching: method.

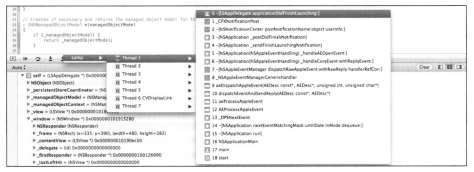

FIGURE 9.3 Viewing the call stack in the Threads and Stacks navigator

WORKING IN THE CONSOLE

FIGURE 9.4 The debugger console

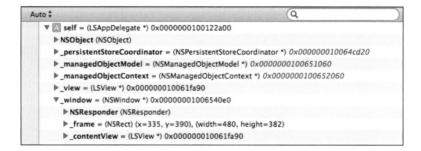

```
All Output ◆                                              Clear  [ ▯ ][ ▦ ][ ▯ ]
(lldb) po event
$2 = 0x000000010063e740 <Event: 0x10063e740> (entity: Event; id: 0x10063cd70 <x-
coredata:///Event/t087A876B-3153-484D-82A7-206024B5BA852> ; data: {
    switchedOn = nil;
    timeStamp = "2013-04-02 20:34:59 +0000";
})
(lldb) |
```

FIGURE 9.5 The Variables pane

```
Auto ◆                                          ( Q                    )
  ▼ Ⓐ self = (LSAppDelegate *) 0x0000000100122a00
    ▶ NSObject (NSObject)
    ▶ _persistentStoreCoordinator = (NSPersistentStoreCoordinator *) 0x000000010064cd20
    ▶ _managedObjectModel = (NSManagedObjectModel *) 0x0000000100651060
    ▶ _managedObjectContext = (NSManagedObjectContext *) 0x0000000100652060
    ▶ _view = (LSView *) 0x000000010061fa90
    ▼ _window = (NSWindow *) 0x00000001006540e0
       ▶ NSResponder (NSResponder)
       ▶ _frame = (NSRect) (x=335, y=390), (width=480, height=382)
       ▶ _contentView = (LSView *) 0x000000010061fa90
```

The console (**Figure 9.4**) displays the console output of your application and, while debugging, serves as a command-line interface to the debugger.

The output can be filtered to show only debugger or target output using the pop-up menu in the upper-left corner of the console area. The debugger prompt is available only when the application is paused in debug mode. When the prompt is available, you can click to the right of the text prompt and input debugger commands, such as the LLDB command po (print object).

The panel to the left of the console area, the Variables pane (**Figure 9.5**), shows the current variables and registers when the debugger is paused. The pop-up button in the upper-left corner of the pane can be used to choose all variables, those that were recently accessed (the default "Auto" setting), or variables local to the current scope only.

The console and the Variables pane can be set to use the entire width of the Debug area using the segmented control at the top right (seen in Figure 9.4). Click the left segment to show only the Variables pane, the right segment to show only the console, and the middle segment to show both.

USING BREAKPOINTS

Breakpoints are used to pause the application (or perform other actions) in the debugger when a particular instruction (point in code) is reached. There are several ways to manage breakpoints in Xcode 4.

ENABLING BREAKPOINTS

For Xcode to stop at breakpoints in the debugger, breakpoints must be active. You can use the Breakpoints button at the top of the project window to activate or deactivate all breakpoints. If this button is not selected, the debugger will stop only when a program signal (such as a memory-management–related crash) is encountered. Alternatively, you can press Command+Y to toggle breakpoints.

MANAGING BREAKPOINTS IN THE SOURCE EDITOR

You can set breakpoints in the Source editor by clicking the gutter on the left edge of the editor beside an instruction. A blue marker appears, showing that a breakpoint is set at that location (**Figure 9.6**).

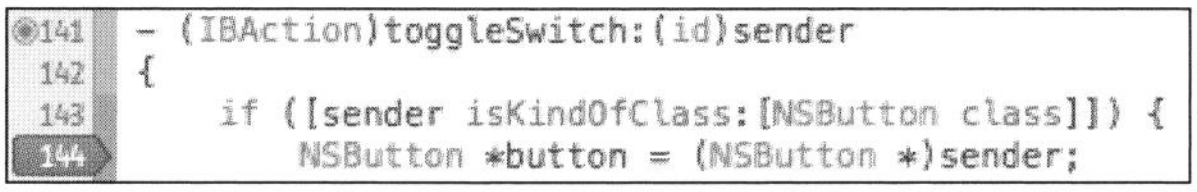

```
141  - (IBAction)toggleSwitch:(id)sender
142  {
143      if ([sender isKindOfClass:[NSButton class]]) {
144          NSButton *button = (NSButton *)sender;
```

FIGURE 9.6 A breakpoint set in the -toggleSwitch: action of Lamp

You can toggle individual breakpoints in the editor by clicking them once. The breakpoint will turn lighter, appearing translucent when inactive. To remove a breakpoint entirely, you can drag it from the gutter and release it. It will disappear in a puff of animated smoke to indicate it has been deleted. To adjust the location of a breakpoint, drag it up and down the gutter.

You can also set breakpoints in the editor with a keyboard shortcut. Command+\ (Command and the backslash character) will set a breakpoint at the current line in the code. If a breakpoint already exists, the shortcut will remove it.

Right-clicking a breakpoint in the gutter displays a context menu that also allows toggling and removing the selected breakpoint. The Edit Breakpoint option will allow customization of the breakpoint (covered in Chapter 15). The Reveal in Breakpoint Navigator option will cause the Breakpoint navigator to be displayed and the selected breakpoint highlighted.

USING THE BREAKPOINT NAVIGATOR

As you learned in Chapter 2, you can use the Breakpoint navigator to manage individual breakpoints, navigate your project by set breakpoints, or view only active breakpoints. There are a few more important features to note:

- Right-clicking a breakpoint in the navigator and choosing Edit Breakpoint from the context menu reveals a pop-up window that presents a number of options. Customization of breakpoints is covered in Chapter 15.

- Right-clicking a breakpoint in the navigator and choosing Share Breakpoint moves the breakpoint from being stored in your user data to being stored in shared data. Shared data can be read by other users who are working on the same project. You can make a breakpoint private again by right-clicking it and choosing Unshare Breakpoint.

- You can set exception or symbolic breakpoints using the + button at the bottom of the Breakpoint navigator. Exception breakpoints are particularly useful for determining the point at which an unhandled exception was thrown.

INTERACTING WITH THE SOURCE EDITOR

While the application is paused, you can interact with the debugger directly in the Source editor in several helpful ways.

INSPECTING VARIABLES IN THE SOURCE EDITOR

The Variables panel isn't the only way to examine the state or content of variables in the debugger. While the application is paused, you can hover the mouse pointer over a variable to examine it as long as it is within the current scope. A yellow box will appear, showing the details of the inspected variable (**Figure 9.7**).

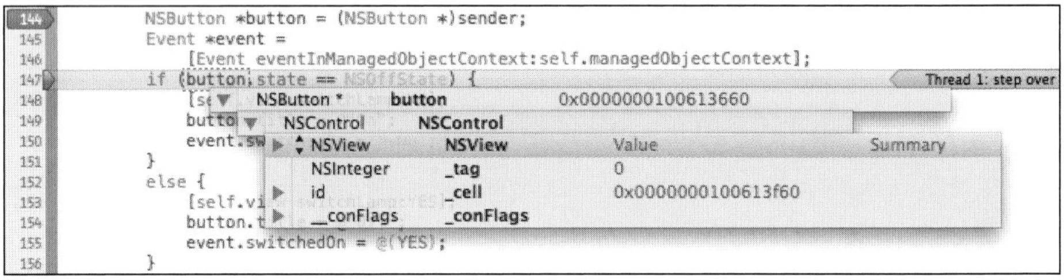

FIGURE 9.7 Examining a variable in the Source editor

NOTE: You've seen that pointers to Objective-C objects can be examined in the Source editor, in the Variables panel, and when using the print object command in the console. The information that is displayed is the result of calling the -description method, inherited from the NSObject class.

USING CONTINUE-TO-HERE

Sometimes it may be advantageous to continue to a point in your code farther down from where you're currently paused or to continue through a loop back to the top. You can continue execution to the desired point using the continue-to-here command.

To continue execution to a chosen instruction, hover your mouse pointer over the gutter next to the instruction. A green button will appear (**Figure 9.8**). Click the button to execute until that instruction.

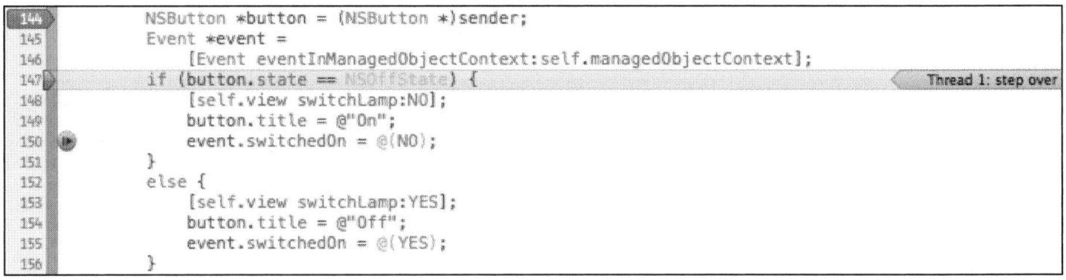

FIGURE 9.8 The continue-to-here button

MOVING THE EXECUTION POINTER

You can drag the execution pointer to anywhere within the local scope. You can use this to skip parts of code or to jump backward to repeat instructions. To move the execution pointer, grab the green arrow along the left edge of the Source editor and drag it to the desired instruction.

Moving the execution pointer backward to repeat instructions will not undo the instructions that were just executed. It will execute them again when you continue or step through your code. If you are new to debugging, missing this distinction can be confusing.

USING THE DEBUG NAVIGATOR

As you learned in Chapter 2, the Debug navigator shows the threads and stacks when execution is paused in the debugger. This view represents the same information found in the Threads and Stacks navigator in the Debug bar. You can organize the navigator by thread or by Grand Central Dispatch queue. Right-clicking a thread allows you to suspend or resume the thread, depending on its current status.

DEBUGGING FLASHLIGHT

You may recall that you finished Chapter 7 with a Flashlight app that contained a bug—when the app first opens, it should have a black background to represent the off state. The view is being set to white at some stage, and you need to know where, and if it is safe to set it to black instead.

BREAKING AND ENTERING

To determine the color of the Flashlight app's background, you need to know a little about the life cycle of the iOS view controller. Fortunately, we know enough to point you in the right direction—when the view controller's view has finished loading, the -viewDidLoad method is executed. To determine what color the view has at that point, you need to set a breakpoint in that method.

Open the LSViewController.m file, and navigate to the -viewDidLoad method. Set a breakpoint on the line containing the code [super viewDidLoad] by clicking in the gutter (**Figure 9.9**).

```
15    @implementation LSViewController
16
17    - (void)viewDidLoad
18    {
19        [super viewDidLoad];
20        // Do any additional setup after loading the view, typically from a nib.
21    }
```

FIGURE 9.9
A breakpoint in the -viewDidLoad method

Using the scheme selector in the toolbar, choose the Flashlight scheme and the iPhone 6.1 Simulator run destination, then click the Run button on the toolbar. Flashlight should start running in the simulator until it hits the -viewDidLoad method, at which point the Debug navigator should appear in the navigator panel, the Debug area should appear below the editor, and the LSViewController.m file should appear with the green execution pointer arrow indicating that the application has been paused on a breakpoint (**Figure 9.10**).

FIGURE 9.10
The Flashlight app
paused at a breakpoint

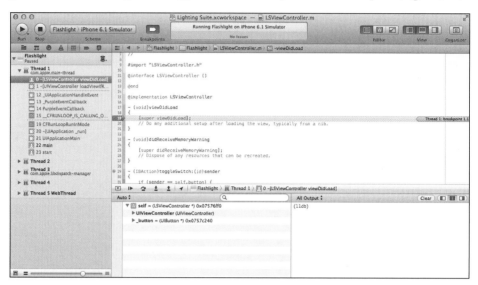

Even though the app has been paused in the -viewDidLoad method, it still hasn't executed the call to the superclass. The background color may or may not be set up in that call, so you need to step over that instruction. You can do so by pressing the Step Over button in the Debug bar, and the instruction pointer should move past the instruction. If there were more code in the method, it would move to the next instruction, but in this case it moves to the closing curly brace to indicate that the method is about to complete.

INSPECTING DATA

Armed with knowledge of the view controller, you can inspect the current state of the main view, a property of the UIViewController class named view. The view is an instance of the UIView class, which itself has a property named backgroundColor. To quickly inspect the value, click in the console section of the Debug area (anywhere near the (lldb) prompt), then enter the following command:

```
po self.view.backgroundColor
```

```
All Output ⬍                              Clear  ⬜ ⬛ ⬜
(lldb) po self.view.backgroundColor
$0 = 0x07640010 UIDeviceRGBColorSpace 1 1 1 1
(lldb)
```

The output should look like that in **Figure 9.11**. You can tell that the background color has a valid value at this point, and is in fact set to white. This should be a good point in code to set the initial color to be black, but to test this theory, you can modify the currently running application state. To do so, enter the following at the prompt:

```
expr self.view.backgroundColor = [UIColor blackColor]
```

Continue the execution of the code by pressing the Continue button in the Debug bar. The app should continue running and display a black background instead of white. Update the -viewDidLoad method as follows:

```
- (void)viewDidLoad
{
    [super viewDidLoad];
    self.view.backgroundColor = [UIColor blackColor];
}
```

This was a very basic debugging example (it is, after all a very basic application), but it hopefully has illustrated a number of techniques—the ability to break, to step through code, and to inspect and modify the data in a running app. For more information on debugging, see Chapter 15.

STATIC ANALYSIS

In Xcode, errors, warnings, and analyzer results are collectively called *issues*. Xcode is constantly compiling and checking your code for issues. Errors are red, warnings are yellow, and potential issues identified by the static analyzer are blue. Like any modern integrated development environment, Xcode flags issues by highlighting them directly in the source code (**Figure 9.12**), with a corresponding icon in the gutter along the left edge of the Source editor. In addition to the immediate issues in the selected source file, all issues Xcode finds in your entire workspace are displayed in the Issue navigator (as described in Chapter 2).

```
31
● 32       if ([sender isKindOfClass:[WibblyButton class]]) {
33                                  ● Use of undeclared identifier 'WibblyButton'
```

FIGURE 9.12 A compiler issue highlighted in the Source editor

USING THE STATIC ANALYZER

Xcode integrates the Clang static analyzer, which goes a step beyond basic compiler errors and warnings. It knows enough about C, Objective-C, and Cocoa patterns to find memory management problems, unused variables, and more. Its integration with Xcode means it can show an impressive amount of detail, including the path of execution leading to the problem and the conditions that caused it along the way. It is called a static analyzer because it performs its analysis without the application running. To analyze a running application, you can use Instruments instead (Chapter 15).

> **NOTE:** You can learn more about the Clang static analyzer at http://clang-analyzer.llvm.org.

You can invoke Xcode's Analyze action by pressing and holding the Run button and choosing Analyze from the pop-up menu, or by choosing Product > Analyze from the main menu. When invoked, the analyzer works to identify problems with your code. If an issue is found, it is flagged in the Source editor and in the Issue navigator alongside errors and warnings (**Figure 9.13**). Clicking the issue in the editor or the Issue navigator reveals details about the issue in the editor, including helpful blue lines indicating the problematic code path, with descriptions of your errant actions along the way.

FIGURE 9.13
A static analyzer issue expanded into steps

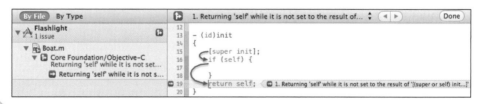

> **TIP:** The Clang static analyzer can be run as a standalone tool, providing textual output of its analysis results. Its integration with Xcode is what provides the much nicer graphical interface.

For issues that are spread over longer bodies of code, following all the curved blue lines can be confusing. Xcode helps you with this in two ways. First, expanding an analyzer issue in the Issue navigator reveals the individual points in the problematic code path. Second, and by far more helpful, an analyzer results bar (similar to a search bar) appears at the top of the editor (**Figure 9.14**). This bar lets you navigate the analyzer issue step by step so it's easier to follow along with the analyzer's complaints.

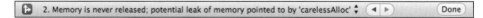

FIGURE 9.14 The analyzer results bar atop the Source editor

You can find some of the following issues with Instruments (see Chapter 15) and by using draconian warning levels, but the analyzer can find them while you're coding and show you exactly where and how you went wrong. Apple's own documentation suggests that you get into the habit of analyzing early and often.

EXPLORING ANALYZER RESULTS

Following are a couple of examples of the static analyzer output, with a walk-through of each result.

MEMORY LEAKS

A simple description of a memory leak in a Cocoa application is that it is an object to which you've lost any references and which thus can no longer be told to release its memory and go away. In this sense, the object's memory is "leaked" because it cannot be reclaimed for the remainder of the application's lifetime. Further, the object keeps living, which, depending on what the object does, can cause unexpected and sometimes very bad behavior.

Figure 9.15 shows an analyzer result for a memory leak in an example project that does not use automatic reference counting (ARC). In this case, an NSString is leaked. From the top of the -hole method, the execution path is followed through the method. The issue is broken down into the two "steps" in the code that caused it.

FIGURE 9.15 A memory leak highlighted by the static analyzer

In the first step, the instruction on line 15 returns an object with a +1 retain count (which, in a memory-managed environment, makes you responsible for properly releasing the object when necessary). In the second step, the method returns without releasing (or autoreleasing) the NSString instance beforehand. This means the NSString instance has been leaked at this point.

This is a contrived example, because we disabled ARC for the project. ARC itself uses the static analyzer while building your code to insert retain and release instructions on your behalf. Memory leaks with ARC are still possible (by creating a strong reference cycle, for example), so it is still advisable to use the static analyzer frequently to catch these.

> **NOTE:** The static analyzer is smart enough to know when your code uses ARC or Objective-C garbage collection and adjusts accordingly for memory-management–related issues.

LOGIC ERRORS

Logic errors can cause crashes or more subtle problems. In complex code, they can be easy to miss and difficult to debug, but the static analyzer picks them up and highlights them easily. Although Xcode runs the analyzer and compiler constantly to highlight issues like uninitialized variables or syntax errors "as you type," it requires the deliberate act of performing the Analyze action to make it check all possible code-paths to detect complex logic errors.

One type of logic error is using an uninitialized variable. A variable declared without an initial value can point to any old garbage lying around in RAM. Attempting to access that variable gives you undefined or garbage values. **Figure 9.16** demonstrates this problem in a basic scenario (the fourth step is highlighted in the figure).

FIGURE 9.16 A logic issue flagged by the static analyzer

On line 24, a BOOL variable named positiveFlag is declared with no initial value. Because the code inside the if/else if blocks (lines 26–31) may not be executed, the positiveFlag may never have a defined value assigned to it before the value is returned in line 32.

This is a good demonstration of the power that the static analyzer puts in your hands. It can follow all possible paths through your code, highlighting a problem if one series of logical branches is followed.

WRAPPING UP

You should now have a firm grasp of the basic debugging facilities that Xcode 4 offers. As well as assisting you in debugging, Xcode can also perform detailed analysis of code on your behalf, flagging potential logic and resource problems that you may not have noticed.

In the next chapter, you'll explore methods for distributing your app via Apple's channels and directly to your users.

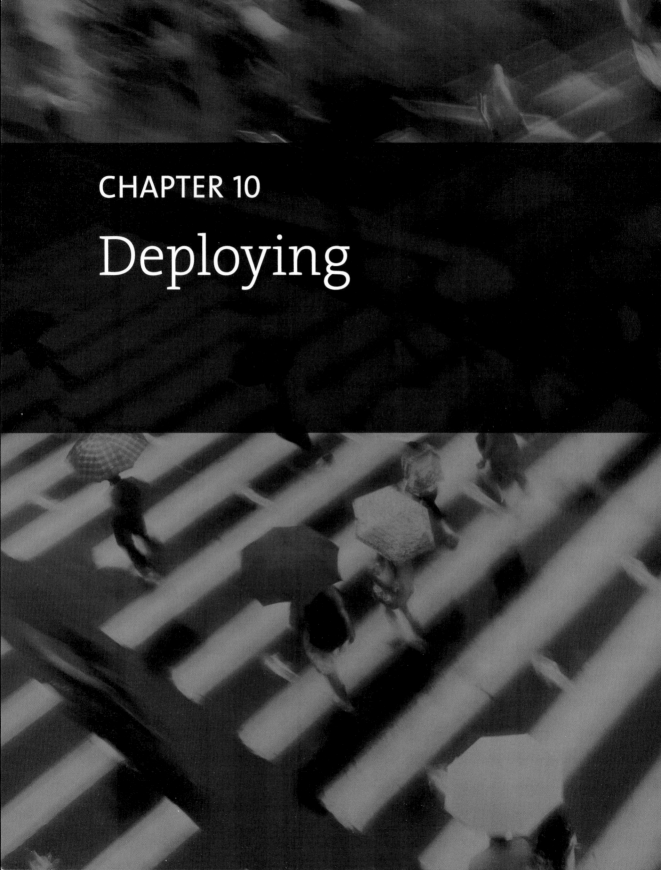

CHAPTER 10

Deploying

To deploy an application, you must build it in Release mode. Whether you're turning the application over to an employer, selling it on your own website, submitting it to Apple's App Store, or just sharing it with a friend, your application must be built for release. In Xcode 4, this is accomplished most directly with the Archive action.

ARCHIVING

There are certain steps that should be taken when preparing an app for deployment—building with optimizations, stripping debug symbols, or digitally signing the executables, to name a few. To simplify switching between the standard build configurations—Debug and Release—Xcode provides an Archive action that produces a Release build by default.

CREATING THE ARCHIVE

Open the Lighting Suite workspace, if it's not already open. Using the scheme selector, choose the Lamp scheme and the My Mac 64-bit run destination. To perform the Archive action, choose Product > Archive from the main menu. Xcode will build in Release mode and then archive any built products that are part of your project or workspace in addition to their corresponding dSYM files.

NOTE: A dSYM file is a copy of the debugging symbols from an application. Storing them in an external file allows you to strip them from your release build but still have the symbols for debugging purposes.

FINDING THE ARCHIVE

The Archives tab of the Organizer (**Figure 10.1**) serves as a collection point and browser for the archives you create. Using the Organizer, you can annotate the archives as well as share them with others or submit them to the App Store. To open the Organizer, click the Organizer button in the toolbar or choose Window > Organizer from the main menu.

FIGURE 10.1
The Lamp archive in the Organizer

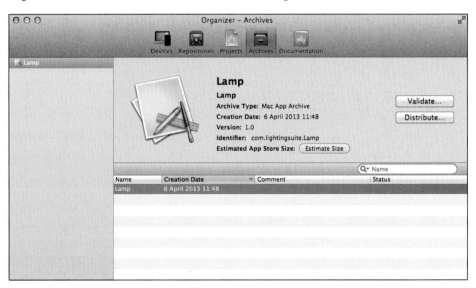

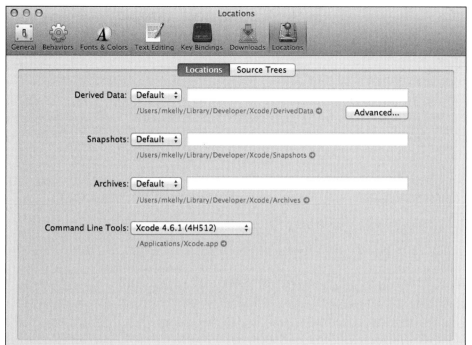

FIGURE 10.2
The Locations prefer-
ences panel

When the Organizer window appears, select the Archives tab. Xcode helpfully presents the Organizer window open to the Archives tab when it performs a successful Archive action configured through the build scheme—see Chapter 13 for information on how to disable this feature if you wish to do so.

The archives of any given project are stored in the default Archives folder that Xcode creates. The default folder is ~/Library/Developer/Xcode/Archives. You can change this and other locations in the Locations panel of Xcode's preferences (**Figure 10.2**). Archives are stored at the path labeled Archives—you may wish to change this if you want to store archives in a shared location. Click the arrow button to the right of the path to open the folder in the Finder. Archives are organized by date (under folders named in YYYY-MM-DD format) and then by project name.

EXAMINING THE ARCHIVE

Currently the only available archive format is the Xcode archive (.xcarchive) format. An Xcode archive file is a *package* (a folder that appears in the Finder as a single file). This means you can view its contents in the Finder by right-clicking (or Control-clicking) the archive file and choosing Show Package Contents from the context menu.

Inside the package, you'll see the dSYM folder, the Products folder (where the built appli-cation resides), and an Info.plist file. The .plist (property list) file, which can be opened in Xcode's Property List editor, contains a description of the package's contents.

FIGURE 10.3
The Lamp.app bundle in
the Xcode archive file

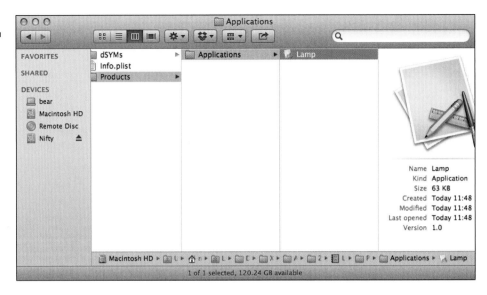

To find the application (Lamp.app), navigate through the Products folder. The products are placed in a folder structure mirroring that of the Installation Directory build setting for the target (see Chapter 13). When you get to the end of the trail of folders, you should see the Lamp application bundle (**Figure 10.3**).

TESTING THE APPLICATION

A lot can be said on the subject of thoroughly testing an application before deployment, but that is beyond the scope of this book (except unit tests, which are covered in Chapter 15). For now, you can verify that the application launches (by double-clicking it in the Finder) and that it performs the functionality you added in previous chapters. When you're satisfied that Lamp does exactly what it did when run directly from Xcode, quit the application. You're ready to think about distribution.

VALIDATING YOUR APPLICATION

Archives in the Organizer are displayed with a pair of action buttons, one of which is named Validate. Depending on your intended method of distribution, there may be a number of conditions that have to be satisfied. The Validate button is a quick way to check that you've got some of the basics in place.

The action of the Validate button varies according to the archive type. Open the Organizer to the Archives tab, and select the Lamp archive you created earlier. To the right of the archive details (Figure 10.1), click the Validate button. The next screen presents you with a

FIGURE 10.4 Validation options for a Mac app archive

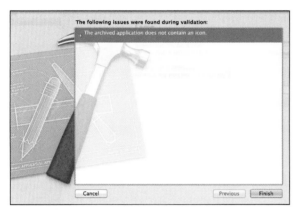

FIGURE 10.5 Archive validation failure

FIGURE 10.6 Archive validation success!

choice of validations (**Figure 10.4**). Choose the Direct Distribution option, and click Next. Xcode will proceed to validate your archive against the criteria it believes are valid for a Mac app distributed directly from your website.

In this case, validation will quickly fail because you do not have an icon set for your app (**Figure 10.5**). Add an icon file to your project by dragging it into the Project navigator. Then open the Lamp project settings, and select the Lamp target and the Summary tab. Drag the icon from the navigator into the App Icon image well. Perform the Archive action again for Lamp, and click the Validate button as before. This time everything should validate fine (**Figure 10.6**).

> **NOTE:** Icon files for Mac applications are a special file type called `.icns`, which can be created using any of a number of third-party applications available in the Mac App Store. We've provided a basic icon file at http://xcodebook.com/lamp.icns if you don't want to make your own.

Selecting the Mac App Store validation option for a Mac app or clicking the Validate button for an iOS app will cause the validation process to prompt you to log in to iTunes Connect using your Apple ID.

To proceed past this point, you need to have a record for your app in iTunes Connect, Apple's online portal for managing app distribution. This is your chance to perform a validation before submitting your app for review—take this opportunity, because it will save the disappointment of submitting an app that is going to fail the review process at the first hurdle.

Once your app is past the validation stage, you are ready to distribute.

DISTRIBUTION CHANNELS

Xcode supports app distribution via a number of mechanisms—the one you choose will be dictated partly by your own needs, partly by the platform you develop for, and partly by Apple's restrictions. Much of the iOS and Mac App Store distribution process is dependent on iTunes Connect and the iOS provisioning portal. As a result, the following material is simply an overview to the distribution types and general requirements rather than a step-by-step guide on how to release an app.

PROVISIONING PROFILES AND CODE SIGNING

For some of the distribution methods, you will need to specify provisioning profiles and code signing identities as part of your build process.

PROVISIONING PROFILES

A provisioning profile is a cryptographically signed document that specifies a range of permissions that dictate the extent to which an application can be provisioned on devices. All iOS apps require some form of provisioning profile in order to be installed on devices, and OS X apps that are distributed through the Mac App Store also require a provisioning profile.

Provisioning profiles are created and maintained through the iOS or Mac provisioning portals. For more information about creating profiles, look for the online help in the provisioning portal itself. Once you have created a profile, you need to import it into Xcode for it to be used with your apps.

The most direct means of importing a provisioning profile to Xcode is through the Devices section of the Organizer. In the sidebar, select the Provisioning Profiles entry under the Library section (**Figure 10.7**), then click the Refresh button in the bottom toolbar. After entering your Apple ID and password, Xcode will contact the provisioning portal on your behalf and download any available profiles to your developer account.

FIGURE 10.7 The Provisioning Profiles section of the Devices Organizer

Alternatively, provisioning profiles can be downloaded from the provisioning portal and imported into Xcode. To import a downloaded profile, locate the file in the Finder and double-click it—Xcode will handle the rest.

CODE SIGNING

When you're building an app for distribution through the App Store, the app must be digitally code signed. To code sign your application, click the project name in the Project navigator, then select the Build Settings tab in the Project Settings editor. Scroll down to the section marked Code Signing, and click the value for the setting Code Signing Identity in order to display a list of valid identities that you can use to code sign the application (**Figure 10.8**).

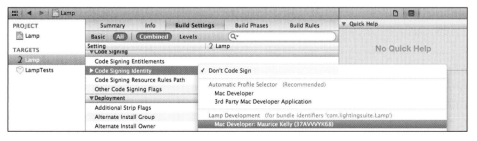

FIGURE 10.8 Selecting an identity to code sign an application

The list of identities can be quite long, and many of them are grayed out to indicate that they are not suitable. The reasons for not being suitable are many and varied, but the list can include identities for the wrong platform, identities that are expired, or identities that are for the wrong bundle identifier.

Figure 10.8 shows the selection of an identity to sign the Lamp application. In this case, we are selecting a Mac Developer identity (highlighted in blue). The line above the identity indicates the name of the provisioning profile associated with this identity (called Lamp Development) and the bundle identifiers that the profile accepts. This profile is specific to one app—com.lightingsuite.Lamp—though it is possible to create provisioning profiles that apply to a number of apps by using a wildcard identifier; for example, we could have created a profile using the bundle identifier com.lightingsuite.*.

Xcode provides a number of automatic identities (for example, iPhone Distribution or Mac Developer) that can be selected as a code signing identity. Sometimes this can be helpful, but it is often a source of more confusion. When you select an automatic identity, Xcode will choose what it considers to be the most appropriate identity. This may be right for your build today, but the creation of a new identity in the future may cause the automatic choice to change.

There are also points in the archiving process where Xcode will prompt you to choose an identity to re-sign your application and will present you with a default that it believes is correct. It is always wise to check that Xcode has truly selected the correct identity before proceeding.

Don't worry if you find that code signing and provisioning profiles are confusing and don't always work as you would expect. It's not unusual for experienced developers to scratch their heads when an application fails to build because of a code signing error. With time, you will come to learn the subtleties and how to diagnose problems.

IOS APP DISTRIBUTION

iOS app distribution is a tightly controlled affair. The locked-down nature of the iOS platform means that it is not possible to simply post an app on your website and allow anyone to come along and install it. Before it can be installed on a device, your app must be digitally signed and include a provisioning profile. The scope of the provisioning profile determines how widely your app can be distributed.

IOS APP STORE DISTRIBUTION

The widest level of distribution for an iOS app is via the iOS App Store. Inclusion in the App Store means that your app can be installed on any device whose owner browses the store and decides they like the look of it. The downside is that your app will only be accepted to the App Store if it meets the standards set out by Apple's app review process. This may seem unfair, but for the most part the app review policies are there for the benefit of the end user. Whatever your position on app review, the boundaries have been set and must be worked within.

The prerequisites for an App Store distribution are:

- A Personal or Corporate iOS developer account
- An App Store distribution provisioning profile
- An iTunes Connect entry for the app
- An app that won't be rejected by app review

To use App Store distribution, first log in to the online Apple Developer Center. In the Certificates, Identifiers & Profiles area, create a new distribution provisioning profile and choose the App Store type. The resulting profile can be downloaded directly into Xcode from within the Devices section of the Organizer, or it can be downloaded from the provisioning portal and imported into Xcode.

You must code sign your app with a certificate that is included in this provisioning profile, selecting it as part of the code signing identity for the Release build configuration. You also need to ensure that there exists an entry in iTunes Connect for you to upload your app against.

When your project has been archived successfully, you will be able to click the Distribute button on its Archives page in the Organizer. Xcode will ask what distribution method you wish to use (**Figure 10.9**). Choose "Submit to the iOS App Store" and click Next. You will be prompted to log in to iTunes Connect, after which Xcode will perform some processing and, all being well, your app will be uploaded and placed into the queue for the review process. Further management of the process, such as choosing when and where to release your app, must be carried out using the iTunes Connect online portal.

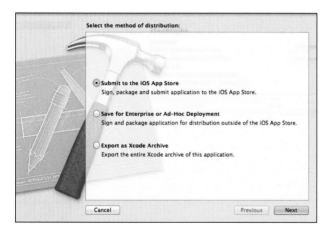

FIGURE 10.9 Selecting your iOS distribution method

AD-HOC DISTRIBUTION

Ad-hoc distribution is the best way to distribute test versions of your app to your testers. An ad-hoc distribution provisioning profile is limited to a range of known devices. An iOS developer account can register up to 100 devices a year, so unless you plan to have a very small user base, you need to use App Store or Enterprise distribution for anything other than testing.

The prerequisites for an ad-hoc distribution are:

- A Corporate or Personal iOS developer account
- An ad-hoc distribution provisioning profile
- One or more registered device identifiers for test devices

When you intend to use ad-hoc distribution, first log in to the Apple Developer Center. In the Certificates, Identifiers & Profiles area, create a new distribution provisioning profile and choose the Ad-Hoc type. Then specify the devices you wish to include in the profile. The resulting profile can be downloaded directly into Xcode from within the Devices section of the Organizer, or it can be downloaded from the provisioning portal and imported into Xcode.

After a successful Archive action, click the Distribute button on the archive's entry in the Organizer. When Xcode asks you which distribution method you wish to use (Figure 10.9), choose "Save for Enterprise or Ad-Hoc Deployment" and click Next. Xcode will then present you with an opportunity to choose a code signing identity (**Figure 10.10**). Xcode will attempt to choose the most appropriate identity, but can often get it wrong. Click the drop-down menu and inspect the list of options to ensure that the correct code signing identity is set.

**FIGURE 10.10** Choosing a code signing identity

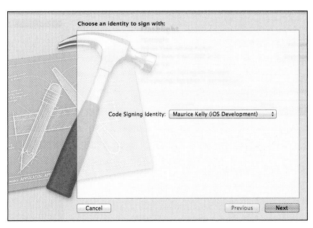

When you click Next, Xcode will present a Save As dialog. Choose a name and location, and click Save to generate the distribution bundle. Xcode will output a file with an extension of .ipa. This file is a bundle of everything that is needed to run the app on the target devices and includes the executable code and the ad-hoc distribution provisioning profile.

The next step is how to get the application bundle onto those devices. The .ipa files can be imported into iTunes and transferred to a device in that way. Alternatively, a number of services have been created as a way to assist developers and their testing with over-the-air distribution. Two such services are TestFlight (http://testflightapp.com/) and HockeyApp (http://hockeyapp.net). If you don't want the full service, there are also apps, like BetaBuilder (https://github.com/HunterHillegas/iOS-BetaBuilder), that can simplify the process somewhat.

ENTERPRISE DISTRIBUTION

Enterprise distribution is intended for companies who wish to develop software for internal use and do not want it to be distributed via the public iOS App Store channel.

The prerequisites for an enterprise distribution are:

- An Enterprise iOS developer account
- An enterprise or in-house distribution provisioning profile

To use enterprise distribution, first log in to the Apple Developer Center. In the Certificates, Identifiers & Profiles area, create a new distribution provisioning profile and choose the In-House type. The resulting profile can be downloaded directly into Xcode from within the Devices section of the Organizer, or it can be downloaded from the provisioning portal and imported into Xcode.

After a successful Archive action, click the Distribute button on its entry in the Archives section of the Organizer. When Xcode asks you which distribution method you wish to use (Figure 10.9), choose "Save for Enterprise or Ad-Hoc Deployment" and click Next. Xcode will then present you with an opportunity to choose a code signing identity (Figure 10.10). Xcode will attempt to choose the most appropriate identity, but can often get it wrong. Click the drop-down menu and inspect the list of options to ensure that the correct code signing identity is set.

When you click Next, Xcode will present a Save As dialog that has a "Save for Enterprise Distribution" option at the bottom. Selecting this option will expand the Save As dialog to show enterprise distribution options (**Figure 10.11**). These options will be used to construct a manifest file for the distribution bundle; all options but Application URL and Title are optional.

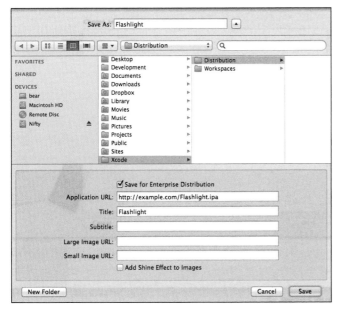

FIGURE 10.11 Configuring the enterprise distribution manifest

In the Application URL field, enter the exact path for your website that the application bundle will be available from—include the full name of the `.ipa` file that will be generated as part of this step. Enter a title for the bundle in the Title field—the name of the app is usually sufficient. The Image URL fields are optional, but should be set to appropriately sized icon files that will display while the app is installing. Click Save when you are ready to produce the app bundle.

The result of this process is a pair of files (`Flashlight.ipa` and `Flashlight.plist`), which should be copied to your web server. Ensure that the `.ipa` file resides in the same location as you stated it would; otherwise, the manifest file (`Flashlight.plist`) will need to be updated. Take note of the path to the manifest file (for example, http://example.com/Flashlight.plist)—this is needed for the install process.

Installing an enterprise distribution build requires that you send the user a special URL containing a reference to the manifest file. The general form of the special URL is as follows:

```
itms-services://?action=download-manifest&url=<manifest-file-url>
```

For *manifest-file-url* insert the path you noted when placing the manifest file on your web server. For our example, the installation URL will become:

```
itms-services://?action=download-manifest&url=http://example.com/
→ Flashlight.plist
```

Alternatively, your corporate IT department may wish to deploy your app to many internal users by using a deployment tool like the iPhone Configurator Utility.

XCODE ARCHIVE DISTRIBUTION

Technically, this is not really a form of app distribution, but it is possible to package your Xcode archive in a distributable format that can be sent to another Xcode user. This method can be used to pass a build on to a user who is responsible for all app distribution. To do so, click the Distribute button on the archive's entry in the Organizer, and when prompted choose "Export as Xcode Archive" (Figure 10.9). A standard Save As dialog will appear, allowing you to export the archive.

If you receive such an archive (indicated by the `.xcarchive` extension), simply double-click it to import it into Xcode, where it will appear in the Archives section of the Organizer.

MAC APP DISTRIBUTION

There are two main methods of app distribution for Mac apps—the Mac App Store and direct distribution. Submitting to the Mac App Store requires a similar review process to the iOS App Store. Direct distribution has been complicated slightly by the introduction of Gatekeeper in OS X 10.8 (and the latest versions of 10.7).

Gatekeeper is a means to protect users from running applications that have not been digitally signed. To sign your application, you must pay an annual subscription to the Mac Developer Program and generate code-signing certificates in a process that is similar to that forced on iOS developers.

MAC APP STORE DISTRIBUTION

Like the iOS equivalent, the Mac App Store requires that submitted apps go through a review process to ensure that they adhere to Apple's guidelines (such as sandboxing).

The prerequisites for Mac App Store distribution are:

- A Mac developer account
- A Mac Submission certificate
- A Mac Installer certificate
- An entry for your app in iTunes Connect
- An app that meets review criteria

The quickest and easiest way to generate the Mac Submission and Installer certificates you need is to open the Devices section of the Organizer and choose the Provisioning Profiles entry in the sidebar (**Figure 10.12**). Click the Refresh button at the right side of the bottom toolbar.

FIGURE 10.12 Choosing a code signing identity

If you don't already have one, Xcode will helpfully suggest that it request a Mac Development certificate on your behalf. Click Submit Request to accept. Xcode will then check if you have a Mac Submission certificate, and then a Mac Installer certificate. In both cases, click the Submit Request button to have Xcode do the hard work for you.

Xcode will also offer to obtain a Developer ID Application certificate and a Developer ID Installer certificate—you don't need these for Mac App Store submission, but they can be used for direct distribution (for example, to beta testers), so it is still worth having Xcode obtain them for you. Once again, click Submit Request for both of these, or click Cancel to defer obtaining them until you need them.

All the certificates can be generated (or revoked and regenerated) through the Certificates, Identifiers & Profiles section of the Mac Developer Portal, so don't worry if you want to re-do any of these steps.

FIGURE 10.13 Selecting a distribution method for your OS X app

To submit your app to the Mac App Store, switch to the Archives tab in the Organizer, locate your chosen archive, and click the Distribute button. When Xcode asks you which distribution method you wish to use (**Figure 10.13**), choose "Submit to the Mac App Store" and click Next.

You will be prompted for your iTunes Connect login credentials, after which Xcode will package, sign, and send your application installer to iTunes Connect. Further management of the submission process must be carried out through the iTunes Connect web portal.

DEVELOPER ID-SIGNED APPLICATION DISTRIBUTION

Many developers choose either to bypass the Mac App Store in favor of direct sales, or to sell through both channels in parallel. While it is not (yet!) mandatory to code sign applications that are sold directly to users, Macs with Gatekeeper enabled will be presented with an ugly warning when your app is run if it has not been signed.

The prerequisites for Developer ID-signed distribution are:

- A Mac developer account
- A Developer ID Application certificate

The easiest way to obtain the Developer ID Application certificate is to follow the instructions outlined in the previous section through the Devices tab of the Organizer. Otherwise, go to the Certificates, Identifiers & Profiles section of the Mac Developer Portal and create a new distribution certificate of the Developer ID type.

After you've created an archive, click the Distribute button on its entry in the Organizer. When Xcode asks you which distribution method you wish to use (Figure 10.13), choose "Export Developer ID-signed Application" and click Next. Xcode will ask you to choose a Developer ID to sign the application with; check that it has selected the most appropriate ID, and click Next to sign the app.

Finally, Xcode will ask you where you want to save the signed application; choose a location and click Save. To distribute, simply zip up the application bundle and host it on a web server, or send it directly to your testers.

UNSIGNED APPLICATION DISTRIBUTION

It is still possible to build a distribution that is not signed in any way. This is useful if you have not yet paid to join the Mac Developer Program but still want a way to distribute to users who are comfortable manipulating their Gatekeeper settings to run the application. There are no prerequisites other than having an app that builds.

When you produce an archive, click the Distribute button on its entry in the Organizer. When Xcode asks you which distribution method you wish to use (Figure 10.13), choose Application from the Export As pop-up menu and click Next. Xcode will ask you to choose an identity to sign with; choose Don't Re-sign, and click Next. In the Save As dialog that appears, choose an appropriate place and click Save. To distribute, simply zip up the application bundle and host it on a web server, or send it directly to your users.

> **NOTE:** You can run an unsigned application either by setting "Allow applications downloaded from: Anywhere" in the Security & Privacy preferences pane or by right-clicking the app in the Finder and selecting Open from the context menu.

OTHER DISTRIBUTION METHODS

Xcode provides some other distribution methods that are less commonly used. As with the iOS equivalent, you can export a Mac app archive (choose Xcode Archive from the Export As drop-down menu) to send it to another developer to perform the actual distribution.

Or you can choose Mac Installer Package from the Export As drop-down menu. This is actually the recommended way to test your app installation process as it would be carried out when a customer installs your app from the Mac App Store. You could distribute this package to advanced users, but it would not be a good way to distribute your app in general. It also requires that you have a Mac Installer certificate (and therefore a Mac Developer Program membership).

ALTERNATIVES TO ARCHIVING

Although the Archive action makes App Store submission easier, it makes getting at your built application to package it for other purposes slightly less convenient. Independent Mac developers, for example, have their own staged archive folders into which they dump the latest release build. This folder may include a "quick start guide" in PDF format, a .webloc (web location file) shortcut to their site, and other marketing goodies. This folder is archived as a zip file or disk image to form a user-friendly downloadable file.

Xcode 4's Archive action does not currently provide enough options to support this level of customization. The best way to achieve this is to create your own scheme to perform all of this staging with your own custom packaging and accoutrements. Alternatively, you can add minimal convenience in the form of a script at the end of the Archive action, which opens the built product's enclosing folder within the archive in a Finder window.

All is not lost, however. An important set of environment variables was added to Xcode's build system that can be used within build scripts to manipulate aspects of the build environment. These are ARCHIVE_PATH, ARCHIVE_PRODUCTS_PATH, and ARCHIVE_DSYMS_PATH. Arguably ARCHIVE_PRODUCTS_PATH is the most important, since it makes it relatively easy to extend the Archive action to build your own custom archives alongside those that Xcode curates.

See Chapter 13 for an overview of the new schemes system and Chapter 16 for more ideas regarding how to customize the build process to perform extra tasks.

WRAPPING UP

In this chapter, you learned how to create a release build of your application and archive it for sharing or App Store submission. You also learned how to use Xcode to perform submission to the Mac or iOS App Store and how to perform other types of direct distribution.

In the next section of the book, you will explore some of the more advanced features of Xcode, starting with using older projects within Xcode.

PART III

Further Exploration

CHAPTER 11

Using Older Projects in Xcode 4

Xcode has evolved rapidly in recent years, and despite stepping through five major releases in less than two years, it is still known as version 4. In this chapter, you'll learn how to work with projects created in older versions of Xcode and how to update your projects to use the latest features of Xcode and Objective-C.

PROJECT MODERNIZATION METHODS

It is a fact of developer life that at some stage you will inevitably have to dig out an old project and do more than just gaze longingly at it. Maybe you want to make a simple bug fix to an application that was created using a much older version of Xcode. Or you might want to revitalize your app and give it a complete overhaul for the modern age.

Whatever your reason for blowing the dust off the archives, there is a good chance that you won't have access to the development environment you first used to create the application. If you do still have it lying around, it may not be suitable for producing apps for the modern Mac and iOS app stores, or you might simply not want to go back to using older tools that are stone age by comparison.

Fortunately, Apple predicted these situations and included project modernization facilities in Xcode 4. The easiest way to take advantage of Apple's efforts is simply to open your legacy project. On opening, Xcode will examine the project, and if it suspects that your project needs a makeover, it will add to the Issue navigator an entry like the one shown in **Figure 11.1**.

Clicking the Validate Project Settings warning will cause Xcode to display an action sheet listing the build and project settings it intends to update to bring your project up to speed (**Figure 11.2**).

FIGURE 11.1 Issue navigator output

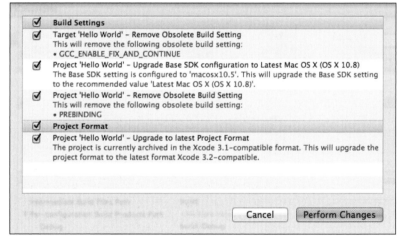

FIGURE 11.2 Validate settings for a Mac application

WAIT! DON'T PRESS THAT BUTTON JUST YET

Before you perform any modernization operation that will change your project forever, ask yourself a few questions:

- Will I ever need to go back to the antiquated version of the project?
- Do I have colleagues who are unable to upgrade to the latest version of Xcode?
- Will I be cutting off any of my users if I take advantage of the latest features?

If the answer to any of these questions is yes, then you may want to consider your decision to modernize your project a bit more carefully. All is not lost, however, because there are still options available to you. If you use any kind of version control system, you could create a new branch for your project. Branching is a worthwhile endeavor prior to making any major changes, and modernizing in this way certainly counts as a major change. If you aren't working with a source code management system, there is still Xcode's safety net: snapshots. Xcode will prompt you to create snapshots (**Figure 11.3**) unless you have turned them off. We covered snaphots in Chapter 6 if you want to go back and turn them on again.

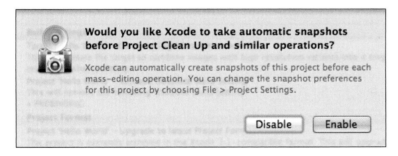

FIGURE 11.3 Creating an automatic snapshot

If you need to make an update to an app that must continue to run on an older version of OS X or iOS, then you may need to locate and install an older version of Xcode, which Apple makes available through its developer site. Unfortunately, some older versions of Xcode will not run on modern versions of OS X, so you may need to dig out your old install disks and investigate the use of virtualization to get older versions of Xcode running. A further caveat if you intend to virtualize an older version of OS X: the Apple license agreement allows only Mac OS X Server versions of Leopard (10.5) and Snow Leopard (10.6) to be run in this way.

MODERNIZING YOUR APP

Once you have read through the list of modernizations that Xcode has proposed—and are happy with them—click the Perform Changes button to start the modernization process. You will be prompted to create a snapshot, and then Xcode will perform its magic.

The process usually works smoothly, but there's always a chance that, for whatever reason, your project may not be fully built and functioning at this stage. Remember that the changes carried out by these operations are based on Xcode's best guesses at how your project should be updated. These guesses may be incorrect, or they may not be able to take you all the way to a functioning project again. It is worth examining the build settings in conjunction with any error output to fully restore your project.

The next sections explain some of the operations that Xcode might be carrying out on your behalf. You can use this information to manually modernize your project or to diagnose what may have gone wrong.

THE MODERNIZATION OF A MAC APP

The best way to make sure your Mac app will build again is to make sure that sensible values have been chosen for the build settings—particularly in the Architectures section. To tune these values, open the Project editor, choose the Build Settings tab, and change the filter from Basic to All (**Figure 11.4**).

A modern Mac will almost certainly contain a 64-bit processor, so it is worth changing the Architectures setting to 64-bit Intel and making sure the Valid Architectures setting includes x86_64 (for example, i386 x86_64). i386 is the setting Xcode uses to represent the 32-bit processor architecture used in older Macs. Unless your code needs to run on very old hardware, you should consider dropping support for this architecture.

The Base SDK setting should also be updated. It represents the most recent version of OS X supported by your code. Consider setting it to Latest OS X unless you need to target an older version of OS X. The Supported Platforms setting should be set to OS X unless you are modernizing a library or framework that is intended to work across OS X and iOS.

If you make changes to the Base SDK setting, you should ensure that the OS X Deployment Target setting has also been updated; this setting specifies the oldest version of OS X supported by your code and should be set to the oldest SDK version that your code will support.

THE MODERNIZATION OF AN iOS APP

As with a Mac app, it is important to ensure that the build settings for an iOS app are set to sensible values. To view the current settings, open the Project editor, choose the Build Settings tab, and change the filter from Basic to All.

As you can see in **Figure 11.5**, the settings for this iOS project are a little mixed up. The Base SDK setting has been detected as iOS 3.1.2 (from the days when it was still known as iPhoneOS), but the Architectures, Supported Platforms, and Valid Architectures settings indicate that Xcode sees this as an OS X project. The best way to fix this is to choose a new Base SDK setting. "Latest iOS" is a good option, though you can specify an explicit version if you need to. Xcode doesn't come with many iOS SDKs installed, but you can get older options by opening File > Preferences and selecting the Downloads pane.

Choosing an updated version of iOS will fix the Architectures, Supported Platforms, and Valid Architectures settings.

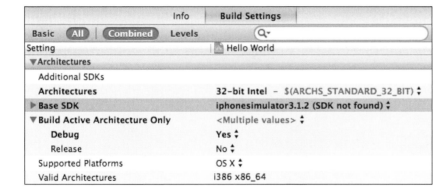

FIGURE 11.5
Build settings for an iOS 3.1.2 app

MODERNIZATION IS FOR SOME OTHER SUCKER

You might think that your project is too young and hip to need modernization—after all you only created it in version 4.2 and that ain't so long ago, right? Don't get cocky, kid!

Apple is updating Xcode features rapidly, and it's always worthwhile to make sure that you are using every potential trick in the bag to get your work done more efficiently. Whenever you open a project in a new version of Xcode, check the Issue navigator to see if Xcode has noticed any potential issues.

CODE MODERNIZATION METHODS

It isn't just Xcode that has improved with age—the underlying technologies that make up the Xcode tool chain have been steadily evolving as well.

UPDATE YOUR TOOLS

In the first edition of this book, Apple had just introduced the low-level virtual machine (LLVM) compiler and the LLDB debugger. Although they were available to use, they were not selected by default and were intended for the developers who wanted to try the future tools rather than for the general populace. Cut to the present, and Apple has already announced that Xcode 4.6 will be the last version of Xcode to support the LLVM-GCC compiler and the GDB debugger.

If your project was using the GCC compiler, then it can use the LLVM-GCC compiler for compatibility. To future-proof your project against the deprecation of LLVM-GCC, you can quickly switch the entire project (or maybe just individual targets) to use LLVM instead. In the File navigator, ensure that the project item is highlighted. In the Project editor, select the project name, choose the Build Settings tab, and change the filter from Basic to All. Type **compiler** into the search bar, and in the results choose Compiler for C/C++/Objective-C. If LLVM GCC 4.2 is selected in the resulting menu, then change it to Apple LLVM compiler 4.2 (**Figure 11.6**).

FIGURE 11.6 Changing the compiler to LLVM

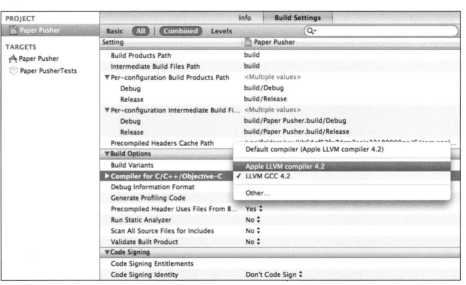

To change your project to use LLDB (the companion debugger to the LLVM compiler), you need to edit your scheme. Click the appropriate name in the Scheme toolbar menu, select Edit Scheme from the menu, and then choose the Run command. The panel on the right (**Figure 11.7**) will display a number of parameters, including the currently selected debugger. From the Debugger menu, choose LLDB. One word of warning: You can set the Test and Run commands differently, so you may want to update both. Unlike with the compiler settings, unfortunately, it isn't possible to update the debugger for every scheme in one fell swoop, so if you have a large number of schemes, you have a bit of clicking ahead of you.

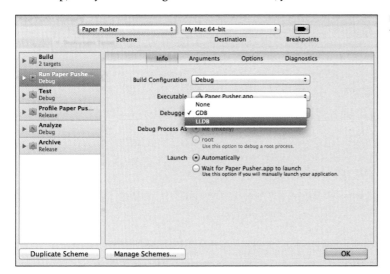

FIGURE 11.7 Changing the debugger to LLDB

UPDATE YOUR CODE

Apple has been actively extending the abilities of the Objective-C programming language. Over the years, they have made it more "normal" by allowing the use of niceties like dot-notation. Perhaps in response to reducing the use of square brackets, Apple has recently introduced a new syntax for creating literals such as numbers and Booleans. The syntax also extends to creating, accessing, and modifying arrays and dictionaries—Objective-C now uses a subscript notation like many other languages.

We're all familiar with this sort of literal syntax, because we use it extensively when creating strings. The following method of string creation is perfectly valid:

```
NSString *myString = [NSString stringWithFormat:@"Long-winded string
→ creation"];
```

Using literal syntax, this becomes:

```
NSString *myString = @"Short-form string creation";
```

We can now take a similar approach to the creation of numbers. In the past, if you wanted to store a number in an NSNumber variable (for example, to subsequently store it in an array), you would use the following syntax:

```
NSNumber *myNumber = [NSNumber numberWithFloat:42.0f];
```

With the new literal syntax, this becomes:

```
NSNumber *myNumber = @42.0f;
```

If you want to use an expression, including variables, then surround the expression with parentheses:

```
NSNumber *myNumber = @(42.0f - anotherNumber);
```

Similarly, to store a Boolean in an NSArray, it needs to be boxed into an NSNumber. The old way to do that was:

```
NSNumber *myBool = [NSNumber numberWithBool:YES];
```

In this new age of enlightenment, we can simply use:

```
NSNumber *myBool = @YES;
```

While these extensions to the language are appealing in themselves, there is also an added bonus in the form of subscript notation for array and dictionary manipulation. Previously to create an array, you would use a long-winded construct such as the following:

```
NSArray *myArray = [NSArray arrayWithObjects:myString, myNumber, myBool, nil];
```

And heaven help you if you forget the nil at the end (technically known as the sentinel). Now you can relax and use:

```
NSArray *myArray = @[myString, myNumber, myBool];
```

That's right—it's shorter, it's more obviously an array, and you don't have to worry about the sentinel. You'll be even more pleased to know that dictionary creation has been given the same sort of simplification. Remember this?

```
NSDictionary *myDict = [NSDictionary dictionaryWithObjectsAndKeys:
                      → @"Value1", @"Key1", @"Value2", @"Key2", nil];
```

Yep—the unnecessarily long method name, values preceding keys, checking that you had the right number of arguments, and that sentinel nil. All things of the past with this as a replacement:

```
NSDictionary *myDict = @{ @"Key1": @"Value1", @"Key2": @"Value2"};
```

No sentinel required, the keys precede the values, and the separator between keys and values is now a colon, allowing for easy visual pairing. It's a thing of beauty.

It doesn't end there, however: Not only is creation simplified, but the process of accessing and manipulating values in arrays and dictionaries has become even easier with subscripting. **Table 11.1** summarizes the changes.

TABLE 11.1 Array and dictionary access with subscripting

OLD STYLE	NEW STYLE
[myArray objectAtIndex:0]	myArray[0]
[myArray replaceObjectAtIndex:0 withObject:newValue]	myArray[0] = newValue
[myDict objectForKey:@"Key1"]	myDict[@"Key1"]
[myDict setObject:newValue forKey:@"Key1"]	myDict[@"Key1"] = newValue

HOW TO DO IT

In isolation, these syntax changes seem like trivial enhancements, but multiply them over a large project and they can save some serious typing. And more to the point, they make your code much easier to read and, thus, maintain. If you're writing new code, it makes sense to use the new syntax. But what if you have a large older project that you'd like to update to the new syntax?

Thankfully, Apple has included functionality to convert an older project to use some (but not all) facets of modern Objective-C. To convert a project, choose Edit > Refactor > Convert to Modern Objective-C Syntax. You'll see an action sheet telling you what it plans to do—in summary, it is going to update some of the code for specific targets, and update some of the build settings for those targets. If you are happy with that, click Next to select the targets you want to modernize. If you are not happy at any stage, click Cancel.

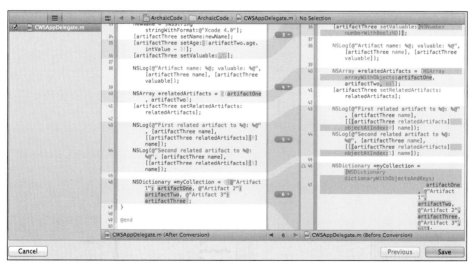

FIGURE 11.8
Previewing proposed modernizations

Once you have selected your targets, click Next to generate a preview of the changes that Xcode is proposing to carry out (**Figure 11.8**). The preview takes the form of a three-pane view: a list of files that will be modified and two editor views indicating the changes as a diff view. This is your opportunity to look through the proposed changes (on the left) and sanity-check them before committing to the process. You can deselect files to exclude them from being changed, or you can discard individual changes within a single file. If you want extra-fine control, you can even make code changes within the left editor view. Once you are happy with the changes, click Save to roll with them, or click Cancel to discard everything.

GET ON THE ARC

In Xcode 4.2, Apple introduced Automatic Reference Counting (ARC) to Objective-C for use with Mac and iOS. ARC takes away the tedium of explicitly sending messages such as retain, release, and autorelease to manage memory. The messages are still sent but are now inserted directly into the code by the compiler. This means that best practices are followed, and there is less chance of mistakenly omitting a release statement.

Mac developers who were using garbage collection (GC) may be disappointed to find that it has been deprecated as of OS X 10.8. If you invested heavily in GC, you are going to need to convert your applications to use ARC in the future.

Whether you are switching from GC or simply want to strip out all manual reference counting in your code, Apple has added a tool to do all of this for you—select Edit > Refactor > Convert to Objective-C ARC to start the process.

FIGURE 11.9
Converting targets to ARC

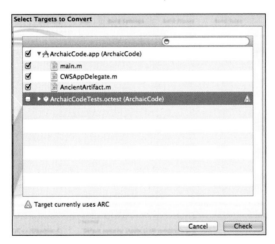

The first step is to select the targets in the current project that you wish to convert to ARC. As shown in **Figure 11.9**, the tool will detect if a project already uses ARC so that you don't needlessly try to convert it again. You can also expand each target to show the source files that are contained in it. ARC can be deselected on a per-file basis, so if you have specific source files that are causing problems with ARC, you can exclude them from conversion at this point.

Click Check to process your selected targets and files—this will kick off an analysis of your code to ensure that there are no issues before processing, because existing build issues may affect the ARC conversion process. If everything is ready, you will be presented with an action sheet explaining the rest of the process. After reading it through, click Next to continue.

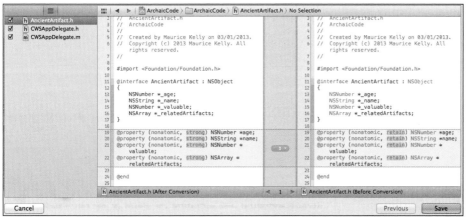

FIGURE 11.10 Previewing the ARC conversion

The next step (**Figure 11.10**) displays a preview containing a list of files to be modified, and two editor views indicating the changes as a diff view. You can review and adjust the proposed changes at this point. If you are happy with the changes, click the Save button to proceed, or click Cancel to go back to manual reference counting or GC.

WHAT CHANGES DOES IT MAKE?

Having an automatic conversion tool is great, but it is still worthwhile knowing what it is going to do behind the scenes. That way, you will know what it's done on your behalf and what to fix if it went slightly wrong.

- The build setting Objective-C Automatic Reference Counting is changed from No to Yes. This is the most important change, because it determines whether or not the compiler automatically inserts the `retain`, `release`, and `autorelease` messages on your behalf.

- The Garbage Collection setting GCC_ENABLE_OBJC_GC is removed.

- The `retain`, `release`, and `autorelease` messages in your code are removed.

- The NSAutoreleasePool class is replaced with the ARC-friendly `@autoreleasepool`.

- Instances of toll-free bridging between Cocoa/Cocoa Touch and Foundation classes are updated.

WRAPPING UP

You now know how to modernize your older projects. Although the built-in tools are very helpful, there are plenty more ways to modernize Objective-C code that you can employ yourself. If you are a member of the Mac or iOS developer programs (http://developer.apple.com), you should take a look at the latest WWDC videos. In the next chapter, you'll discover some more features available to you in the Source editor.

CHAPTER 12

Advanced Editing

In Chapter 5, you explored the Source editor and some of its features. In this chapter, you'll explore a few more powerful features and familiarize yourself with some additional tips and tricks to make better use of the editor.

RENAMING SYMBOLS

The Edit All in Scope command is a simple and often overlooked editor feature. As its name suggests, you can edit a symbol name and automatically change each instance of it within the current scope at the same time.

Consider a local variable named bob. You've decided a variable should sound more formal, so you want to change bob to robert. Assuming bob is reused throughout the current scope of a long method, it would be tedious and error-prone to find and rename each instance, even though they're temporarily underlined when you select an instance or simply put the insertion point within an instance. To formalize bob, move the insertion point inside the symbol, and all instances of bob within the current scope then appear with a dotted outline (**Figure 12.1**).

If you hover your mouse pointer over any highlighted bob, you'll notice that a button appears immediately to its right. Click this button to open a context menu, and select Edit All in Scope; if you prefer to use keyboard shortcuts, you can press Control+Command+E. Xcode responds by highlighting each bob in the current scope, ready to edit them all. Begin typing to replace the text, or move the cursor around within the highlighted text to modify it. In this example, every instance of bob has been renamed robert (**Figure 12.2**).

To end editing, click to place the text insertion point somewhere outside the symbol, or navigate away using the arrow keys. Note that only the symbol name changed; it remains a pointer to the string literal @"Bob". You could further edit the symbol to give robert a sex change. Repeat the procedure, but instead of replacing the text, place the cursor after the *t* in robert and then add an *a*. The symbol should now be roberta, who is suddenly in need of a new wardrobe or at least a new string literal.

It's important to note that this operation works only within the current scope. You cannot use this feature to rename an instance variable or a method.

```
148     NSString *bob = @"Bob";
149     NSLog(@"My name is %@", bob);
```

FIGURE 12.1 All instances of the symbol bob outlined

```
148     NSString *robert = @"Bob";
149     NSLog(@"My name is %@", robert);
```

FIGURE 12.2 In the current scope, bob is now robert.

REFACTORING

The programming term *refactor* is perhaps overused but in general means to "repurpose" or "reengineer" code or even architecture. Xcode's Refactor tools allow you to modify code in an intelligent way.

In the previous section, you learned how to rename symbols within a given scope. The Edit All in Scope tool is a more surgical approach than a blind search and replace, since replacing all instances of the common iterator i, for example, would likely make a mess of anything containing the letter *i*. Still, renaming symbols is limited to the current scope, so you cannot rename an instance variable.

The Refactor tools go a step beyond Edit All in Scope, using knowledge of your code base to make more intelligent decisions about your code, and simplifying common but error-prone refactoring tasks.

REFACTORING TOOLS

You can find the various types of refactoring that Xcode can automate for you in the Edit > Refactor menu. The first six tools are also available in a context menu if you right-click anywhere in the Source editor.

RENAME

Rename works in much the same way as Edit All in Scope, with one exception: It is not limited to scope. This distinction means you can rename an instance variable. In the case of an Interface Builder outlet (see Chapter 7), Rename will update the outlet in your xib as well (a huge time-saver). If you are renaming a class, Rename will also update the filenames for the interface and implementation files to match.

Note that the Rename operation must be carried out on a single symbol that is defined within your project. This means you cannot carry out the Rename operation if you select multiple symbols, a word from comments, a literal string, or a symbol defined in the Mac or iOS SDKs. When you carry out the operation, you will be presented with an action sheet (**Figure 12.3**) where you can define the new name for the symbol, and optionally rename files if you are changing a class name. When you are satisfied with your name, click Preview to show the changes that will result.

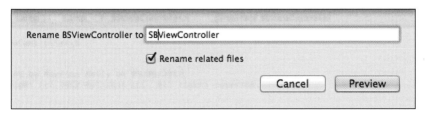

FIGURE 12.3 The Rename action sheet

EXTRACT

Extract takes a selected block of code and creates a method or function (depending on your choice) with it. If the code block depends on local variables, they will be converted to arguments of the method or function. When using the Extract tool, you should try to select a block of code that is reasonably self-contained. Although it is possible to perform the operation on a single line, it is rarely beneficial to do so.

On executing the Extract tool, you will be presented with an action sheet showing the proposed signature of the extracted code (**Figure 12.4**). Xcode will look for variables that it can place as parameters to be passed into the extracted method. You can rename these and the method name, as well as decide whether to extract the code to an Objective-C method or a regular C function. When you are happy with your changes, click Preview to inspect the results.

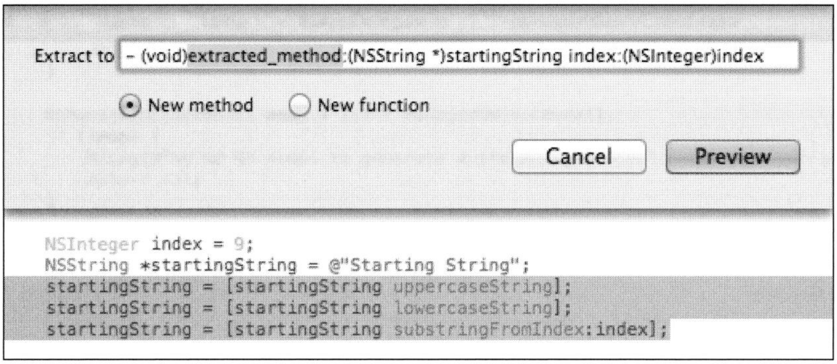

FIGURE 12.4 The Extract action sheet

CREATE SUPERCLASS

Create Superclass does just as the name suggests—it creates a superclass from the selected class. To use it, you need to highlight the name of a class that you have defined within your project. For example, you can superclass your own subclass of NSViewController, but you cannot make a superclass of NSViewController itself. When you execute the tool, you will be presented with an action sheet (**Figure 12.5**) that allows you to define the name of your superclass and allows you to choose to place the declaration and implementation in the selected class's files or in their own new files.

FIGURE 12.5 The Create Superclass action sheet

```
Create superclass of BSViewController named: SuperBSViewController

    ● Create files for new superclass
    ○ Add superclass to BSViewController's files

                          Cancel      Preview
```

MOVE UP/MOVE DOWN

If you have created yourself a new superclass, or you already have a convenient class hierarchy lying around, you can use the Move Up tool to move a method or instance variable from the subclass to the superclass. Obviously you must "own" the superclass—you cannot move a method into a superclass that belongs to the SDK. The Move Up action sheet (**Figure 12.6**) allows you to decide if you want methods that make direct access to the item to be moved with it (for example, accessor methods). If you decide not to move these methods, Xcode will display a warning in the Refactor preview sheet if it believes the methods are needed.

Move Down is the companion that allows you to move a symbol from a superclass to one or more subclasses. Again, you must own the superclass to perform this operation. Move Down has the most boring of all the Refactor action sheets, with no opportunity to do anything except move on to the preview sheet (where you can select which subclasses you want the symbols to be moved to).

Move managedObjectContext from PPDataStore to DataStore

☐ Move related methods

Cancel   Preview

FIGURE 12.6 The Move Up action sheet

ENCAPSULATE

As properties become more common, it is less likely that the Encapsulate tool will be much use. If you have old code that relies heavily on instance variables, Encapsulate creates accessor methods (getters and setters) for a selected instance variable and changes all direct references to them so that the accessors are used instead. When you're executing the tool, the action sheet (**Figure 12.7**) will allow you to define the getter and setter names—it usually chooses sensible values, but you might want to adjust them to taste (for example, many developers like to use more descriptive terms, like isActive or hasDownloaded, for their BOOL instance variables).

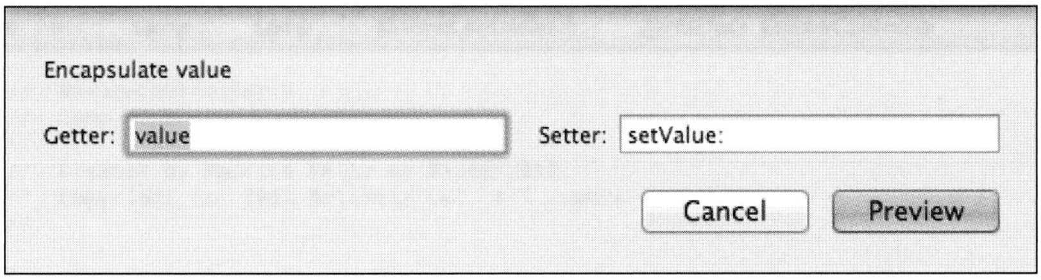

Encapsulate value

Getter: value   Setter: setValue:

Cancel   Preview

FIGURE 12.7 The Encapsulate action sheet

CONVERT TO OBJECTIVE-C ARC

Convert to Objective-C ARC (not available in the Refactor context menu) will update your project settings and the source files to use Automatic Reference Counting. This option has far-reaching consequences for your project and is covered in depth in Chapter 11.

CONVERT TO MODERN OBJECTIVE-C SYNTAX

Convert to Modern Objective-C Syntax (not available in the Refactor context menu) will update large swaths of your project to use features like literal syntax and subscript notation. This refactoring tool replaces an older action called Convert to Objective-C 2.0 but unfortunately no longer performs updates to older loop syntaxes or properties. It is covered in Chapter 11.

THE REFACTOR PREVIEW

As you have seen, most of the Refactor tools operate in a similar fashion—you select the code that you want to refactor, and then you choose the operation you wish to perform on that code. In the next step, Xcode analyzes your code and displays a three-pane preview sheet (**Figure 12.8**) that allows you to verify and cherry-pick individual replacements.

FIGURE 12.8 The Refactor preview sheet

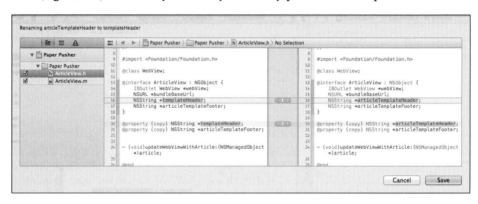

FIGURE 12.9 The Refactor preview controls

You can use the list on the left side of the window to jump directly to each instance that will be renamed. Each item has a check box that lets you choose whether that file will be included in the renaming changes. Notice that there are three controls at the top of this list (**Figure 12.9**). From left to right, these controls allow you to view the list of affected files as a tree, to view the affected files in a flat view, and to view any issues in your project that may affect the proposed refactor.

The middle and right panes show two versions (an "after" and a "before") of the file selected in the left pane. Between the two versions, you will see a sequence of numbered controls representing each change Xcode is proposing to make. You click the small arrow on the right of each of these controls to include or exclude that change. If you are not happy with simply including/excluding files or specific changes, you can even use the middle pane as an editor to customize your refactor—just in case Xcode gets it wrong.

If you are happy with the changes that Xcode proposed (and that you have tweaked), click Save, telling Xcode to apply them. If you have automatic snapshots enabled (see Chapter 6), one will be taken at this point, in case you change your mind.

ORGANIZING WITH MACROS

Xcode includes CPP, the C preprocessor, through which your code runs just prior to compilation. The preprocessor transforms your code wherever macros are encountered. For example, when it encounters an #import directive, the preprocessor replaces it with the referenced file (nearly always a header file) so its contents are available to the compiler.

A less obvious use of preprocessor macros is for organization within a graphical editor. Using the #pragma mark directive, you can define areas within your source file. When you have this file open in the Source editor, the last segment of the jump bar (which, as you'll recall, lists class members for easy navigation) will reflect your marks by grouping them in its pop-up menu. For example, **Figure 12.10** shows one possible organization of a source file.

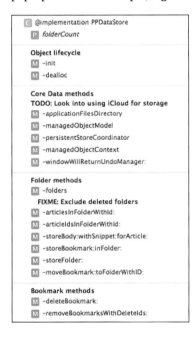

FIGURE 12.10 Organizing the jump bar pop-up

To use the directive, just place it (along with a name for the section) on a blank line by itself:

```
#pragma mark Constructors / Destructors
```

You can go a step further and place a separating line in the menu by using a dash:

```
#pragma mark -
```

For convenience, you can even combine them into a single line:

`#pragma mark - Constructors / Destructors`

There is no defined standard dictating how you should use this directive, nor does it have any effect on your compiled code (it is not part of the compiled code). Although it's easy to get carried away and pepper your code with marks, take a minimalist approach and group methods by their primary function.

The jump bar can also include comments that begin with the words `TODO:` or `FIXME:`. These can be helpful, ever-present reminders of tasks that you need to get finished, or that a collaborator needs to do.

CHANGING EDITOR KEY BINDINGS

Although the focus of the Key Bindings preferences panel (**Figure 12.11**) is not limited to the Source editor, it's worth pointing out that you can use it to customize even the most basic OS X text-editing and menu keyboard shortcuts in Xcode 4. Developers familiar with the shortcuts of other environments will find this invaluable.

To open the Key Bindings preferences panel, choose Xcode > Preferences from the main menu and then select Key Bindings from the toolbar. The left side of the panel provides controls for managing command sets you create or customize. The right side lets you locate and customize shortcuts.

FIGURE 12.11 The Key Bindings preferences panel

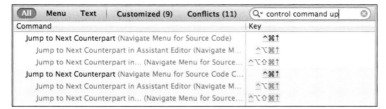

FIGURE 12.12 Filter commands by short-cut keys.

Shortcuts are divided into two main groups: menu shortcuts and text shortcuts. Menu shortcuts are further divided into subgroups according to main menu items such as File and Edit. Text shortcuts are grouped loosely by function, such as Selection and Deletion. You can filter the list using the search bar at the top. As well as searching by the command name, the search bar will filter by key name. For example, to find all commands that use the Control key, Command key, and Up arrow key, just type **control command up** in the search bar (**Figure 12.12**).

To the far left of the search bar, you can choose to show only menu or text-editing short-cuts. When you have customized shortcuts or have conflicts with your custom shortcuts and the defaults, an additional pair of filter buttons will appear to left of the search bar.

> **NOTE:** The shortcut for most any item in Xcode's menu can be customized (or added if none yet exists). The list of customizable shortcuts is extensive, and it's worth a few minutes of your time to browse it.

MANAGING COMMAND SETS

You can think of command sets as keyboard shortcut profiles. For example, if you were nostalgic (or stubborn), you could create a command set whose text shortcuts match those of Emacs or CodeWarrior.

Use the + (plus) and − (minus) buttons at the bottom of the Command Sets list (Figure 12.11) to create or remove command sets. Although it's not really obvious, the currently selected command set is the one currently in effect and is persistent. To switch to a different command set, just select it.

If you have a particularly well-loved and finely tuned command set, you might want to take it with you between Macs. There is no way to export a command set from Xcode, but fortunately the command sets exist as easily portable files. To copy a command set to your home directory, use the following command at the terminal (where Custom is the name of the command set):

```
cp ~/Library/Developer/Xcode/UserData/KeyBindings/Custom.idekeybindings ~/
```

To use the command set in Xcode on another Mac, just copy the command set to the other machine and use the following command:

```
cp ~/Custom.idekeybindings ~/Library/Developer/Xcode/UserData/KeyBindings
```

You will need to restart Xcode for the change to take effect.

CUSTOMIZING SHORTCUTS

To customize a shortcut, double-click the field in the Key column next to the shortcut. The field will become highlighted, and + and – buttons will appear near its right side. The – button removes a shortcut, and the + button lets you add shortcuts (so multiple shortcuts can fire the same action). To set a shortcut, press the key combination you'd like, and then click outside the field to end editing (or press the + button to add another).

ADJUSTING PROJECT SETTINGS

When you create a new project, Xcode will re-use some of the details you used when creating a previous project. Sometimes as you work on a project you might want to change some of those details. For example, you might want to develop under a different organization for personal rather than professional projects. You may want to adjust (or remove) the class prefix that is applied to the suggested name of future classes you create in that project— for example, you may not wish to have class prefixes prepended to all of your data model subclasses.

It is possible to change these details (and more) by selecting the project entry in the File navigator and opening the File inspector (**Figure 12.13**). From there, you can rename the project, change the organization and the class prefix, and adjust the text settings and the source control.

FIGURE 12.13 The File inspector

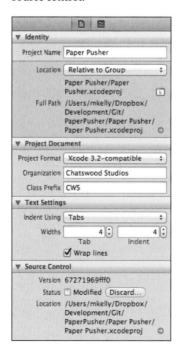

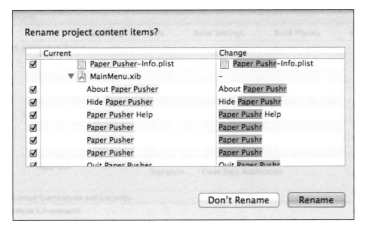

FIGURE 12.14 Renaming project content

Renaming the project is a far-reaching action—when you do so, Xcode will search through your project to find instances to rename for you. When it has done so, it will present an action sheet detailing the changes (**Figure 12.14**) and allow you to select all, select some, or simply not rename anything but the project and its targets.

USING THE SEARCH NAVIGATOR

Initiating a basic search is simple—type a term into the familiar search box at the top of the Search navigator and press Return. If you are not currently in the Search navigator, you can get there quickly by choosing Edit > Find > Find in Workspace from the main menu, or by pressing Command+Shift+F at any time.

The results are displayed in the Search navigator outline (**Figure 12.15**), organized by source file. Selecting a file or a matching line within a file will cause Xcode to navigate to it in the appropriate editor. It will flash in yellow to grab your attention, and it will then show as a regular text selection. The search results themselves can be further refined by typing an additional term in the filter field at the bottom of the Search navigator.

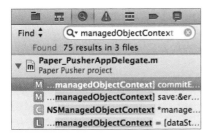

FIGURE 12.15 Search navigator showing matching results

FIGURE 12.16 Search options context menu

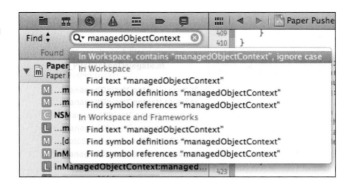

The basic scope of the search can be selected as you are typing the search term, before you press Return. A context menu will appear as you type (**Figure 12.16**), allowing you to limit the scope to your project/workspace or to your project/workspace and all frameworks, and allowing you to choose a type of search: symbol definitions or symbol references.

"Symbol definitions" will filter the search to include only matches that define a symbol (such as a property or method name) containing the search term. "Symbol references" will filter the search to include only matches that use a symbol containing the search term. These are helpful because they can refine searches to exclude symbol names appearing in comments. You can select one of these options by using the mouse or by using the Up and Down arrow keys and then pressing Return; pressing Return without using the Up arrow key always chooses the first option in the list.

USING THE FIND OPTIONS

A number of options are available to specify your search. Click the magnifying glass icon at the left edge of the top search field to reveal a context menu. Choose Show Find Options, and the Find Options panel will display (**Figure 12.17**). The context menu also gives you quick access to recent searches if you need to repeat one.

FIGURE 12.17 The Find Options panel

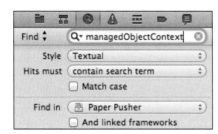

USING THE STYLE OPTION

The Style option allows you to specify a textual search, a regular expression search, a symbol definition search, or a symbol reference search (as described in the previous section). A textual search matches the literal text term you type. A regular expression (or regex) search will search for patterns using the regular expression syntax.

Although you can perform reasonably complex changes with carefully chosen search-and-replace strings, regular expressions are a far more powerful pattern-matching tool. Support for regex is built directly into many modern APIs and text editors. Although the subject is beyond the scope of this book, an abundance of books and online tutorials exist on the topic.

USING THE HITS MUST OPTION

This option allows you to specify the location of the search term within the searched items. That is, you can choose to view any results containing the term, only those that begin with the term, ones that exactly match the entire term, or only those that end with the term.

USING THE MATCH CASE OPTION

This option lets you choose whether the search is case sensitive. For example, with Ignore Case selected, the term `managedObjectContext` would successfully match any instance variables in your project and any usage of the class name `NSManagedObjectContext`. If you choose Match Case, it would match only `managedObjectContext` and not `NSManagedObjectContext`.

USING THE FIND IN OPTION

This option lets you narrow the scope to specific projects in a multiproject workspace or any custom scope you define. Workspaces are covered in detail in Chapter 4; custom scopes are covered in the next section. You can also choose to include any frameworks that your project links by selecting the "And linked frameworks" check box.

CREATING CUSTOM FIND SCOPES

This powerful feature lets you define search scopes with user-defined rules that can match locations, names, paths, extensions, or file types. To define a custom scope, choose Custom from the Find In pop-up menu under Find Options. A sheet will appear listing custom scopes (empty by default) and their associated rules (**Figure 12.18**).

FIGURE 12.18 The Find Scopes sheet

A good use case for a custom scope would be to narrow it to only HTML files within the workspace. This can be useful if you include an HTML-based Mac Help Book with your application and need to find all references to a feature you intend to rename or expand upon.

To create a custom find scope, make sure the Find Scopes sheet is open and then click the + button at the lower-left edge of the sheet. A new scope will be created with a basic rule ("Location is within workspace"). Double-click the My Scope entry in the scopes list, rename it something useful (such as HTML Source), and press Return.

Since the default rule narrows the scope to matches anywhere within the current workspace, you need only one additional rule to narrow it to HTML files. To add this rule, click the + button to the right of the first rule ("Location is within workspace"). A new default rule will appear ("Name is equal to"). Click the Name menu and select Type. Click the "any" menu and select html. Your Find Scopes sheet should now look like **Figure 12.19**.

FIGURE 12.19 A new custom find scope

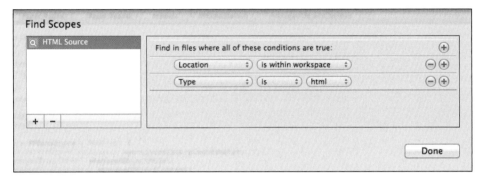

NOTE: Help Book is Apple's term for the application's documentation. Application Help Books are accessed through the application's Help menu.

Click Done to close the sheet. The new scope is now selected in the Find In menu and will remain as one of the available search scopes. You can edit or delete it or add new scopes at any time by choosing the Custom option from the Find In menu.

REPLACING TEXT

To the left of the top search field is a pop-up button with Find selected. Click the pop-up and choose Replace. More options are revealed below the search field (**Figure 12.20**). An additional field, in which you can specify the replacement term, accompanies three buttons (Preview, Replace, and Replace All). When the navigator area is not wide enough to contain all three buttons, the Preview button is represented by an icon representing a loupe.

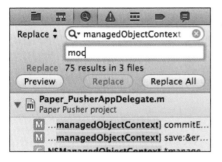

FIGURE 12.20 The Replace options

NOTE: The additional Find options that are revealed when you choose Show Find Options from the search field's magnifying glass menu are also available when you perform a Find and Replace.

You can replace specific instances by selecting them (Command-click to select multiple non-contiguous results) and clicking the Replace button. This will replace only those instances with the replacement term. To replace all instances, click Replace All. Xcode will replace the desired instances, and the changes will be saved automatically when you build or close your project.

Xcode has a visual replacement preview interface for previewing replacements. When you click the Preview button, a sheet similar to **Figure 12.21** appears. The preview sheet lets you cherry-pick the replacements you want, and you can view the effect each change will have before you apply it. Do this by placing a check mark next to the desired matches in the left-side outline view or by flipping the switches to the right in the preview panel.

Clicking the Replace button in the lower-right corner of the sheet will apply your changes. You may be prompted to take a snapshot of the project so you can revert the changes. Snapshots are covered in Chapter 6.

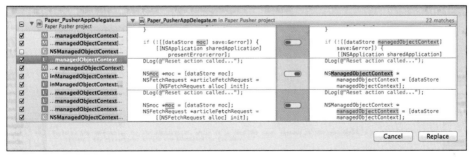

FIGURE 12.21 The Replace preview sheet

SEARCHING WITHIN FILES

You can also perform a search or a search and replace within the currently selected source file in the Source editor. The simpler UI works much the same way as the Search navigator, including additional options (by clicking the search field's magnifying glass icon) and a Replace field (**Figure 12.22**).

FIGURE 12.22 The Source editor Find panel

To find a word or phrase, select Edit > Find > Find from the main menu or press Command+F. Enter a search term and press Return. You can navigate through the matches within the file using the back and forward buttons to the left of the search field, or you can press Command+G to go to the next match and Command+Shift+G to go to the previous one.

Although there is no preview as with a project-wide search and replace, you can choose Replace All to replace all matches, Replace to replace the current selection, or Replace & Find to replace the current selection and select the next match. Pressing the Option key will change the Replace All button to the In Selection button—this allows you to apply the replacement only to a selected portion of the text.

Click Done to close the Find panel.

> **TIP:** A handy shortcut for finding quickly is to highlight a portion of text and press Command+E. This will populate the Find field with the selected text whether or not the Find bar is visible. Pressing Command+G will then navigate through the matches.

WRAPPING UP

This gentle introduction to the more advanced (or simply less common) aspects of Xcode 4 has given you a handful of powerful Source editor features. These features offer elegant solutions to tedious and error-prone editing tasks that developers encounter when writing or maintaining code.

You've seen how you can search and replace within your project or the currently selected file. The comprehensive set of options—including user-customizable, rules-based scopes—is flexible enough to help you find exactly what you're looking for. The preview system lets you cherry-pick exactly what you want to replace.

In the next chapter, you'll learn about Xcode 4's schemes system and how to customize the build and archive process, set up target dependencies, and more.

CHAPTER 13

The Build System

Xcode 4 offers for its build system a powerful user interface that de-emphasizes switching between separate build configurations for debug and release and focuses more on what developers spend most of their time doing within the IDE: coding and debugging.

AN OVERVIEW

Let's take a brief tour of the terminology before exploring each term in depth. The result of a build is some sort of product—an application, a plug-in, a command-line program, a framework, or a library.

TARGETS

A *target* describes a product (an application, a plug-in, a library, a unit testing bundle, or an aggregate of other targets) to be built and the instructions for building it. The instructions specify build settings, phases, rules, and source code and resource files within the project. A project might contain more than one target. For example, a project might contain targets for a desktop application, a companion command-line program, and a library of shared code used by both. A target can also specify another target and a script to run, giving you the ability to create a "deployment package" target.

SCHEMES

A *scheme* describes one or more targets to build, a configuration to use when building them, custom build scripts to execute, and tests to execute against the target (see Chapter 15). Xcode allows you to perform a number of build actions against a scheme, such as Run, Test, Profile, Analyze, and Archive. A project will have at least one scheme but can contain as many as you need. A scheme can be shared with other developers who use the project or workspace and can be exported for use in other, unrelated projects to save the trouble of re-establishing settings used commonly in your organization. Xcode can also create new schemes as you add targets. Schemes (and a corresponding run destination) are selected when building and running applications to specify which target and dependencies to build with what configuration, and in what environment to run the built product.

BUILD SETTINGS

Build settings include the target architecture and SDK, the location of intermediate build files, compiler selection, linker settings, search paths, and more. The settings can be project-wide or target-specific, and a separate value can be defined for a given configuration (Debug versus Release, for example).

CONFIGURATIONS

A *configuration* describes a collection of build settings for the build environment. By default, an Xcode project has two configurations: Debug and Release. The configuration Xcode uses when performing a given action (such as Run, Analyze, or Archive) is dictated by the settings in the active scheme. For example, the Run action of the default scheme of a Cocoa application project would use the Debug configuration, and the Archive action would use the Release configuration. Common configurations can be exported and imported to enable sharing and reuse among an organization's projects.

RUN DESTINATIONS

A *run destination* describes the environment in which to run an executable product (that is, a target that specifies an application or command-line program). The environment can be your Mac (in 32-bit or 64-bit mode), the iOS Simulator, or an actual iOS device. The available run destinations shown in the Scheme controls are determined automatically by the build settings specified for the associated target—specifically, the combination of settings specified in the Supported Platforms, Architectures, and Base SDK build settings.

BUILD PHASES

A *build phase* is a stage in the build process of the current target (dependencies, compile, link, copy resources, run a postprocessing script, and so on). In addition to the standard compile, link, and dependencies phases, you can add phases to a target, such as Copy Files or Run Script. This can be a simple way of adding an additional step to the target's build process, such as copying an embedded framework into an application bundle. It can also provide a hook for more complex manipulations during the build process using shell scripts. See Chapter 16 for more details regarding customizing the build process.

BUILD RULES

A *build rule* defines associations between a type of file (such as a C or Objective-C source file) and the program used to compile or process it. The default build rules for common file types are target-independent, but you can define target-specific rules as well. You might define a custom build rule for a new file type that Xcode does not know how to handle or to specify an alternative tool to use (or the same tool with different arguments) when handling that file type.

WORKING WITH TARGETS

Since a target represents a built product (or an aggregate of other targets), it's an "end result" of your coding efforts. Xcode 4 provides template targets for the most common types of target, such as Mac or iOS applications, command-line programs, frameworks, and so on (**Figure 13.1**).

FIGURE 13.1 The template chooser

Numerous other target templates exist for less common tasks as well. These include system plug-ins for Spotlight importers, screen savers, device drivers, and others (**Figure 13.2**). Templates exist for specific applications bundled with OS X as well, including Address Book and Automator. They can't be created as part of a new project but can be added to an existing project (see "Adding New Targets" later in this chapter).

FIGURE 13.2 Other target types

FINDING YOUR PROJECT'S TARGETS

When you create a new Xcode project, an initial target is created and configured for you; it shares the name you specified for your project. You can find every project's targets by selecting the project itself in the Project navigator (**Figure 13.3**).

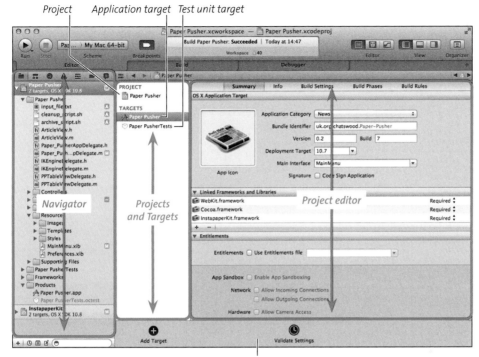

Project   Application target   Test unit target

Navigator

Projects and Targets

Project editor

Add Target

Validate Settings

Settings toolbar

FIGURE 13.3 Selecting a project's target

If during the creation of your project you selected the Include Unit Tests check box, then you may have another target in the list. This particular target produces an `.octest` bundle, which Xcode uses to run unit tests (see Chapter 15). Note the different icon—a building block signifying a plug-in bundle.

PROJECT-WIDE SETTINGS

Selecting your project under the Project group reveals project-wide settings. These settings serve as the global settings used by all the targets defined within it. The Info tab reveals three main groups: Deployment Target, Configurations, and Localizations.

The Deployment Target group currently holds only one setting (depending on the platform—Mac OS or iOS): the minimum OS version for which your project's targets are built.

The Configurations group lets you define the configurations available to your targets. As mentioned at the beginning of the chapter, Xcode creates Debug and Release configurations (and appropriate build settings for each) by default. Here you can add, rename, or remove configurations as desired. At the bottom of this group is an option to specify which configuration command-line builds use when builds are initiated using Xcode's command-line interface (see Chapter 17).

The Localizations group lets you specify to which languages your Cocoa applications are localized, which helps you automatically manage the individual copies of user interface and other resource files that are specific to a language. Localization is beyond the scope of this book.

Below the Project editor is a toolbar containing two buttons: Add Target and Validate Settings. We will discuss adding new targets later in this chapter. The Validate Settings button will cause Xcode to analyze your project and determine if its settings are up to the standards it decrees to be modern. If your project doesn't pass muster, Xcode will offer to modernize it for you. See Chapter 11 for more details on project modernization.

EXPLORING A TARGET

Application targets (a standard Mac or iOS Cocoa application bundle) have the most settings, so these make a great starting point for exploring the range of potential target settings. Create a new project using the OS X Cocoa Application template, select the Include Unit Tests check box, and name the project **TargetExplorer**. Once it has been created, select the project in the Project navigator. In the Project editor, select the TargetExplorer target. Let's explore each tab along the top of the editor, starting with the Summary tab.

THE SUMMARY TAB

The Summary tab displays basic information—mostly reflecting the options you chose when you created the project—in the top panel, OS X Application Target. The Application Category menu is used to categorize the application if you plan to sell it in Apple's App Store. The Bundle Identifier field is the canonical name you chose (which should correspond to your organization's domain name in most cases). The Version number is the string that the Finder and the application's About panel display for the application. The Deployment Target specifies the version of OS X for which your application is built. The Main Interface menu allows you to choose a xib file to load on application startup. The App Icon image well holds the application's icon and sets its corresponding configuration entry when a new image is dragged into it. The Build field allows you to specify a build number for the application—many developers increment this frequently while maintaining the same version number in order to have a differentiator between different test builds.

The next section, Linked Frameworks and Libraries, displays (and lets you edit) the frameworks and libraries to which your application is linked. This affects the Link Binary With Libraries build phase in the Build Phases tab. The Add (+) and Remove (−) buttons let you edit this information directly. Clicking the Add button reveals a searchable list of libraries and frameworks available on your computer from which you can choose (**Figure 13.4**). You can also choose Add Other from this sheet to locate a library or framework not present in the default locations that Xcode knows to search.

FIGURE 13.4 Choosing frameworks and libraries to link against

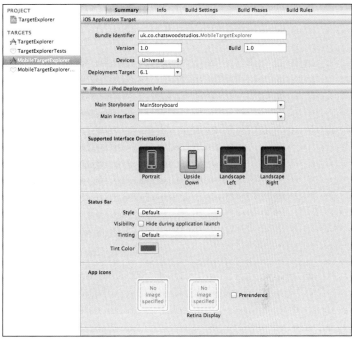

FIGURE 13.5 The Summary tab for iOS targets

The Entitlements section allows you to configure your OS X app to use sandbox entitlements or to take advantage of Apple's iCloud service. It is mandatory to use entitlements if you are planning to sell your app in the Mac App Store. To develop with entitlements enabled, you will also need to code-sign your application. For more information about entitlements, see the "Entitlements and Sandboxing" section later in the chapter.

If you are developing an iOS application, the Target Summary tab contains a lot more information. To see it, add a new target to the TargetExplorer project. Click the Add Target button at the bottom of the Summary screen, choose the iOS Master-Detail Application template, and name the target **MobileTargetExplorer**. When it is created, you will have another pair of targets—MobileTargetExplorer and MobileTargetExplorerTests.

For iOS targets, there are some differences in the Summary tab. In **Figure 13.5**, notice the Devices menu under the iOS Application Target section. This lets you select whether your project produces an application for iPhone, iPad, or both (a Universal application). Under the Deployment Info section, you'll see options (enabled by clicking them) to specify which orientations your application supports—that is, which directions your applications will follow when the user rotates the device. You will also find options for changing the appearance of the status bar.

The App Icons wells work the same way as the App Icon well in an OS X target, except that the second well (Retina Display) holds a high-resolution version of the icon, appropriate for the high-resolution Retina display in newer devices. The plethora of Launch Images wells are used to specify the images used at launch time. For the iPhone and iPod touch, there are three wells: one for non-Retina devices, one for 3.5" Retina devices, and one for 4" Retina devices. For iPads, there are four wells: one for non-Retina portrait orientations, one for Retina portrait orientations, one for landscape non-Retina, and one for landscape Retina.

The section Linked Frameworks and Libraries functions exactly as per its OS X counterpart described earlier. The Entitlements section allows you to use features like iCloud integration, and as of iOS 6 there is now a Maps Integration section. If you are creating an app that offers transit routing information, it can be configured to work with Apple Maps in this section.

THE INFO TAB

The Info tab (**Figure 13.6**) lets you edit the information contained in the app bundle's `Info.plist` file—the file that Cocoa bundles use to describe themselves to the operating system. This file contains some of the information you can manage on the Summary tab, but it has a great deal more responsibility.

Summary	Info	Build Settings	Build Phases	Build Rules

▼ Custom OS X Application Target Properties

Key	Type	Value
Bundle versions string, short	String	1.0
Bundle identifier	String	uk.co.chatswoodstudios.${PRODUCT_NAME:rfc1034identifier}
InfoDictionary version	String	6.0
Bundle version	String	1
Executable file	String	${EXECUTABLE_NAME}
Principal class	String	NSApplication
Bundle OS Type code	String	APPL
Icon file	String	
Bundle creator OS Type code	String	????
Main nib file base name	String	MainMenu
Minimum system version	String	${MACOSX_DEPLOYMENT_TARGET}
Localization native development region	String	en
Bundle name	String	${PRODUCT_NAME}

▶ Document Types (0)
▶ Exported UTIs (0)
▶ Imported UTIs (0)
▶ URL Types (0)
▶ Services (0)

FIGURE 13.6 The Info tab

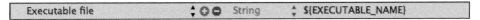

Executable file	$\updownarrow$ $\oplus$ $\ominus$	String	$\updownarrow$ ${EXECUTABLE_NAME}

FIGURE 13.7 Info property entry

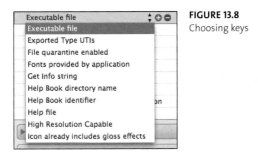

FIGURE 13.8
Choosing keys

The Custom OS X Application Target Properties section lists all the basic parts of the property list that define your unique application (including version number, the principal class used to load the application, the main nib file to use, and so on). Some of the information is duplicated between here and the Summary tab, so changes in one will reflect in the other. Selecting an individual row reveals more aspects of the editor (**Figure 13.7**). Each row's type (the key used to specify its corresponding value) can be edited by clicking the arrows to reveal a list of other available keys (**Figure 13.8**). Double-clicking a key or value lets you edit it directly. See the "Bundle Structures" section of the Bundle Programming Guide in Apple's documentation for more information about the keys used and their meaning.

The Document Types section holds any document types defined for your application. If your application is not document-based (like our TargetExplorer example), this section is empty by default, however non-document-based applications can be given document types that they can recognize. **Figure 13.9** shows a sample document type configuration for an imaginary document type called TargetFile. In this case, we've declared our application to be an editor for the document type, but you can also declare your application to be just a document viewer.

FIGURE 13.9 An imaginary TargetFile document type

The Exported UTIs and Imported UTIs sections let you define any UTIs (Uniform Type Identifiers) your application imports or exports. Defining UTIs here is a way of letting your application "claim" (and provide icons or system services for) a particular data type as well as define new data types and lineage that your application provides. See the Uniform Type Identifiers Guide in Apple's documentation for more information.

The URL Types section allows you to define the URL schemes that your application understands. An example might be a URL that takes the form of `targetexplorer://targetid` and causes your application to be launched and display the task with the specified `targetid`. See the Launch Services Programming Guide in Apple's documentation for more information.

The Services section lets you define system services (such as Insert Employee ID Here), which can be accessed from other applications. See the Services Implementation Guide in Apple's documentation for more information.

THE BUILD SETTINGS TAB

The Build Settings tab contains all the build settings for the selected target, grouped by category. The simplest view, as shown in **Figure 13.10**, can be seen by setting the filter bar (just beneath the tab bar) to show Basic and Combined. This instructs the editor to show you only the most commonly used settings and only the values for the selected target.

FIGURE 13.10 The Build Settings tab

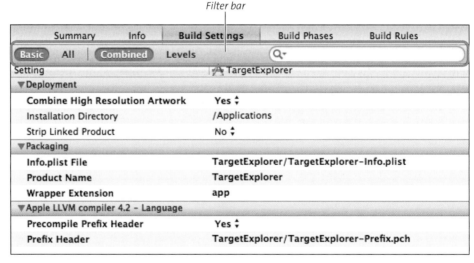

For each setting, you can edit the matching value under the column that displays the name of your target. Some values are simple strings, while others are presented in a pop-up menu. In cases where you can make more than one selection (such as the Architectures setting), you can select Other from the menu, and you'll be presented with a pop-up window (**Figure 13.11**) that allows you to add multiple selections. In the figure, an environment variable is used that, to Xcode, means the standard 64-bit universal binary. To add further selections, click the Add (+) button; click the Remove (–) button to remove a selection.

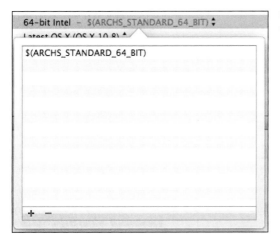

FIGURE 13.11 A multiple selection pop-up window

You can also have per-configuration settings; that is, separate settings for Debug versus Release configurations (or any others you define). In **Figure 13.12**, you see that the Build Active Architecture Only setting has an open disclosure triangle next to it and has separate settings for the two configurations—Debug and Release. When you're building an application, it is possible to build binaries for all the valid architectures (for example, i386/x86_64 for OS X, or armv7/armv7s for iOS). This makes sense for a release build, but during the development process it makes sense to build only for the active architecture, saving the time taken for a build and debug cycle.

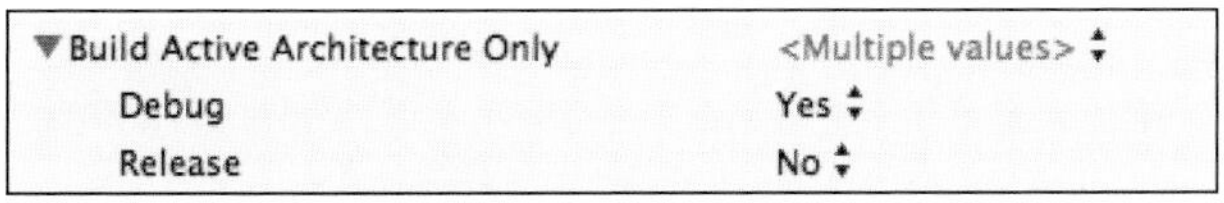

FIGURE 13.12 Per-configuration settings

NOTE: The disclosure control appears permanently only for settings that already have per-configuration values defined. Otherwise, it will appear only when hovering the mouse pointer over the row.

FIGURE 13.13 Build set-
tings arranged by level

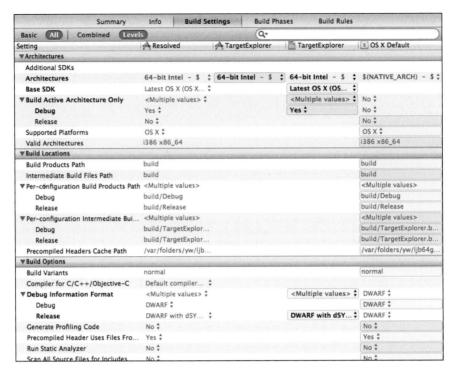

Setting	Resolved	TargetExplorer	TargetExplorer	OS X Default
▼Architectures				
Additional SDKs				
Architectures	64-bit Intel – $ ⎮	64-bit Intel – $ ⎮	64-bit Intel – $ ⎮	$(NATIVE_ARCH) – $ ⎮
Base SDK	Latest OS X (OS X... ⎮		Latest OS X (OS... ⎮	
▼Build Active Architecture Only	<Multiple values> ⎮		<Multiple values> ⎮	No ⎮
Debug	Yes ⎮		Yes ⎮	No ⎮
Release	No ⎮			No ⎮
Supported Platforms	OS X ⎮			OS X ⎮
Valid Architectures	i386 x86_64			i386 x86_64
▼Build Locations				
Build Products Path	build			build
Intermediate Build Files Path	build			build
▼Per-configuration Build Products Path	<Multiple values>			<Multiple values>
Debug	build/Debug			build/Debug
Release	build/Release			build/Release
▼Per-configuration Intermediate Bui...	<Multiple values>			<Multiple values>
Debug	build/TargetExplor...			build/TargetExplorer.b...
Release	build/TargetExplor...			build/TargetExplorer.b...
Precompiled Headers Cache Path	/var/folders/yw/ljb...			/var/folders/yw/ljb64g...
▼Build Options				
Build Variants	normal			normal
Compiler for C/C++/Objective-C	Default compiler... ⎮			
▼Debug Information Format	<Multiple values> ⎮		<Multiple values> ⎮	DWARF ⎮
Debug	DWARF ⎮			DWARF ⎮
Release	DWARF with dSY... ⎮		DWARF with dSY... ⎮	DWARF ⎮
Generate Profiling Code	No ⎮			No ⎮
Precompiled Header Uses Files Fro...	Yes ⎮			Yes ⎮
Run Static Analyzer	No ⎮			No ⎮
Scan All Source Files for Includes	No ⎮			No ⎮

For projects with multiple targets (or workspaces with multiple projects), you may need finer control than you get by choosing Combined rather than Levels in the filter bar. Choosing Levels reveals multiple columns after the Setting column, showing what the settings are for each level (**Figure 13.13**). From right to left, the columns represent global defaults down to project- and target-specific settings.

Starting from the right and working to the left, you see the default settings for the platform (OS X Default). These settings cannot be edited because they are the same for every OS X target, and all levels below this one inherit its settings. Project and workspace-level settings come next, then target-level settings. The Resolved column shows the final state of all inherited settings for the selected target.

When you're viewing settings arranged by level, values are shown at all levels for which they have been defined. If a value is overridden farther down the hierarchy (working toward the left), that value is also outlined in green. This helps you determine the level at which a setting is customized and, when considered with the Resolved column, lets you easily determine the precise setting for your individual targets.

In **Figure 13.14**, the Product Name field for TargetExplorer is defined only at the target level and does not have a system-wide default. This makes sense: All targets must be uniquely named and cannot share a default. In **Figure 13.15**, the Wrapper Extension field for the TargetExplorerTests is defined at the target level. You can see that on a system-wide basis, a bundle will have an extension of .bundle by default, but in this case it has an .octest extension. Xcode set this up when it was creating a unit-test bundle.

Setting	Resolved	TargetExplorer	TargetExplorer	OS X Default
Product Name	TargetExplorer	**TargetExplorer**		

FIGURE 13.14 The Product Name field needs to be defined at the target level.

Setting	Resolved	TargetExplorerTests	TargetExplorer	OS X Default
Wrapper Extension	octest	**octest**		bundle

FIGURE 13.15 The Wrapper Extension field is overridden at the target level.

You can also add user-defined build settings by using the Add Build Setting button in the toolbar below the Project editor. This lets you further customize the build process by passing custom settings not shown in the editor. User-defined settings appear at the bottom of the list, in a group called User-Defined.

There are many settings in this tab that affect the build environment, the built product, and even what kinds of errors and warnings the build system should respect or ignore. The depth and breadth of these settings is beyond the scope of this book, but it's worth noting that the Quick Help pane of the Utility area will give you detailed information on each. Just select the setting in the editor, and the Quick Help pane will provide an overview of the setting, its options, and its implications.

THE BUILD PHASES TAB

The Build Phases tab (**Figure 13.16**) lets you manage, add, and remove build phases for your target. The available phases depend on the type of target you are building. For example, only bundles can have bundle resources (such as images, sounds, Help Book files, and so on), so the build phase would not be used for a command-line tool.

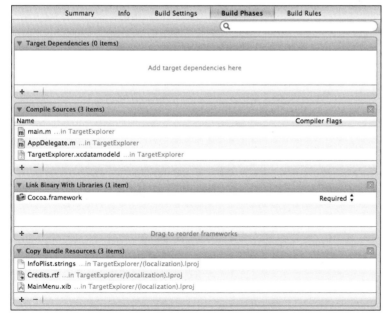

FIGURE 13.16 The Build Phases tab

You can add phases using the Add Build Phase button at the bottom of the editor. Those that are removable can be removed by clicking the remove (x) button in the upper-right corner of the phase's table.

The first build phase—Target Dependencies—is the one phase that cannot be removed. This special phase lets Xcode know of other dependencies (such as a framework or plug-in for an application) that must be built before the currently selected target can be built. This build phase defines explicit dependencies as opposed to allowing Xcode to determine target dependencies automatically (an option you can enable and disable in the Scheme editor). You can add and remove targets (any target except the one currently being edited) for this phase by using the Add (+) and Remove (–) buttons at the bottom of the phase's table.

The Compile Sources phase compiles any source files belonging to your target using the appropriate compiler for the file type as defined in the Build Rules tab. You can set compiler flags (such as optimization settings) for each individual file by double-clicking in this phase's Compiler Flags column, typing the flags, and then pressing Return. (When you enable or disable ARC on a per-file basis, this is where Xcode makes the change; see Chapter 11 for more information about using ARC in your project.) You can add source files to and remove source files from this phase using the Add (+) and Remove (–) buttons at the bottom of the phase's table. This phase seems like it should not be optional, but if you recall that there can be aggregate targets and other types, you can see why this phase is not always necessary.

The Link Binary With Libraries phase lets you control which libraries your product is linked against using the linker. While it's true that you don't have to use a library or framework in your source code to make use of it in your application (because it might be used from an instantiated object in your xib), you'll always have to link against it if you use it at all. By default, all Cocoa applications are linked against the Cocoa framework, which explains the framework's presence in the TargetExplorer target. You can add and remove linked libraries and frameworks for your product using the Add (+) and Remove (–) buttons at the bottom of the phase's table. Clicking the Add button reveals the same Frameworks and Libraries sheet you saw in Figure 13.4, from which you can select the library or framework to which to link.

The Copy Bundle Resources phase copies any resources included with your bundle into the Contents/Resources folder (the standard location for resources in any type of Cocoa bundle). Resources include application and button icons, Interface Builder xib files, video and sound clips, template files, and so on.

There are three other types of build phases that you can add to your target using the Add Build Phase button at the bottom of the editor. These phases don't show up by default for a standard Cocoa application target.

The Copy Files phase (**Figure 13.17**) lets you identify a path into which to copy the files you specify. You can choose a predefined destination path from the Destination menu, or you can specify a custom path. Most often, a Copy Files phase would specify a location within a bundle (the bundle built by the target), but this phase can be used to copy files or even built products to a variety of locations. Predefined paths include a bundle's Resources or Frameworks folder, the Shared Frameworks system path, and more. It's not uncommon to have multiple Copy Files build phases in a target. For example, you may specify a framework you either built yourself or are including from a third-party source, and choose to copy it into the application bundle's Frameworks path so the framework is available to the application at runtime (see Chapter 14). You might also add a Copy PlugIns build phase, with which you can copy a set of built plug-ins included with your main application into the application bundle's PlugIns folder. The Subpath field lets you append a subpath to whichever path you selected in the Destination menu. The "Copy only when installing" check box instructs Xcode to copy the files only when your current scheme's build settings include the Install flag. The Add (+) and Remove (–) buttons work the same way as in the other phases, allowing you to specify the files that are copied to the selected location.

FIGURE 13.17 The Copy Files build phase

The Copy Headers phase (**Figure 13.18**) lets you specify header files and their visibility for products such as frameworks, plug-ins, and drivers. The scopes (Public, Private, and Project) determine the visibility of the header in the built product. A public header is included in the product as readable source code; a private header is included in the product but is marked as private so clients know not to use its symbols directly; a project header is not included in the product and is meant to be used only by the project when building the target. The Add (+) and Remove (–) buttons work the same way as in the other phases, but in this case, when you add you'll see a sheet similar to Figure 13.4, but which lets you select only header files. Once added, a header will first appear in the Project scope. You can then drag it into the Private or Public scope, as desired.

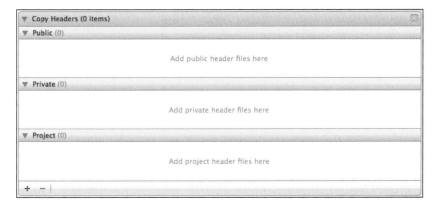

FIGURE 13.18 The Copy Headers build phase

The Run Script phase lets you run any script (by typing in the script editor field or dropping a script file into the field). This is an extremely powerful feature of the Build Phases tab, and we will cover this in much greater detail in Chapter 16.

THE BUILD RULES TAB

Xcode maintains a default list of predefined (system) rules that determine which file types are processed by which script or program during the build process. This is found under the Build Rules tab (**Figure 13.19**). For example, C source files are compiled using the default compiler (Clang in Xcode 4.6), and Core Data model files are compiled using the data model compiler. The Build Rules tab lets you customize these rules or define new ones for the selected target.

With the filter bar set to All, you see all the default system build rules and any target-defined rules. Set the Build Rules tab's filter bar to Target to see the rules overridden or defined only for the target (that is, to filter out the default system rules).

To customize a system build rule for a given file type, locate it in the list and click its Copy to Target button. The new custom rule will be added to your target, ready for you to specify the script or predefined program to use to process the file type. You can also add a rule to your target for a file type not covered by the system rules by clicking the Add Build Rule button at the bottom of the editor.

It's easy to see how much power this simple feature, hidden away as it is, can give you. With this feature, you can teach Xcode how to handle other types of files automatically during the build process.

FIGURE 13.19 The Build Rules tab

ADDING NEW TARGETS

There are several reasons why you might want to add multiple targets to a project. Earlier in this chapter you added a pair of extra targets to the project when creating an iOS application target (plus associated unit tests), though in a real-world scenario it is probably advisable to create a separate project for different platforms.

Your application might need a Spotlight plug-in (kept in its bundle's Resources subfolder so OS X can find it easily). A Spotlight importer plug-in can be kept in a separate project, but it makes more sense to keep it within the same project as its parent application. Therefore, your project might have a separate target to build that plug-in (which would be a dependency of the application's target and would be included in a Copy Bundle Resources build phase that copies the built plug-in into the app bundle's Resources folder when it is built). The same applies to other plug-ins, libraries, bundles, and so on.

Another example might be two separate builds of the same application: a free version and a paid Pro version. Both applications might share 95 percent of the source code and resources and differ only in that the Pro version has the ability to access certain features, or in that the free version expires 30 days after its first launch. Or, because of Apple's App Store policies, you might choose to link against, include, and use your own registration system in one build of your app, while using the App Store receipt validation process in an App-Store-only build.

You might also add a unit test target that executes unit tests against your code. Unit tests are covered in Chapter 15.

To add a new target, use the Add Target button at the bottom of the editor while a target or project is selected. A sheet appears (**Figure 13.20**), similar to the one that appears when creating a new project. In the figure, a Spotlight Importer target (for teaching the OS X Spotlight searching facility how to index your application's information) is selected.

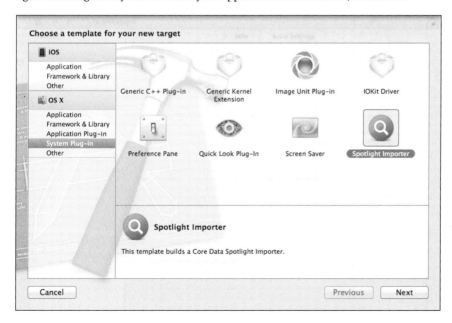

FIGURE 13.20 Spotlight Importer in the target template sheet

FIGURE 13.21 The new
target's resources

If you were to click Next and continue defining the target to add to the TargetExplorer
project, you'd be prompted with much the same line of questioning as when you created
the project (which was necessary to create the TargetExplorer application bundle target).
In the case of a Spotlight Importer target, you only need to give it a sensible name (such as
TargetImporter) and a company identifier (preferably the same as that of your application).
Xcode will add the target to the project's targets list (complete with build settings appropriate to the target type), create a separate build scheme for the target, and add the necessary
source and resources to the project, as seen in **Figure 13.21**.

NOTE: The New Target sheet is similar to the New Project sheet primarily
because Xcode needs to know what kind of target (or targets) to add to your
newly created project.

For distribution purposes, it makes sense to bundle the TargetImporter Spotlight plug-in
with the TargetExplorer application—you could distribute them independently, but why
make life more difficult for your customers? To accomplish this, you need a way to copy the
build product of the TargetImporter target into the TargetExplorer app bundle at the end
of the build process. We saw earlier that the Build Phases tab for the TargetExplorer target
contains a default phase called Copy Bundle Resources, which can be used to accomplish
what we need.

To hook this up, expand the Products group in the Project navigator so that you can
see the product named `TargetImporter.mdimporter`. Select the TargetExplorer target
in the Project editor, and ensure that the Build Phases tab is selected. Expand the Copy
Bundle Resources phase. Drag the `TargetImport.mdimporter` product into the Copy Bundle
Resources build phase (**Figure 13.22**).

FIGURE 13.22 Drag the
TargetImporter product
to the Copy Bundle
Resources build phase.

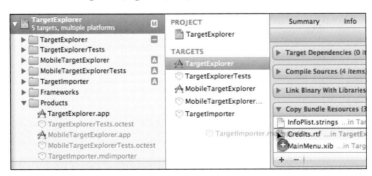

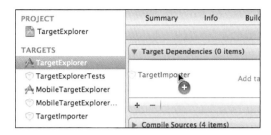

FIGURE 13.23 Establishing a target dependency

You're not done yet. If the TargetImporter target has been built, it will successfully copy into the app bundle. If you haven't yet built it, then the Copy Bundle Resources build phase will report an error. To ensure that the TargetImporter target is built first, expand the Target Dependencies build phase and then drag the TargetImporter target into the Target Dependencies area (**Figure 13.23**).

> **NOTE:** The code and knowledge necessary to customize the importer is beyond the scope of this book. Search in the Organizer's documentation tab for "Spotlight Importer Programming Guide" for more information.

SHARING FILES BETWEEN TARGETS

Sometimes you will find that you have source code files that are needed by more than one of your targets. For example, your application might have a model class that is used by the main application but is also needed by a plug-in. When you're creating new source files, Xcode gives you the opportunity to assign them to one or more targets (**Figure 13.24**). When you do this, the source file will be added to the Compile Sources build phase for all of the targets you select.

If you have an existing source file that you have since decided needs to be available to both targets, there are two ways to achieve this. The simplest way is to select the file in the Project navigator and then open the File inspector. Under the Target Membership section, you can select the check boxes for the targets you wish to build the file (**Figure 13.25**). Alternatively, if you are already working in the Project editor you could ensure that your target is selected and that the Build Phases tab is displayed; then drag the source file onto the Compile Sources build phase.

FIGURE 13.24 Pick your target at file creation time...

FIGURE 13.25 ...or you can update the targets later on.

WORKING WITH SCHEMES

You learned that schemes tie together one or more targets with a build configuration and run destinations. There is no hard set of rules that determines how many schemes a target can belong to or how many targets belong to a scheme. Schemes are meant to be a simple system for switching between conceptual sets of these items—sets that make sense to your project and workflow.

There are many ways you might use the system, but the simplest example is creating separate schemes for an App Store build of your application and a build that uses your own customer relations and registration management system. You might have a separate scheme to run, analyze, test, and deploy a server-side registration key generator—a command-line program that is called from your web store's server upon successful payment. In Chapter 16, we will show you how to use a scheme to produce a beta version of your app for distribution to testers. Any way you look at it, schemes are meant to give you an extra layer of flexibility as well as a collection point for these conceptual products and code/build/run/test/distribute scenarios.

FINDING YOUR PROJECT'S SCHEMES

`TargetExplorer ) My Mac 64-bit` Unlike many of the target-related settings, schemes are right in front of you at all times. The Scheme control (a pop-up menu in the top left of your toolbar) lets you select schemes and destinations and allows you to manage, edit, and create schemes. The first (leftmost) segment of the Scheme control lets you choose between the schemes defined within your project or workspace, and allows you to edit, create, and manage schemes. The second (rightmost) segment selects the destination (Mac, device, simulator, and so on) available for the selected scheme.

The run destinations for each scheme are dynamically determined from the targets that make up the scheme. If your scheme contains a target that has an Architecture setting of 64-bit Intel and is a Mac app, then the scheme will gain a run destination of "My Mac 64-bit." If one of the scheme's targets is a Universal iOS app, your scheme will gain run destinations including iPad and iPhone simulators, as well as any physical iOS devices attached to your Mac.

MANAGING SCHEMES

Xcode automatically creates a scheme for each target, with the exception of unit-test targets created at the same time as a Mac or iOS app target. If you have been following along with the TargetExplorer project from earlier in the chapter, you should by now have three schemes—TargetExplorer, MobileTargetExplorer, and TargetImporter.

Choose Manage Schemes from the Scheme control pop-up menu to display the sheet shown in **Figure 13.26**. The sheet lets you create, duplicate, delete, reorder, rename, and generally wrangle schemes within the current workspace.

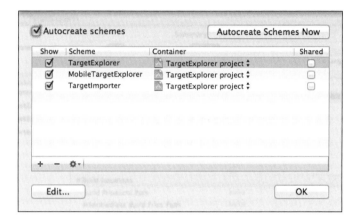

FIGURE 13.26 The Scheme Manager sheet

CREATING SCHEMES

You can create a scheme by clicking the Add (+) button at the bottom of the schemes table. A sheet (**Figure 13.27**) will appear asking for a target and a name. As you recall, schemes are linked to targets, so a new scheme must be given a target when created. Once you give the scheme a target and a name, click OK and you're finished.

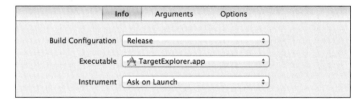

FIGURE 13.27 The New Scheme sheet

REMOVING SCHEMES

To remove a scheme, just select it and click the Remove (−) button. You'll be prompted for confirmation before the scheme is removed, because this cannot be undone. If you're certain you want to remove the scheme, click Delete to confirm and the scheme will be removed.

REORDERING SCHEMES

You can reorder schemes by dragging them into the desired order in the list. This affects the order in which they appear in the Scheme control.

DUPLICATING SCHEMES

To duplicate a scheme, select it in the list, click the Action button (located to the right of the Remove button), and then choose Duplicate from the menu. The duplicate scheme will be created, and the editing sheet (discussed in the "Editing Schemes" section) will appear.

IMPORTING AND EXPORTING SCHEMES

You can also import and export schemes to share across unrelated projects by using the Action button to the right of the Remove (–) button. You'll be prompted with a standard save panel for export or a standard open panel for import.

DEFINING A SCHEME CONTAINER

In the scheme table, you will see that the third column is named Container. A scheme has to belong to a container, which by default is the project to which its initial target belongs. For single-project setups, there is only one project to choose, but if you use workspaces containing multiple projects you will be able to choose to stash your scheme in any of the projects or in the workspace itself. This may seem like an insignificant difference, but if one of your projects is a framework that was checked out from a different SCM repository, you should probably keep schemes relating to it in the appropriate project.

SHARING SCHEMES

Like the villain who tells all to the superhero, you can also share your schemes. On the far right of the scheme table is a column called Shared, which contains a check box for each scheme listed. Making a scheme shared does not seem to do much, but under the hood Xcode has performed some migrations for you. Each user has their own set of schemes (tied to their username), and there is a set of shared schemes. If you and a colleague both work with the same project (either on disk or from an SCM system), then you each will see only your own schemes and the shared schemes. If you create a useful scheme, you need to select the Shared check box if you want your teammates to benefit as well.

AUTO-CREATING SCHEMES

As mentioned previously, Xcode can create schemes automatically as targets are created or duplicated within the project. This feature is active by default so that appropriate schemes will be created for targets in projects created by previous versions of Xcode and opened in Xcode 4.

To prevent Xcode from automatically creating schemes, deselect the Autocreate Schemes check box. If you want to have Xcode generate schemes automatically only when you want it to, open the Manage Schemes sheet and click the Autocreate Schemes Now button. Otherwise, you can leave this feature disabled and manage schemes manually.

Xcode does not remove schemes for deleted targets regardless of the auto-create setting; you must remove schemes manually.

EDITING SCHEMES

To edit a scheme, you can double-click it in the table in the Manage Schemes sheet, select it in the table, and press the Edit button; or you can select it in the Scheme control (remember to click the scheme name on the left part of the control; the right side chooses the destination) and then choose Edit Scheme from the menu. The Scheme Editor sheet will appear. This is the same edit sheet that appears when duplicating an existing scheme, though the scheme name is editable when in duplication mode.

THE SCHEME CONTROLS

The main scheme controls (**Figure 13.28**) are shown across the top of the editor sheet. These controls match the functionality of the Scheme control pop-up as well as of the Breakpoints button next to it. The behavior of these controls can be confusing.

The Scheme pop-up in the editor changes the scheme currently being edited as well as the active scheme in the Scheme pop-up. Its purpose is primarily to allow you to move between schemes without closing the editor sheet. Be aware that it also affects the active scheme even after you close the editor. The Destination pop-up also directly sets the active destination in the main Scheme control but does not appear to do anything more.

The buttons along the bottom of the editor sheet let you duplicate the current scheme, go back to the Scheme Manager sheet, or dismiss the editor sheet (using the OK button, which should probably be a Done button).

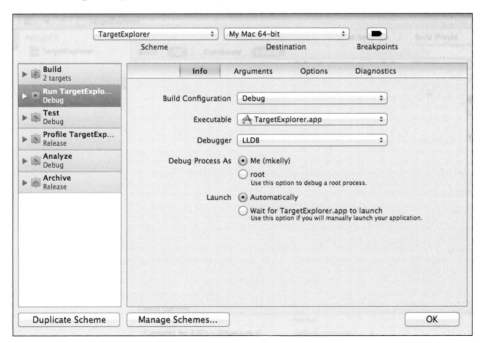

FIGURE 13.28 The Scheme Editor sheet

In the middle of the sheet are two panels, used to edit the settings of each action for the scheme. The left panel shows a list of actions corresponding to those found under the Product menu in the main menu. Selecting each action reveals that action's scheme settings in the right panel.

THE BUILD ACTION

The Build action serves as the basis for the rest of the actions. It is necessary to build a product before it can be run, tested, or profiled, so the Build action is always performed before performing any of the other actions that need a built product. To edit this action, select it from the list on the left of the Scheme Editor sheet. **Figure 13.29** shows the settings for the Build action.

FIGURE 13.29 The Build action's options

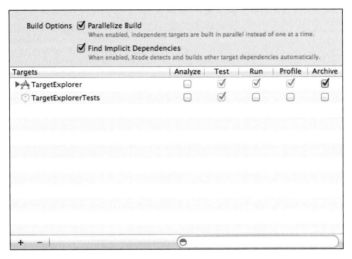

Two build options are visible at the top of the editor. The Parallelize Build option allows Xcode to build multiple independent targets—targets that do not depend on other targets—in parallel, taking advantage of your modern multi-core Mac. The Find Implicit Dependencies option allows Xcode to try identifying dependencies automatically. That is, if one target's product is linked against or copied into the resources of another, Xcode can probably figure out this dependency automatically. This lets Xcode build the targets in the necessary order without your having to define the dependencies yourself.

The complicated-looking table beneath the build options lists all the targets that are to be built for the current scheme. Note the columns with check boxes that correspond to each of the remaining actions. These check boxes control whether the target is built automatically (if necessary) before each action runs. In the figure, two targets are listed—the TargetExplorer application itself and the tests bundle. Notice that the check box for the Test action is selected and disabled so you cannot deselect it. Likewise, TargetExplorer's Test, Run, and Profile actions are selected and disabled. This indicates that the action uses the TargetExplorer target. To deselect these actions, you need to go to the Info tab for the action and stop the target from being used.

You can use this table to define dependencies directly (especially useful in complex situations where Xcode is unable to determine the dependencies itself). Use the Add (+) button at the bottom to choose another target within the workspace (including multi-project workspaces). You can drag the dependencies into the required order if necessary (just remember to deselect the Parallelize Build option if order truly is important).

As you begin to use the Scheme editor, you will start to find that there are actions you cannot carry out, and some that, once carried out, have strange results. For example, you can remove targets from the list in the Build action, though they must not be in use in any of the other actions—if they are in use, this is indicated by the inactive check boxes. Similarly, if you were to change the target product to be executed in the Run action (say from TargetExplorer.app to MobileTargetExplorer.app), you will suddenly find that a new target has appeared in the list.

There's one other item of interest hiding in the Build action's settings. Notice the disclosure triangle beside the TargetExplorer target. If you expand it, you'll see the TargetImporter target you created earlier in the chapter. Because you placed the Spotlight Importer product into the TargetExplorer target's Target Dependencies build phase, it has been automatically included in the list.

THE RUN ACTION

The Run action specifies the executable to run, the debugger to use, arguments to pass, and some environmental settings when you ask Xcode to run with the active scheme. **Figure 13.30** shows the Run action's multi-tab editor.

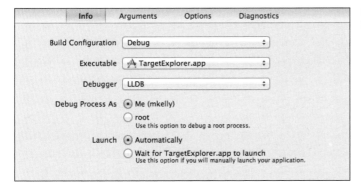

FIGURE 13.30 The Run action's Info tab

The Info tab (Figure 13.30) holds the basic settings for the Run action. The Build Configuration menu lets you select the configuration (such as Debug or Release) to use when running. The default is the Debug configuration so that the debugger can be used. The Executable menu, predictably, lets you choose the executable to run—changing this to a product whose target is not currently included in this scheme will cause that target to be added. Targets without executables (such as our Spotlight Importer) will have their executable set to None, because they can't run on their own. The Debugger menu lets you choose among installed debuggers. LLDB is the default, and although GDB is still available, it may not be for long. The Debug Process As option (for Mac apps only) allows the process to be run as your own user (the default) or as the root user. This is needed when you're debugging processes that will normally be running as root. The Launch options instruct Xcode either to launch the executable automatically when the Run action is evoked (the default and most common behavior) or to wait for you to launch it yourself before running, attaching the debugger, and so on.

The Arguments tab (**Figure 13.31**) lets you control the launch arguments and environment variables. The Arguments Passed On Launch list lets you use the Add (+) button to add specific arguments to be passed when the application launches. This makes the most sense when running command-line programs. You use the Add (+) button in the Environment Variables list to add or override the environment variables present (such as USER) in the application's environment. The Expand Variables Based On menu specifies which executable's specific environment variables (as seen in the run logs) are to be used when expanding those that Xcode supplies (such as ARCHS).

FIGURE 13.31 The Run action's Arguments tab

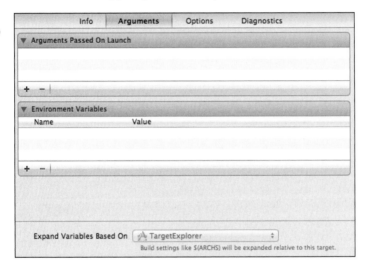

The Options tab is for the more general runtime options. While most of the tabs are fairly consistent for OS X and iOS targets, the Options tab is starkly different. For Mac targets (**Figure 13.32**), the Persistent State option disables the restoration of an application's persistent state (an API added to OS X in 10.7). The Document Versions option turns on additional debugging support for browsing versions in the document versions API. The Working Directory option lets you specify a custom working directory for the executable at runtime.

FIGURE 13.32 The Run action's Options tab for Mac targets

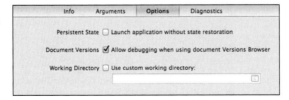

For iOS targets (**Figure 13.33**), the iPhone/iPad Simulator Display options allow you to define the screen resolution to use when running your application. The default is "Last used," but if you find yourself frequently having to set your simulators to specific resolutions, this is a good place to alleviate the frustration. The Core Location option allows you to simulate the acquiring of location information in your simulators, with the Default Location menu providing predefined co-ordinates for some major cities, or you can load a GPX file containing custom location information.

The Application Data setting allows you to preload data from your project into your application. The Routing App Coverage File setting is for working with transit apps and lets you specify within the project a GeoJSON file that details the geographical areas your app covers. The OpenGL ES Frame Capture option provides debugging support for OpenGL applications, and the Enable Performance Analysis option enables performance analysis for iOS apps.

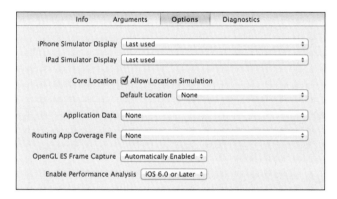

FIGURE 13.33 The Run action's Options tab for iOS targets

The Diagnostics tab (**Figure 13.34**) specifies a number of options for memory management debugging, logging details, and debugger behavior during runtime. The specifics of these options are beyond the scope of this book, but we do recommend checking Apple's documentation for details.

FIGURE 13.34 The Run action's Diagnostics tab

THE TEST ACTION

The Test action specifies the unit-test bundle (or bundles) to use for the scheme. **Figure 13.35** shows the Info tab of the Test action editor. When you created the TargetExplorer project, you chose to include unit tests. This caused Xcode to create a unit-test bundle for the TargetExplorer product and add it to the tests to be run in this action.

The test bundles in the list can be expanded to show the individual test classes contained in the bundle and can be further expanded to list the individual tests within the test classes. It is possible to enable or disable tests at any level of granularity by using the Test check boxes; entire bundles can be disabled, or a single test can be enabled from an otherwise disabled test class. To add or remove test bundles from the list, use the Add (+) and Remove (−) buttons at the bottom. The Add (+) button will display a list of all test bundles in the current project or workspace.

The Build Configuration menu defaults to the Debug configuration—builds carried out with the standard Release configuration will have debugging symbols stripped and compiler optimizations enabled, making them more difficult to debug. The Debugger menu works the same way as in the Run action—it specifies the debugger to use when running unit tests.

The Arguments tab (**Figure 13.36**) allows you to specify options similar to those of the Run action. The only difference is the check box at the top ("Use the Run action's arguments and environment variables"). This check box is selected by default and, when active, disables the Test action's own arguments controls, using those defined in the Run action instead. Deselect this to specify a separate set of arguments and environment variables for testing.

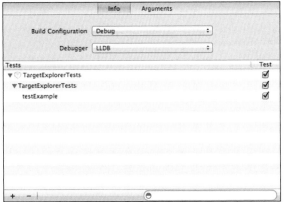

FIGURE 13.35 The Test action's Info tab

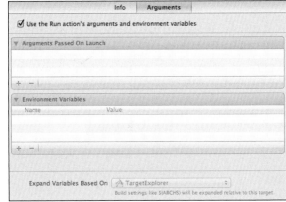

FIGURE 13.36 The Test action's Arguments tab

THE PROFILE ACTION

The Profile action is Xcode's gateway to launching Instruments, Apple's code-profiling tool (covered in Chapter 15). **Figure 13.37** shows the Info tab of the Profile action editor. The Build Configuration and Executable settings all work the same as in previously discussed actions. The key setting here is the Instrument menu. The Ask on Launch setting will open Instruments' Trace Template sheet (**Figure 13.38**), prompting you to choose a trace instrument to use when profiling your executable. All other settings in the menu launch the executable within Instruments, with the chosen trace instrument selected.

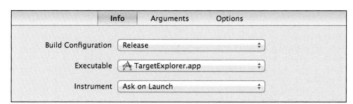

FIGURE 13.37 The Profile action's Info tab

FIGURE 13.38 Instruments templates

The Arguments and Options tabs work in the same way as those of the Test action. That is, you can specify arguments and environment variables or use the Run action's settings. If you are profiling an iOS target, the Options tab will not be available.

NOTE: If you've selected Ask on Launch and Instruments is already running (that is, you've already selected a trace instrument), subsequent calls to the Profile action will immediately run your executable using the previously chosen instrument without asking again. Close the Instruments window to be prompted again the next time you select the Profile action.

THE ANALYZE ACTION

The Analyze action runs the static analyzer (introduced in Chapter 9) against the targets specified in the Build action.

The editor has only one option: the Build Configuration menu. As with other actions, use this to specify the configuration (usually the default Debug or other debugger-friendly configuration) to use when analyzing the built target(s).

THE ARCHIVE ACTION

The Archive action, covered in Chapter 10, is responsible for creating an archive of all built targets and their debugging symbols (stored in dSYM files). The archives are suitable for submission to Apple's (Mac and iOS) App Stores.

The editor (**Figure 13.39**) has only three options. The first, Build Configuration, works as expected. A Release build makes the most sense and is the default, but you're free to create your own release-friendly configurations for use here. The Archive Name field lets you specify a name to use for the created archives. The Options check box lets you specify that you'd like Xcode to reveal the archive in the Archives tab of the Organizer (also mentioned in Chapter 10) when the action is complete.

FIGURE 13.39 Archive action options

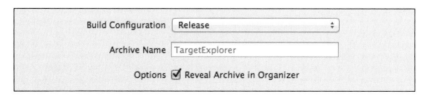

PRE-ACTIONS AND POST-ACTIONS SCRIPTS

You may have noticed the disclosure triangle next to each action in the Scheme editor's actions list. When a disclosure triangle is expanded, you'll see three entries (**Figure 13.40**). When you select the action, you're viewing the options for the action itself (the middle item in the expanded action's children), but what about the Pre- and Post-actions items? Pre-actions are things that can be done prior to the start of an action. Post-actions are done after. If you select one of them, you'll see an empty list into which you can insert actions.

FIGURE 13.40 Extra action options

There are two different pre/post action types you can insert: execute script or send email. Using the Add (+) button, you can add one or more of either type of action to customize your build process. **Figure 13.41** shows a simple set of actions that notifies the pathetic humans (and their pointy-haired masters) of the completion of an Archive action.

These extra hooks into Xcode's main actions open the possibilities for process customization considerably. See Chapter 16 for more ideas regarding interesting ways of taking advantage of Xcode's various scripting hooks.

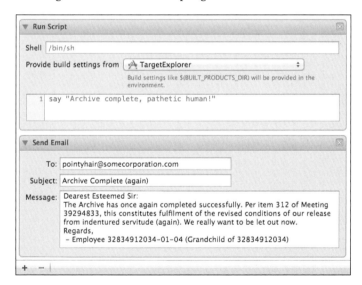

FIGURE 13.41 Some example post-actions

ENTITLEMENTS AND SANDBOXING

Application sandboxing is a security concept introduced in Mac OS X 10.7, and although it was an optional process, it has now become mandatory for all applications submitted to the Mac App Store. Opting into this system makes your application more secure by limiting its access to various system resources unless specifically requested in the application's entitlements. Mac developers who sell outside the confines of the Mac App Store are free to opt out. Sandboxing has always been a feature of iOS development, and there is no opt out.

Because of the flexibility and openness of an Objective-C application, foreign code can be injected into the application and the application's binary can be modified. This code would run with the same privileges your application enjoys. By voluntarily limiting your application's system access to only those resources it actually needs, you are reducing the chances for malicious code to achieve whatever goal it has in its evil little bytes. Much could be said on the topic and likely will be by plenty of other books, but as always, this book's focus is on the IDE, not the technologies it helps you control.

Xcode makes managing your application's entitlements easy. To find their settings, navigate to the desired build target and click the Summary tab. The Entitlements section (**Figure 13.42**) contains check boxes and menu choices.

FIGURE 13.42 The OS X target Entitlements controls

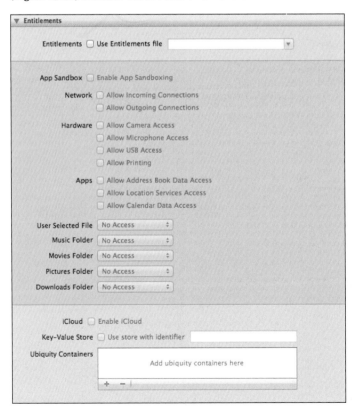

CODE SIGNING

iOS developers have lived with the challenges of code-signing their applications since the iOS SDK was first opened to third-party developers in 2008. The principle behind code signing is simple: An app is digitally signed by a developer so that it can be shown to come from a trusted source. The developers request a certificate from Apple that they use to sign their app. Because only signed apps can be run (more on that in a second), users can feel safe in knowing that the app must have been produced by a developer known to Apple.

Code signing is used for all Mac and iOS apps sold through the App Stores, but it is an opt-in feature for Mac apps sold direct from developer to customer. With the release of OS X 10.8 (Mountain Lion), Apple introduced a new OS-level feature called Gatekeeper. The default setting on new Macs is to warn users who attempt to run an app that has not been code-signed. While it is easily by-passable through System Preferences, many Mac developers have opted to code-sign their apps to make life easier for their customers.

To code-sign your apps, you will need to have a paid developer account with Apple. The personal and payment details required to sign up for such an account have been deemed by Apple to be enough information to verify your identity to sign your apps. The process for creating the necessary certificates and code-signing applications is covered in Chapter 10.

ACTIVATING ENTITLEMENTS AND SANDBOXING

You can turn on entitlements for your app by selecting the Entitlements check box at the top of the list in the Entitlements section. You then choose an entitlements file from the Use Entitlements File menu. Xcode helpfully creates one matching the name of your target and adds it to your project (**Figure 13.43**). The file is a simple property list. You can edit it by selecting it using the Property List editor, but it is easier to use the Entitlements section that you're exploring now.

FIGURE 13.43 The Entitlements file

To sandbox your application, select the App Sandbox check box. Now you must grant your application access to the functionality it needs.

SETTING SPECIFIC ENTITLEMENTS

The remaining settings in the Entitlements section grant specific entitlements to your application. When you enable sandboxing, all the settings are disabled by default and must be explicitly enabled.

NETWORK
Use the Network check boxes to allow incoming or outgoing connections. If your application is some sort of server process intended to receive requests, then you need to enable

incoming connections. If your app is intended only to act as a client, you should allow only outgoing connections—the data that comes back as part of a client request is not considered to be incoming.

HARDWARE

Use the Hardware controls to allow access to cameras, microphones, USB devices, and printers attached to or accessible by the system.

APPS

Use the Apps controls to allow access to the user's Address Book and Calendar data as well as to location services.

FILE SYSTEM

Sandboxed apps are limited as to where they can read and write data. Each app has its own container—an area deep within a user's home directory dedicated to the app and into which it can read and write data without having to request permission. To go beyond the container, you need to grant access in five categories.

The first category—User Selected File—will allow the app to provide a standard filesystem open panel so that the user can navigate to any file. The reasoning here is that if the user decides that they want to access that file, then the application is allowed to do so. This can be limited to No Access (the default), Read Access, or Write Access.

The other four categories provide access (or not) to the standard `Music`, `Movies`, `Pictures`, and `Downloads` folders in the user's home directory. The level of access for these locations can be individually set.

iCLOUD

The final part of the Entitlements section (the only part for iOS targets) provides access to iCloud settings. iCloud is Apple's attempt to put user documents in the cloud so that their data can "be everywhere" (hence the gratuitous use of the word "ubiquity" when it comes to iCloud). Adopting iCloud is beyond the scope of this book, but should you venture down this path, here is where you can enable it for your app.

WRAPPING UP

This chapter covers a lot of material, but Xcode's build system is easily the most important and arguably the most difficult concept to understand. An IDE is an environment that helps the developer manage the most basic actions performed during the course of development: building, running, debugging, testing, and deploying a product.

In the next chapter, you'll expand on this knowledge by exploring the concept of frameworks a bit further.

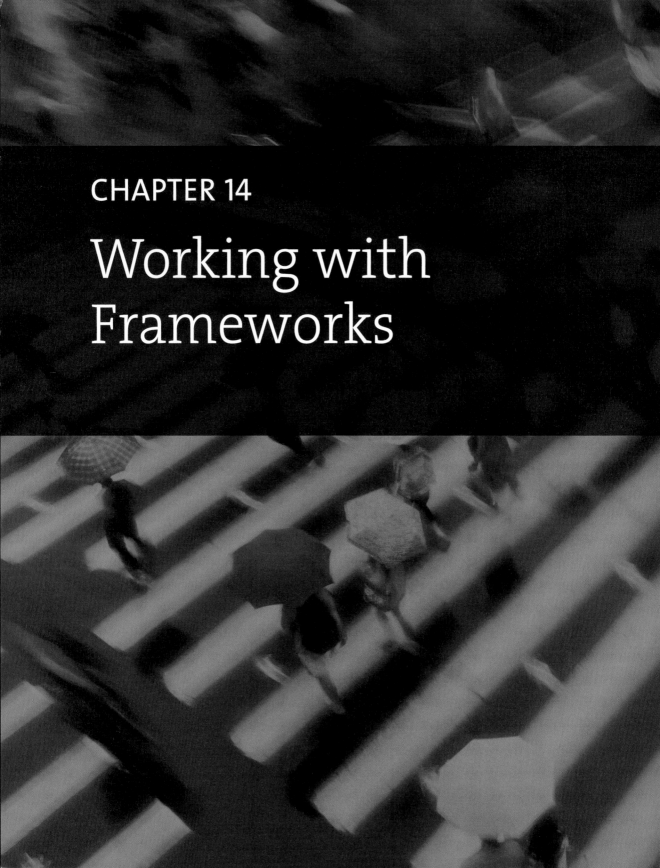

CHAPTER 14

Working with Frameworks

During our explorations we've seen that Xcode provides templates for a variety of project types. You also learned that the project templates dictate the types of targets that will be set up for you. There's a rich world full of products beyond applications. Not only can you write them yourself, but you can also use the work of others in the form of third-party plug-ins, libraries, and frameworks. In this chapter, you'll explore the distinctions between these things and learn how to use them or build your own.

WHAT ARE LIBRARIES, FRAMEWORKS, AND BUNDLES?

Libraries, frameworks, and bundles are similar in that you can think of them as prepackaged code meant to be used from within another library or application. They're all meant to improve or expand the functionality of an executable (including those that are part of the operating system) by making their code available to it. Plug-ins, which we've discussed in previous chapters, are a specific type of bundle. Purists may take exception to the oversimplified descriptions that follow, but because this is a book about Xcode, we'll keep things simple and leave the details (or extreme accuracy) for programming books.

LIBRARIES

The term *library* has the same meaning on every platform. A library is the most basic form of prepackaged, shared code meant to be reused in multiple applications. OS X and iOS come with a number of standard C libraries and libraries specific to the operating system. In the Mac and iOS world, static libraries have the .a extension (a static object code library archive), and dynamically loaded libraries have a .dylib extension. If you're coming from the world of Linux, you may be used to .so files, or if you're a former Windows developer, you might call them DLLs.

STATIC LIBRARIES

Static libraries are linked into the executable by the linker at build time. That is, the code in the library is un-archived and copied into the executable along with your program's compiled object (.o) files. Static libraries result in a larger executable because the library's code isn't shared but merely "available to copy." An example of a common static library is libc.a, the standard C library.

DYNAMIC LIBRARIES

Dynamic libraries can be loaded at launch time or when needed at runtime. The code from the library is shared and is not part of the executable. This gives the potential for faster launch times, smaller executables, and less wasted space (as a result of many executables carrying the same code linked from a static library). An example of a popular dynamic library that Cocoa developers use every day (perhaps without realizing it) is libobjc.a.dylib, which contains the Objective-C runtime library.

> **NOTE:** Dynamic libraries are a luxury that are available only to OS X developers. While it is technically possible to use dynamic libraries with iOS, it will more than likely result in an App Store rejection if you try to use them in a shipping app.

FRAMEWORKS

A framework is a bundle of files and folders that can contain dynamic shared libraries, Interface Builder files, localized (translated) strings, headers, and media resources. It could contain nothing but a dynamic library or nothing but resources. If you've used Cocoa, you've used a collection of frameworks already.

You've likely heard Cocoa being called "the Cocoa frameworks." That's because `Cocoa.framework` is actually an "umbrella framework" that encompasses a number of sub-frameworks. One such sub-framework is `Foundation.framework`, which gives you basic strings, container classes, and so on. On a Mac, things like windows, buttons, and drawing routines come from `AppKit.framework`, a Cocoa sub-framework. The same goes for AppKit's iOS cousin, `UIKit.framework`.

Unless your Cocoa application is fairly simple, it's likely you'll be using other frameworks, provided by the system or by third parties, that can be linked against to provide functionality not found in the core Cocoa frameworks themselves. At the very least, you may end up using a Cocoa framework that's not normally automatically linked.

iOS developers can link against system frameworks (like `UIKit.framework` and `Foundation.framework`), but it is a bit trickier to create your own frameworks containing static libraries for use with iOS.

LOADABLE BUNDLES

A bundle is a directory structure that appears to the end user as a single file. Applications, frameworks, plug-ins, and kernel extensions are all specific kinds of bundles.

A loadable bundle contains code and resources that can be loaded and unloaded at run-time. This enables developers to divide up their applications into modules and even provide extensibility in the form of plug-ins. For example, the Spotlight search system comes with a core set of plug-ins that teach it how to index various types of files. Third-party developers can create Spotlight importer plug-ins to allow Spotlight to index even more file types (usually files created by their own applications). Screen savers are another example. Each screen saver is a plug-in (a bundle) that teaches the screen saver application how to display yet another form of eye candy, while the screen saver application itself only takes care of loading the effects or stopping them when the user moves the mouse (and possibly provides a password to unlock the screen).

Xcode comes with a dazzling array of bundle types. As you've seen previously, there are templates to create plug-ins for Spotlight, Address Book, QuickLook, System Preferences, Automator, Dashboard, and even the kernel. Alternatively, you can just choose the generic Bundle template (found under the Framework & Library template group) and optionally tack on your own extension (such as `.testappplugin`) to stand out from the crowd.

Loadable bundles are like libraries or frameworks that your users can install and remove by drag and drop. Although things like Spotlight plug-ins often come embedded within an application bundle (which Spotlight automatically finds), their power as standalone plug-ins that a user can add or remove themselves is often overlooked. It's important to be aware that loadable bundles can just as often be a product in themselves as a component embedded in another product.

Once again, you can create and use bundles with iOS applications (say, for collecting groups of resources like images or sound files), but you can't use loadable bundles to run code.

USING EXISTING LIBRARIES AND FRAMEWORKS

Using an existing library or framework is simple in Xcode, especially if it's included as part of the operating system. At a minimum, you need to link your target against the library or framework. You learned how to do this in Chapter 13. To use a framework in code, you may need to include one or more of its shared headers.

If you're using a framework that isn't part of the operating system, you'll have to distribute it with your product. This means you would have to add a Copy Files build phase to the product, specifying the framework to copy into the bundle's Frameworks folder.

SYSTEM FRAMEWORK EXAMPLE

Let's use WebKit.framework as an example of how to use a system framework to add web-browsing capabilities to a product. You'll create a single-window Mac app containing a web view that automatically loads Google's home page.

CREATING THE APPLICATION

Select File > New > Project, and in the project template sheet choose OS X > Application > Cocoa Application. In the project options step, give your project the name **LinkedWeb** and enter your company name and identifier if necessary. Deselect the check boxes for Create Document-Based Application, Use Core Data, Include Unit Tests, and Include Spotlight Importer. Select the check box for Automatic Reference Counting. Save the project and open the xib file named MainMenu.xib. The Interface Builder editor will open with a blank canvas. Display the single window by choosing it from the list of elements in the editor dock bar.

Open the Object library, filter for the word "web," drag a web view to your new window, and position it to taste. You should have something similar to **Figure 14.1**.

FIGURE 14.1 A simple web view

A web view isn't very useful without a website to visit. To save time, assume that your only user is your grandmother, who of course ignores the address bar completely and Googles every web address. You need an IBOutlet that you can use to communicate with the web view, so that you can tell it to load Google.com. Use the Assistant to drag a connection from the web view to the AppDelegate.h file, naming it webView. Xcode will complain that it doesn't know what a WebView is yet, so before the @interface section add the following line as a hint that a WebView is a class (all it needs to know right now):

@class WebView;

When you're finished, you should have things configured as in **Figure 14.2**.

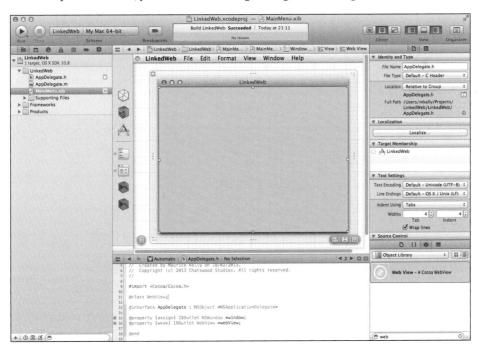

FIGURE 14.2 A fully hooked-up web view

Now you just need to add some code to load Google.com into the web view when the view controller is displayed. Open the AppDelegate.m implementation file, and add the following to the body of the applicationDidFinishLaunching: method:

```
NSURL *googleURL = [NSURL URLWithString:@"http://google.com"];
NSURLRequest *request = [NSURLRequest requestWithURL:googleURL];
[[self.webView mainFrame] loadRequest:request];
```

At this stage, Xcode still does not know what a WebView is (and will not be fobbed off with mere hints). To give it all the information it needs to know about the WebView class, add the following #import near the top of the file:

```
#import <WebKit/WebKit.h>
```

TIP: The WebKit.h header is an "umbrella" header that includes any other headers in the WebKit framework.

That's it. Run the application and watch it…oh. It crashed. You should see a crash output something like the following:

```
2013-02-28 21:20:32.653 LinkedWeb[74077:303] An uncaught exception was raised
2013-02-28 21:20:32.654 LinkedWeb[74077:303] *** -[NSKeyedUnarchiver
→ decodeObjectForKey:]: cannot decode object of class (WebView)
```

Even though you went to the trouble of importing the WebKit headers, you still don't have everything that is needed to take advantage of external code.

LINKING AGAINST THE FRAMEWORK

To link against WebKit, select the project in the Project navigator. Select the LinkedWeb target, then click the Build Phases tab. Expand the Link Binary With Libraries phase and click the Add (+) button. A sheet (**Figure 14.3**) will appear, prompting you to choose from the list of available system or workspace libraries and frameworks or to add another from an alternative location. Type **web** to filter the list, select WebKit.framework, and click Add. In addition to Cocoa.framework, LinkedWeb will now be linked against WebKit.framework to gain all its super web powers (**Figure 14.4**).

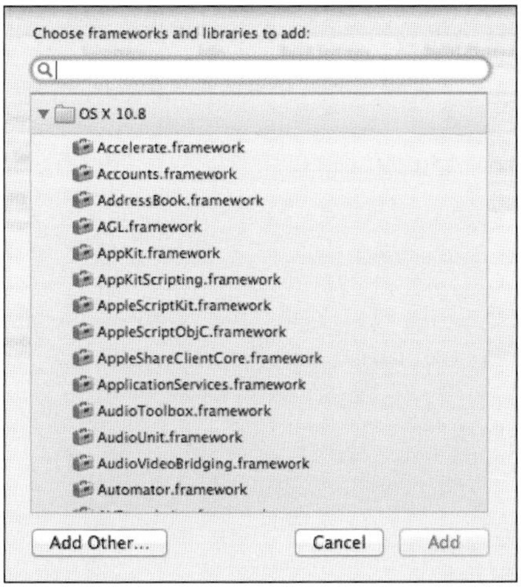

FIGURE 14.3 The framework and library sheet

FIGURE 14.4 The WebKit framework in the linking build phase

Now that it is linked, you can try running the LinkedWeb application again. All being well, you should have a basic browser for your grandmother (**Figure 14.5**).

FIGURE 14.5 A working `WebView` showing Google.com

USING THIRD-PARTY FRAMEWORKS

Third-party frameworks require a little more work to use. Since they aren't a part of the operating system, they must be distributed with the application. The most common way to do this is to embed the framework inside the application bundle so that it goes along for the ride when the user installs your application.

ADDING A FRAMEWORK TO THE PROJECT

Most third-party frameworks are open source, and many must be built before they can be used in your project. For this example, you can download a simple (and almost entirely useless) framework called Bookmarks.framework from this book's website. Its purpose is simple—it provides a simple class that can be used to load bookmarks for the basic web browser we created in the previous section. The direct download URL is http://xcodebook.com/Bookmarks.framework.zip. Download the file and unzip its contents. You should see a folder titled Bookmarks.framework.

> **NOTE:** You can skip copying the framework into the project folder, but you'll have to keep track of where all the pieces necessary to build your project are located. One way to do so is to create a conveniently located folder called Third-Party Frameworks or something similar so you always know where it is, no matter the project.

To add the framework to the project, drag Bookmarks.framework into the Project navigator and drop it inside the Frameworks group (**Figure 14.6**) for neatness (although it doesn't actually matter where you drag it—you can organize your project however it best suits you). The Add Files sheet you encountered in Chapter 5 will appear (**Figure 14.7**). Select the "Copy items into destination group's folder (if needed)" check box, make sure that the LinkedWeb target is selected in the "Add to targets" list, and then click Finish. The framework will be copied into the project folder and appear in the Project navigator.

FIGURE 14.6 Adding the framework to the project by dragging and dropping

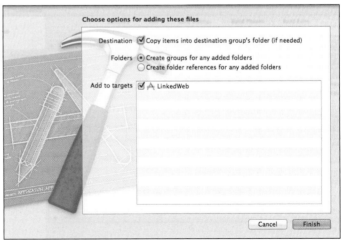

FIGURE 14.7 Copying items into the project folder via the Add Files sheet

LINKING AGAINST THE FRAMEWORK

Unlike in the last example, Xcode has automatically added the framework to the Link build phase of the LinkedWeb target. This was done for you because, as you saw in Figure 14.7, you accepted the default settings for the Add to Targets table (that is, you asked Xcode to add the framework only to the LinkedWeb target). Xcode is smart enough to know that a library should be added to the Link build phase of the selected targets. You can verify this for yourself by examining the target's Link phase (**Figure 14.8**).

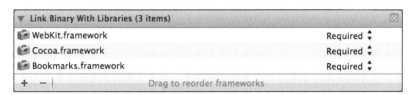

FIGURE 14.8 The Bookmarks framework in the target's Link build phase

EMBEDDING THE FRAMEWORK

To embed the framework within the application, navigate to the Build Phases tab of the LinkedWeb target. Add a Copy Files build phase by clicking the Add Build Phase button at the bottom of the window and selecting Add Copy Files. Double-click the title of the new build phase and change it to **Copy Frameworks** for clarity. Expand the build phase and set the Destination pop-up to Frameworks. Now drag Bookmarks.framework from the Project navigator into the Copy Frameworks phase. Your new build phase should look like **Figure 14.9**.

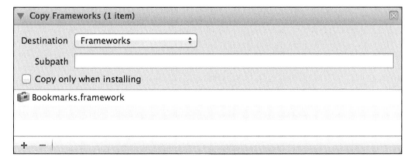

FIGURE 14.9 Adding the Bookmarks framework to a Copy Files build phase with Frameworks as its destination

NOTE: You can opt to install a framework in a shared location, but the ins and outs of framework distribution are beyond the scope of this book. See the Framework Programming Guide in Apple's documentation for more details.

USING THE FRAMEWORK IN CODE

Bookmarks.framework doesn't have any UI components, but it does provide a single class, named Bookmark. The Bookmark class has a class method called predefinedBookmarks, which returns an array of Bookmark instances. We will take advantage of this and load the first bookmark in our browser instead of the Google homepage we loaded in the previous section.

In the AppDelegate.m file, add the following import statement near the import of the WebKit.h file:

```
#import <Bookmarks/Bookmarks.h>
```

In the applicationDidFinishLaunching: method, replace the code we inserted in the previous section (it created a URL then loaded it into the WebView) with the following code:

```
NSArray *bookmarks = [Bookmark predefinedBookmarks];
Bookmark *bookmark = bookmarks[0];
NSURLRequest *request = [NSURLRequest requestWithURL:bookmark.url];
[[self.webView mainFrame] loadRequest:request];
```

TIP: If you're unsure which header to include, you can either use AutoComplete or expand the framework itself in the Project navigator list, open its headers subfolder, and take a look around. Also, most frameworks have an umbrella header named for the framework itself, such as "Bookmarks.h" for Bookmarks.framework or "WebKit.h" for WebKit.framework.

Run LinkedWeb and watch it load the new bookmark; it should open the Apple developer site—exactly what your grandmother needs to get started with app development.

To summarize, the extra steps to use a third-party framework are the following: add it to your project, optionally copy it into the project folder when adding it, and embed it into your application bundle so it's distributed with the application.

CREATING A FRAMEWORK

We used a framework named Bookmarks.framework to provide bookmark support for our browser. You downloaded it to see how you could use third-party frameworks, but in this section we will create the Bookmarks.framework from scratch. It might seem like overkill, but if you regularly re-use large portions of your code across multiple projects, then it can be useful to separate these out into your own framework. That way, all the projects can benefit from improvements and bug fixes from the same source.

CREATE THE PROJECT

To create a new project, choose File > New > Project from the main menu. Choose the Framework & Library group under the OS X section. Select Cocoa Framework from the list, and click Next.

The project options sheet (**Figure 14.10**) will appear. In the Product Name field, enter **Bookmarks** so you can distinguish it from the LinkedWeb project. It's also a good idea to make sure the Company Identifier value is the same as the one you gave for the LinkedWeb project. Select the Use Automatic Reference Counting check box, but for simplicity deselect the Include Unit Tests check box. Click Next.

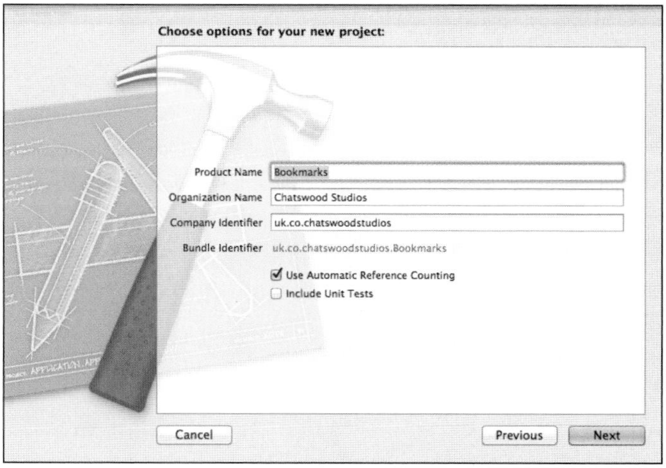

FIGURE 14.10 Creating a new framework project

Select the "Create local git repository for this project" check box, and select the same folder that contains the LinkedWeb project folder (the LinkedWeb folder's parent). Make certain you don't save it in the LinkedWeb project folder, but one level above. Ensure that the Add To pop-up menu is set to "Don't add to any project or workspace," then click Create. When it creates the project, Xcode will open the project window as you would expect but with some slight differences (**Figure 14.11**).

FIGURE 14.11 The new framework project workspace

Firstly, the project target is not an application but is instead a framework (differentiated by the toolbox icon). The target editor no longer has a Summary tab, the Info tab now reports an OS X Framework Target Info section (with no sections for document types or UTIs), and the Build Phases tab has a Copy Headers build phase added by default.

ADD SOME CODE

To start with, a framework should have a simple umbrella header—that is, a header that includes all other headers needed to use the framework and that allows a one-stop import into other classes. The WebKit.h header file that we imported into the LinkedWeb application earlier is an example of an umbrella header. The convention is that the umbrella header is named the same as the framework. A file named Bookmarks.h has already been created for us during the project creation, but we don't need its companion named Bookmarks.m, so it can be safely removed. Right-click the file in the Project navigator, choose Delete, and then choose the Move to Trash option when prompted.

To store a bookmark, we need to create a class named Bookmark that will store the bookmark name and URL. Choose File > New > File from the main menu, and select the Objective-C Class template from the OS X > Cocoa category. Click Next, enter your class name as **Bookmark**, and ensure that the "Subclass of" field contains the NSObject class name. Click Next, select Bookmarks as the Group, and ensure that the Bookmarks option is selected under Targets. Finally, click Create to finish making the Bookmark class.

In the newly created Bookmark.h, add two properties as follows:

```
@property (nonatomic, copy) NSString *name;
@property (nonatomic, strong) NSURL *url;
```

We'll also add a class method named predefinedBookmarks that returns an array of bookmarks (you should recall we used this in the previous section).

```
+ (NSArray *)predefinedBookmarks;
```

We need to flesh out this method in the implementation file Bookmark.m. In the past, we would have needed to have synthesized the properties in the implementation file as well, but the Clang front-end to the LLVM compiler does this for us now. In the implementation file, enter the following method:

```
+ (NSArray *)predefinedBookmarks
{
    Bookmark *firstBookmark = [[Bookmark alloc] init];
    firstBookmark.name = @"Apple developer site";
    firstBookmark.url = [[NSURL alloc] initWithString:@"http://developer.
    → apple.com"];

    Bookmark *secondBookmark = [[Bookmark alloc] init];
    secondBookmark.name = @"Xcode Book";
    secondBookmark.url = [[NSURL alloc] initWithString:@"http://xcodebook.com"];

    NSArray *bookmarks = @[firstBookmark, secondBookmark];
    return bookmarks;
}
```

Now that you have some code in your framework, you need to make it available via the umbrella header file Bookmarks.h. Open the file, and add the following statement to the imports:

```
#import "Bookmark.h"
```

Any other classes you add to your framework can be similarly included in this umbrella header. This way, when your framework is used, there is only one header to import, which brings the headers of any other classes along for the ride.

Try a build (Command+B), and verify that there are no build issues. The framework should build cleanly.

CONFIGURE THE HEADERS

To use a framework's headers, they must be configured in the Copy Headers build phase. To do so, navigate to the project itself and then select the Bookmarks target in the list. Next, select the Build Phases tab, and expand the Copy Headers phase (**Figure 14.12**).

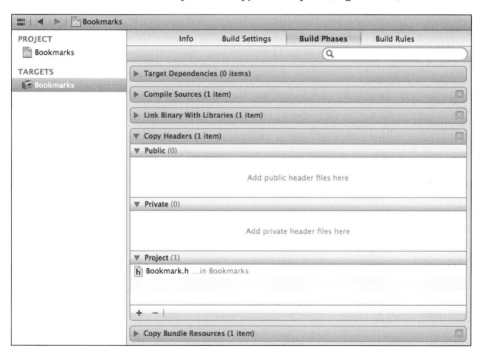

FIGURE 14.12 The Copy Headers build phase

Note that the `Bookmark.h` header file was automatically added to the Project group when it was created. This makes the header available to other projects if they all exist as projects in the same workspace, but does not allow access to the header when used as a framework as described earlier.

To make the framework's code more "visible," its headers must be made public. Drag the `Bookmark.h` header into the Public group. You also need to add the umbrella header to the Public group—you can do so by dragging `Bookmarks.h` from the Project navigator to the Public group. Once you've done so, the Copy Headers build phase should look like **Figure 14.13**.

FIGURE 14.13 The framework's headers made public in the Copy Headers phase

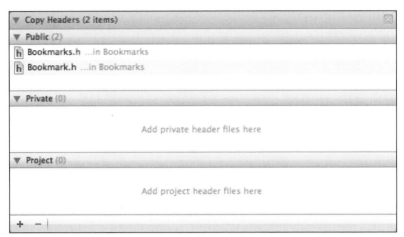

Although the framework seems to be ready to build and use in other projects, there is another tweak we need to make. While you're still in the Project editor, select the Build Settings tab, and in the filter type **INSTALL_PATH**. For the parameter "Installation Directory," set a value of `@executable_path/../Frameworks` (**Figure 14.14**). While the intricacies of this setting are beyond the scope of this book, it basically embeds a setting in the framework so that apps which link against the framework can read. Setting this path tells the apps that they can expect the framework to be embedded in the application bundle.

FIGURE 14.14 Setting the installation directory of the framework

To have a look at the innards of your newly minted framework, build one more time (Command+B), and then expand the Products group in the Project navigator. Right-click (or Control-click) the Bookmarks.framework product, and choose Show in Finder from the context menu. **Figure 14.15** shows the fully expanded folder structure with the code library and its public headers.

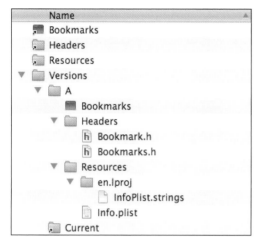

FIGURE 14.15 The built framework's file structure

TIP: If you wanted to use this framework right now, you'd have to archive it or manually create a release build scheme and build it with that scheme. See Chapter 16 for alternative deployment build approaches.

TIP: It's very common (and considered good practice) for developers to create test application targets alongside the framework. This application is used to test your framework as it's being developed.

That's all there is to it. You have a fully functional framework with some custom code that could be shared between multiple projects.

WRAPPING UP

You've seen how to create frameworks and learned how to use them in other projects. In the next chapter, you'll delve into advanced debugging techniques and explore the concept of test-driven development.

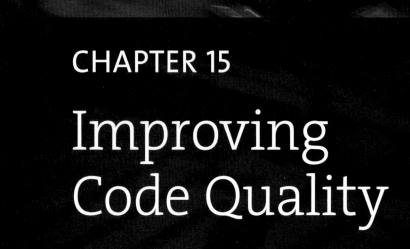

CHAPTER 15

Improving Code Quality

The disciplines of debugging, unit testing, and analyzing your code go hand in hand. Xcode benefits from a powerful set of built-in tools that help you accomplish these tasks without having to leave the application suite. With a mastery of these tools, you will be able to produce higher-quality code that ships with fewer bugs and better performance.

DEBUGGING

In Chapter 9, we took a brief tour into the world of debugging but left some of the more in-depth topics for this chapter. Xcode debugging is built upon the foundations laid by the LLDB debugger, so we will explore some of its powerful console-based features, as well as some that are exposed through the Xcode user interface.

OBSERVING AND MODIFYING VARIABLES

The ability to set a watch on a variable's memory address and be notified when its content changes is a common feature in most any IDE. In Xcode 4, this is done by pausing the debugger and showing the Debug area's Variables view, then right-clicking the variable and choosing Watch "*variableName*" from the menu. This creates a special form of breakpoint called a *watchpoint*.

Try this out by adding the following code to the -applicationDidFinishLaunching: method of a Cocoa application:

```
NSInteger theNumber = 1;
theNumber++;
theNumber = 42;
```

Set a breakpoint on the first line of code, run the application, and wait for it to stop when the breakpoint is reached. In the Variables list of the Debug area, right-click theNumber and select Watch "theNumber" from the menu. Click the Continue button in the Debug bar.

Execution should briefly resume and stop again as soon as theNumber is modified—the watchpoint has been hit. You should also notice that the values of theNumber before and after modification have been printed to the Console section of the Debug area. Click the Continue button in the Debug bar twice more to observe the value of theNumber as you progress through the lines of code (**Figure 15.1**).

FIGURE 15.1 Using watchpoints to monitor variable values

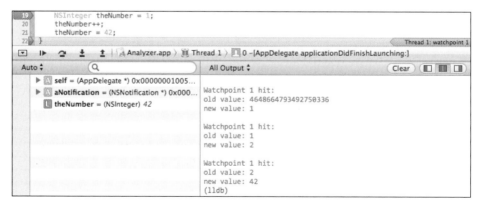

Watching variables (or more precisely, their memory locations) in this way is an effective means of debugging, because you can continue using your applications as normal until a specific variable has been modified. This is particularly useful if a variable is modified only under a specific set of conditions that may not be triggered by slowly stepping through code.

The lifetime of a watchpoint is limited in comparison to regular breakpoints—when you stop running the application, any watchpoints will be removed. If you want to remove them manually, open the Breakpoint navigator, select the watchpoint, and press Delete to remove it.

Sometimes it's not enough to simply observe the value of a variable while debugging. Say, for example, you wanted to test a particular code path without waiting for a contrived set of circumstances to occur by themselves. In that case, you can set a breakpoint prior to the point of interest. When the app runs and the breakpoint is reached, click the variable you wish to modify—or right-click and select Edit Value from the menu—to make the value editable directly in the Variables list. Continue execution to see how your app behavior changes using the new data.

CUSTOMIZING BREAKPOINTS

The basic breakpoint controls are simple—click in the gutter to add a breakpoint, click the breakpoint to toggle it on or off, and drag it up and down the gutter to move it to another line. Right-clicking the breakpoint (in the gutter or in the Breakpoint navigator) reveals another option: Edit Breakpoint. Selecting this option presents a breakpoint editor popover, like the one shown in **Figure 15.2**, containing a number of extra options that you can add to your breakpoints.

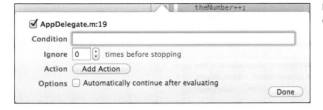

FIGURE 15.2 The breakpoint editor popover

- Enable/Disable. The top line of the breakpoint editor displays the name and line number of the file to which the breakpoint is attached. It also features a check box that allows you to enable or disable the breakpoint.
- Condition. The Condition field allows you to enter a conditional statement that determines whether or not your breakpoint will actually stop program execution. This field accepts simple conditional logic (for example, theNumber == 42) as well as more complex function and method calls within the scope of the breakpoint. When the breakpoint condition is evaluated, the debugger will pause execution if the condition evaluates to YES or a non-zero integer.

- Ignore. The Ignore directive allows code execution to pass the breakpoint without stopping a specified number of times. Use this if you want to let your application run through the code for a while before stopping—this is especially useful for debugging looping code.

- Action. Action is a powerful tool that allows you to execute scripts or generate alerts when a breakpoint is encountered. Clicking the Add Action button presents a drop-down menu that allows you to execute an AppleScript, execute a shell or debugger command, capture an Open GL ES Frame, generate a log message to the console, play a sound, or even speak a message every time the breakpoint is encountered (**Figure 15.3**). While some of these options could be downright annoying if triggered many times during the execution of an application, when combined with a condition an appropriately placed log message could be a helpful aid to debugging. To add even more actions (or remove the existing ones) just use the Add (+) and Remove (−) buttons located to the right of the drop-down menu.

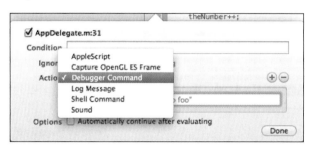

FIGURE 15.3 The available breakpoint actions

- Options. There is currently only one option, but it is a useful one: "Automatically continue after evaluating." This may seem confusing at first—why create a breakpoint that you don't want execution to stop at? When this option is combined with a breakpoint action that performs logging, your application could run continuously in a debug mode, logging whenever your breakpoint is encountered.

USING THE CONSOLE

The debugger console is your command-line interface to the debugger. LLDB provides a command-line interface to the same features that Xcode gives you graphically. Nevertheless, a few quick commands to the debugger via the console can be helpful. To issue commands to the debugger, you must click inside the console window to place the cursor to the right of the debugger prompt ((lldb)). You can give the debugger commands only when execution of your application has been paused. The next sections describe a few common tasks that can sometimes be done more easily with the console.

PRINTING OBJECTS AND VALUES

There are a few ways to print objects and values from the console. The command you use depends on the kind of information you want to see.

"Print object" (po) is the most commonly used debugger command for Cocoa developers. The command will ask Objective-C objects to print the result of their common -description method. Inherited from NSObject, the method returns a string that describes the object. This description is intended to be useful for debugging. When the application is paused in the debugger, all the symbols in the current stack are available to you. This lets you issue a print object command to inspect objects (or other objects to which those objects hold references).

To print an object, you need to pause the application in the debugger using a breakpoint or watchpoint. **Figure 15.4** shows a basic Cocoa application paused in its -applicationDidFinishLaunching: method. This method receives an NSNotification object named aNotification. To print the notification, type the following command into the console and press Return:

```
po aNotification
```

```
29    - (void)applicationDidFinishLaunching:(NSNotification *)aNotification
30    {
31        NSInteger theNumber = 1;                                    Thread 1: breakpoint 1.1
32        theNumber++;
33        theNumber = 42;
34    }
35
36    // Returns the directory the application uses to store the Core Data store file. This code
         uses a directory named "uk.co.chatswoodstudios.Analyzer" in the user's Application
         Support directory.
```

Analyzer ⟩ Thread 1 ⟩ 0 -[AppDelegate applicationDidFinishLaunching:]

All Output ⬍   Clear

```
(lldb) po aNotification
$0 = 0x000000010220f6c0 NSConcreteNotification 0x10220f6c0 {name =
NSApplicationDidFinishLaunchingNotification; object = <NSApplication: 0x102104660>; userInfo = {
    NSApplicationLaunchIsDefaultLaunchKey = 1;
}}
(lldb)
```

FIGURE 15.4 Printing an object in the debugger console

The debugger will respond by logging the string returned when the NSNotification object is asked for its -description. Figure 15.4 also shows the results in the debugger console. You can also print self when stopped within a method belonging to an instance of an Objective-C class. In the current scope of the example, self refers to an instance of the AppDelegate class. **Figure 15.5** shows the result of printing self in this scope. In this case, the AppDelegate class doesn't override -description, so the information displayed is the default description format inherited from NSObject. That is, the class name (AppDelegate) and the memory address of the instance (0x100699690) are printed.

Analyzer ⟩ Thread 1 ⟩

All Output ⬍

```
(lldb) po self
$1 = 0x0000000100699690 <AppDelegate: 0x100699690>
(lldb)
```

FIGURE 15.5
Printing self

Of course, you can also print objects through the accessors of other objects. For example, NSNotification has an NSString property called name. To see the details of the name property, you can issue the following command:

```
po aNotification.name
```

The debugger calls the NSNotification -name accessor method, then calls the returned object's -description and prints the result.

Note that using dot notation works in the console for accessing a property a single level deep, but you must use regular message sending when trying to dig deeper, despite what autocompletion says!

Although many objects in the Cocoa API come with reasonably useful descriptions, it's up to you to override -description in your objects and provide meaningful descriptions for debugging.

The po command works only on objects. What about values of primitives? What if you wanted to know the length of the notification name for some reason? You might expect the following command to work:

```
po [aNotification.name length]
```

But it won't work, because the -length method of NSString returns an NSUInteger—a primitive type, not an object. For primitive values, you use a different print command:

```
p (NSUInteger)[aNotification.name length]
```

The debugger responds with this:

```
(NSUInteger) $1 = 43
```

Let's take a quick look at the structure of the command and its response. The command p (short for print) expects the result of the statement you give it to evaluate ([aNotification. name length]) to be cast to the expected type (NSUInteger) so it knows how to represent it. This type should be the return type of the method or function that ultimately returns the value (the outermost call in nested calls). In the case of NSString's -length method, that's an NSUInteger.

The response is actually more interesting than it looks. The debugger not only prints the result but also kindly assigns it to a local variable for you to use in future evaluations. In this example, the number 43 (the length of the name string) was assigned to the variable $1. To use this is simple. Imagine that you can't work out in your head the math necessary to multiply the length by two. No problem—LLDB can do it for you!

```
p (NSUInteger)($1 * 2)
```

LLDB performs this complex computation and responds with:

```
(NSUInteger) $2 = 86
```

Notice that even that evaluation was assigned to a new variable, $2.

CONTROLLING PROGRAM EXECUTION

You can control program execution from within the console just as you can by using the Debug bar or the menu system. This can be handy if you're working heavily with the console. **Table 15.1** shows a few basic commands.

TABLE 15.1 Console commands

COMMAND	DESCRIPTION
c	Continue
n	Step program
s	Step into
fin	Finish current method

LLDB can also remember your previous commands—use the Up and Down arrow keys to navigate through the command history. Pressing Return with no command causes it to repeat the previous command, which can be very handy.

There are many more execution control commands, but these are the basics you're likely to need most. The debugger itself can offer help.

GETTING DEBUGGER HELP

There are an impressive number of commands available in LLDB, and getting help with these commands is easy. Type `help` in the debugger and press Return for a list of primary commands. Type `help commandname` to list subcommands that apply to the named command, and type `help commandname subcommandname` for help on a specific subcommand. To use one of the previous examples, type the following into the console:

```
help print
```

Remember to use the `help` command to find your way around the debugger's toolkit. If you are familiar with GDB, you might find that LLDB has introduced a lot of its own nomenclature. In many cases, it has aliases from older GDB commands to help people adjust (a complete mapping is listed at http://lldb.llvm.org/lldb-gdb.html), but as time goes on (and the feature set expands) it will be helpful to learn the new syntax.

EXTENDING LLDB USING PYTHON

One of the new commands introduced by LLDB is `script`, a seemingly innocuous command that is in fact the gateway to a world of either productivity or lost time, depending on how proficient you are with the Python scripting language. LLDB has the ability to execute Python scripts and provides a rich API that exposes much of the data available from the debugger. Exploring Python scripting is beyond the scope of this book, but it is an aspect of LLDB that is worth monitoring for the future.

INSTRUMENTS

Instruments is humbly presented as a single application when in fact it is really a collection of diagnostic and analysis tools. These tools can be run against an application or other process to extract sample data that can be displayed and analyzed.

The long list of available instruments continues to grow, and many require a solid grasp of one or more debugging and profiling techniques. An entire book could (and should) be dedicated to Instruments, but this is unfortunately not that book. As a result, we can take you only on a brief tour of how to launch Instruments and of the pertinent parts of the interface.

LAUNCHING INSTRUMENTS

Instruments can be launched in one of two ways: The easy way involves launching it from within Xcode as part of the Profile action; the long way is to open Instruments directly and attach it to an already running process.

THE EASY WAY

The easy way to launch Instruments (for your Xcode projects) is to choose the Profile action from within Xcode. You're already familiar with the Run, Test, and Archive actions. You can trigger the Profile action by choosing Product > Profile from the main menu; by holding the Run button and then choosing Profile from its menu; or by pressing Command+I.

Assuming your project builds successfully, Instruments will launch and prompt you for a template for your new trace document (**Figure 15.6**). Note that the list of templates will be filtered to include only those that are applicable to your current run destination. Take some time to inspect the templates available—clicking a template icon in the upper-right portion of the window will display additional information that will be gathered about your application.

FIGURE 15.6 The template chooser

Once you choose your template, Instruments will launch your application, attach to it, and begin recording the trace.

THE LONG WAY

If you've used Instruments before (or even just seen it in passing), you may be wondering where it has disappeared. In recent versions of Xcode, Instruments has been demoted from a standalone application to being tucked away inside the Xcode application bundle.

To run Instruments independently of a project or workspace, choose Xcode > Open Developer Tool > Instruments from the main menu. Xcode will look inside its application bundle, locate Instruments, and launch it for you. As with the easy way, it will present a list of templates for you to choose (**Figure 15.7**), but this time the list will not be filtered, and will include templates for OS X, iOS simulators, and physical iOS devices.

FIGURE 15.7 The expanded list of templates

> **TIP:** If you yearn for an even more direct method of launching Instruments, then right-click its icon in the dock and select Options > Keep in Dock from the menu.

Choose a template for your document, and click Choose to create a new Instruments document; or click Record to create a document, select a target, and start recording. The next step is to choose the process you want Instruments to attach to or start up. If you clicked Choose rather than Record, then you can select the Target control on the toolbar to find a suitable target (**Figure 15.8**).

FIGURE 15.8 The Target control's menu

The Attach to Process menu item will present a list of all running processes to select from. The Choose Target > Choose Target menu item will present a sheet allowing you to select from applications and other binaries on the system to execute and analyze. This is also the entry point to Instruments if you selected Record from the template chooser sheet.

AN OVERVIEW OF THE INSTRUMENTS USER INTERFACE

When you have launched Instruments and chosen your template, you are presented with a document that is configured with the instrument types that correspond to the template you selected. Depending on how you entered Instruments, it will either be ready to record data or be already in the process of recording. The trace operations are performed inside an Instruments trace document. A document contains the instruments and their configuration as well as every trace session recorded into it. It can be saved for later review, and future trace sessions can be appended to it.

Figure 15.9 shows a trace document with one trace session recorded in it. This document used the Time Profiler template found under the OS X category of the template chooser. A great deal of information is shown here, with all the Instruments main views active.

FIGURE 15.9 An Instruments trace document

TIP: The trace document can be saved and re-opened later. You can also append a new session by using the Record button.

Figure 15.10 shows the expanded Time Profiler (using the disclosure triangle to the left of its name in Figure 15.9). The most recent track is always placed on top. Subsequent sessions will produce additional tracks for each instrument, and they can be reviewed and compared by expanding the disclosure triangle and clicking the track itself. The active track is shaded a darker blue.

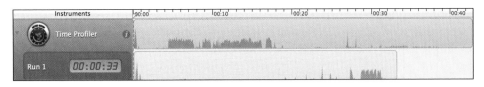

FIGURE 15.10 The Time Profiler showing multiple tracks

There are many more view modes that won't be covered in this chapter. Instead, let's stick to the main views.

THE TOOLBAR

There are some important clusters of controls on the toolbar you'll need to understand. Let's explore each major grouping, starting on the left side of the toolbar.

The Record and Target controls work closely together. Use the Target control to attach Instruments to any running process. Depending on how you launched Instruments, a target (the application you're tracing) may already be selected. Use the Record controls to control the trace. From left to right, there is a Pause/Resume button to pause and resume tracing the running program; the Record button to start and stop recording new tracks; and a Restart button, which stops the current trace and starts a new one (producing a new track). If the program is not running when the Record button is pressed, it will be launched. If the program was launched by the trace session, pressing the Record button while recording will stop recording and terminate the program.

The Inspection Range controls specify the range of time in the track's timeline you want to inspect. Specifically, you can filter out all trace information that is not within the specified range. The left button marks the beginning of the time you want to inspect; the right button marks the end. Setting a beginning point with no end means "start here and show me everything to the end"; setting an end point with no beginning means "show me everything from the beginning up to this point." The middle button clears the selected range.

Although not part of the toolbar, it's important to understand how to specify a point in time. You do this by dragging the scrubber control to the desired location in the timeline. The scrubber control is located in the graduated bar just above the instrument tracks. The term *scrubber* comes from audio/video applications, where the time-pointer control is moved, or scrubbed, across a track to view and listen to the scrubbed region of time.

The status control in the center of the toolbar shows (in hours, minutes, and seconds) the length of the current trace session (by default) or the currently displayed trace session and number of sessions in the document (if there's more than one recorded), and it provides controls (the left and right arrows) to switch between sessions. Click the small icon to the right of the time display to toggle between running time (the session's length) and inspection time (the current position of the scrubber control).

The View controls toggle the three primary views in a trace document's interface. From left to right, the buttons toggle the Instruments, Detail, and Extended Detail views. You'll explore these in a moment.

The Library control toggles the Library panel (**Figure 15.11**), which provides all available instruments. To add a new instrument to the trace, drag it from the Library panel and drop it into the Instruments list.

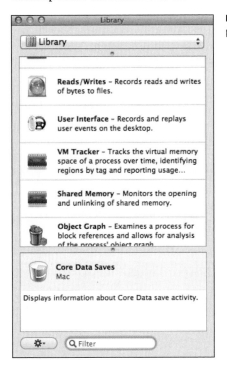

FIGURE 15.11 The Library panel

The Search control filters the displayed trace information by symbol or library (to choose the filter, click the magnifying glass icon in the control's left edge and select from the menu). For example, typing "drawRect" into the field will show only the trace information about the -drawRect: method provided by NSView (and any other methods containing "drawRect" in their names), assuming it's been called during the recorded trace session.

THE STRATEGY BAR

The strategy bar (**Figure 15.12**) gives you three main tracing *strategies* to choose from. The buttons on the left edge of the bar toggle between the (from left to right) CPU, Instruments, and Threads strategies. (All the figures in this chapter thus far have shown the Instruments strategy—the default strategy.) The pop-up menus let you filter by core and process/thread. An additional pop-up appears in CPU and Threads strategies, letting you specify additional chart options.

FIGURE 15.12 The strategy bar

The right-most button pops up a graphical legend (**Figure 15.13**) whose contents depend upon the chart mode (which colorizes the chart information). The legend shows each color used and what it represents in the chart.

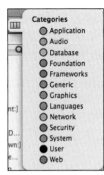

FIGURE 15.13 The status bar legend

Figure 15.14 shows the trace session from Figure 15.9 using the CPU strategy. The application's activity is divided according to the CPU core on which that activity took place. If you have more than one instrument in the Instruments list, use the pop-up below the Instruments list to switch between them and see their collected trace information (**Figure 15.15**).

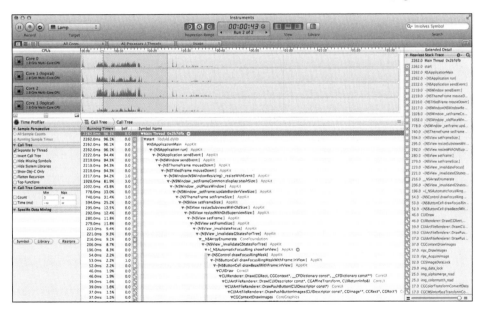

FIGURE 15.14 The CPU strategy

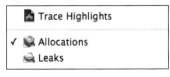

FIGURE 15.15 The instrument chooser pop-up

FIGURE 15.16 The
Threads strategy

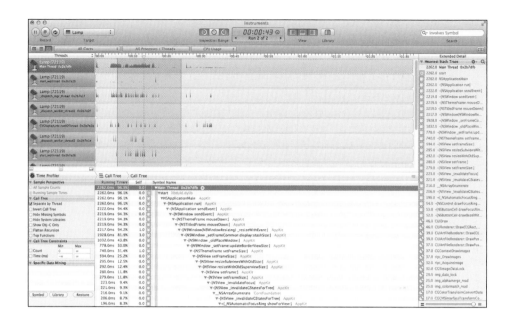

Figure 15.16 again shows the same trace session, this time using the Threads strategy. Here, the application's activity is divided by thread.

THE INSTRUMENTS VIEW

The Instruments view (**Figure 15.17**) shows a list of all instruments (or cores or threads, depending on the selected strategy) in the top list. Each instrument can be selected by clicking it in the list. Once selected, pressing the Delete key will remove the instrument (and its data for all recorded sessions) from the trace document. Click the info button (**i**) to the right of each instrument to reveal a popover that offers more trace recording data and track display options.

FIGURE 15.17 The
Instruments view and
information popover

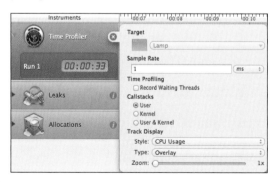

NOTE: The control immediately below the list of instruments zooms in and out of the timeline. It is not actually part of the Instruments view and remains where it is when the view is toggled. Similarly, the instrument chooser pop-up seen in Figure 15.15 belongs to the navigation bar of the Detail view.

THE DETAIL VIEW

Whereas the Instruments view (and the tracks it records) controls and displays the basics of what is collected, the Detail view is where the actual trace information is shown and explored. When you toggle the Detail view using the toolbar View control, the navigation bar at its top always remains visible.

The navigation bar (**Figure 15.18**) is composed of three separate areas. The left-most area is the instrument chooser pop-up control (which you saw in Figure 15.15). This control lets you choose which instrument's trace information is shown in the Detail and Extended Detail views and has the same effect as clicking an instrument in the list. To the right of the instrument chooser, the display mode lets you choose how the trace information is displayed. The list of available modes depends on the selected instrument, but most have the Call Tree and Console modes in common. Finally, the rest of the bar is dedicated to navigational context (much like the jump bar above Xcode's editors), letting you navigate into and out of levels of detail in the current view.

FIGURE 15.18 The Detail view navigation bar

Beneath the instrument chooser control are categorical lists of filters and display options specific to the active instrument (**Figure 15.19**). These controls are visible only when both the Detail and Instruments views are shown, and their content can vary widely from instrument to instrument. A common use case is to run a time profile of your application, choose the Call Tree display mode, and then (under the Call Tree group in the filter and options list) choose to hide missing and system symbols and show only Objective-C information. This gives you a view of only your own code, as opposed to including information about the myriad system libraries against which your code links.

FIGURE 15.19 The active instrument's options list

The main view (usually a table or outline) lists the individual data points that Instruments gathered about your application; the information it shows is specific to the selected instrument. **Figure 15.20** shows the Objective-C–related call tree information collected by the Time Profiler. Note that the call tree has been inverted using Invert Call Tree from the options list. Inverting the call tree is a useful technique that puts the focus on the methods farther down the tree and can save you drilling down.

The top result reveals the method in which Lamp.app (one of our example apps from way back in Part II) spent most of its time during the profiling session: -drawRectAsLayerTree. Considering that the app used NSView's -drawRect: to color the window background, this call tree makes a lot of sense. Double-clicking entries in the list can often drill down into further detail.

FIGURE 15.20 The Detail view showing call tree information

	Time Profiler	≡ Call Tree	Call Tree	
▼ Sample Perspective	Running Time▼	Self	Symbol Name	
○ All Sample Counts	235.0ms 12.9%	0.0	▼-[NSView(NSLayerKitGlue) _drawRectAsLayerTree:] AppKit	
◉ Running Sample Times	235.0ms 12.9%	0.0	▼-[NSView _drawRect:clip:] AppKit	
▼ Call Tree	233.0ms 12.8%	0.0	▶-[NSView _recursiveDisplayAllDirtyWithLockFocus:visRect:] AppKit	
☐ Separate by Thread	2.0ms 0.1%	0.0	▶-[NSView _recursiveDisplayRectIfNeededIgnoringOpacity:isVisibleRect	
☑ Invert Call Tree	122.0ms 6.7%	0.0	▶-[NSApplication nextEventMatchingMask:untilDate:inMode:dequeue:] A	
☐ Hide Missing Symbols	88.0ms 4.8%	88.0	▶+[_NSAutomaticFocusRing showForView:] AppKit	
☐ Hide System Libraries	85.0ms 4.6%	0.0	▶-[NSButtonCell drawBezelWithFrame:inView:] AppKit	
☑ Show Obj-C Only	57.0ms 3.1%	0.0	▶-[NSThemeFrame _drawUnifiedToolbarWithState:inFrame:] AppKit	
☐ Flatten Recursion	44.0ms 2.4%	0.0	▶+[NSScreen screens] AppKit	
☐ Top Functions	29.0ms 1.6%	29.0	▶-[NSView(NSInternal) _recursive:displayRectIgnoringOpacity:inContext:to	
▼ Call Tree Constraints	27.0ms 1.4%	27.0	▶-[NSCGSContext _invalidate] AppKit	
	27.0ms 1.4%	27.0	▶-[_NSArrayM dealloc] CoreFoundation	
☐ Count Min 0 Max ∞	24.0ms 1.3%	0.0	▶-[NSThemeFrame _maskCorners:] AppKit	
☐ Time (ms) -∞ ∞	22.0ms 1.2%	22.0	▶-[NSView _drawRect:clip:] AppKit	
	22.0ms 1.2%	0.0	▶-[NSAutoreleasePool drain] Foundation	
▶ Specific Data Mining	21.0ms 1.1%	0.0	▶-[NSBitmapImageRep _performBlockUsingBacking:] AppKit	
	20.0ms 1.1%	0.0	▶-[NSView _invalidateGStatesForTree] AppKit	
	20.0ms 1.1%	0.0	▶-[NSRegion addRect:] AppKit	
	20.0ms 1.1%	0.0	▶-[CUITextEffectStack newBackgroundPatternColorWithSize:contentScale:]	

THE EXTENDED DETAIL VIEW

The Extended Detail view (**Figure 15.21**) shows extended information about the selected data in the Detail view. As with the rest of the detail-oriented views, its content is instrument specific. In the figure, the view is displaying extended detail about the selected Time Profiler

FIGURE 15.21 The Extended Detail view

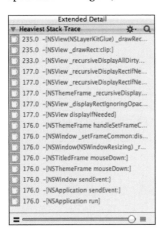

symbol in Figure 15.20. In this case, it's appropriate to show the heaviest stack trace (the stack trace responsible for the bulk of the calls to the selected symbol). This view represents the same information found in the Debug navigator. The slider on the bottom works in the same way as the slider in the Debug navigator as well—it smartly filters out "uninteresting" chunks of the stack trace, depending on its position.

TIME PROFILING AN APPLICATION

Now that you know the Instruments basics, it's time to apply them to a common profiling task. Create a new OS X application by selecting File > New > Project from the main menu, then select the OS X > Application > Cocoa Application template, and click Next. Name your project (we've called ours Molasses), and deselect the Include Unit Tests and Include Spotlight Importer check boxes. Click Next, find a place to save the project, and click Create.

You don't get very far in a moderate-to-complex application without encountering performance problems. Such problems have traditionally been difficult to track down. More often than not, the cause is entirely different from what you suspected. The Time Profiler instrument has an uncanny ability to show you inefficiencies in your code that you may not even have suspected.

To begin, open your AppDelegate.m file and add the following method to the @implementation section:

```
- (void)doSomethingStupid
{
    NSMutableArray *array = [NSMutableArray arrayWithCapacity:10000000];
    for (NSInteger i = 0; i < 100000; i++) {
        array[i] = @(i);
    }
}
```

Now change the -applicationDidFinishLaunching: method so that it calls the new method:

```
[self doSomethingStupid];
```

Taken together, this code creates a mutable array with a capacity of 10,000,000 objects and fills it with 100,000 instances of NSNumber. Not surprisingly, this will take a bit of time and cause the UI to be unresponsive for a short time after launch. Once you have this code in place, press Command+I to invoke the Profile action.

Assuming there are no errors, Instruments will launch and prompt you for a template. Choose the Time Profiler template, and click the Profile button. Your app will launch, but it'll take just a bit longer than usual. Once it launches and shows its window, stop the trace by pressing the Record button. Make sure the Instruments and Detail views are shown and that the Detail view mode is set to Call Tree. Then, under the Call Tree options on the left side of the Detail view, make sure that Invert Call Tree, Hide System Libraries, and

Show Obj-C Only are the only options that are selected. This shows only your app's symbols. You should see something similar to **Figure 15.22**.

FIGURE 15.22 Your app's (sparse) call tree

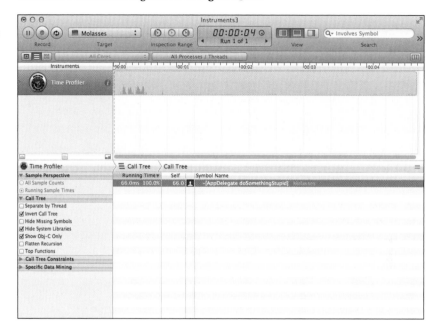

In the figure, only one symbol is shown, and it should be painfully clear that your app spent most of its time doing something stupid. Many developers' knee-jerk reaction would be to blame the tight for loop. Of course it's going to take a while to create one hundred thousand objects. Astute Cocoa/Objective-C developers will know better with such a contrived example, but here's where the Time Profiler really shines. Double-click the -[AppDelegate doSomethingStupid] symbol in the list, and the Detail view will prove its name (**Figure 15.23**).

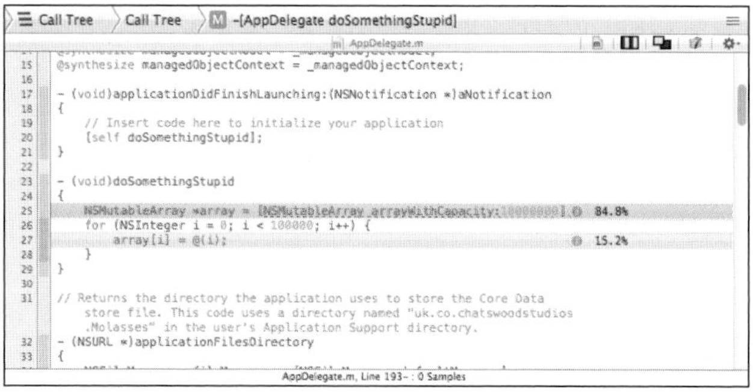

FIGURE 15.23 Source code overlaid with a heat map

In the figure, AppDelegate.m is displayed with some additional information overlaid. Instruments has broken down the time spent in that symbol (the -doSomethingStupid method) to highlight the most time-consuming instructions within it.

To see the percentages (as in Figure 15.23), you may need to click the gear button in the upper-right corner and select View as Percentage from the menu. The overlay is color-coded to serve as a sort of heat map, where the color (ranging from "red hot" to "not-so-hot yellow" and beyond) represents how much time your computer spent executing the most time-consuming instructions.

This makes one thing very obvious: The culprit isn't the for loop, though it certainly takes time. The red-hot instruction (84.8 percent of the method's time in the example) was the line where you allocated and initialized an NSMutableArray. If you don't already know why this is, here's where Instruments gets even better.

Click the Call Tree segment of the Detail view's navigation bar to get back to the list of symbols. Deselect the Hide System Libraries check box to show all the system library calls in addition to those of your app. Your symbols should be gone, replaced by some system library symbols. Because the call tree is inverted, the deepest call in the stack is shown as a top-level object, and the top results are the calls that happened as a result of -doSomethingStupid.

Expand the items until you see something similar to **Figure 15.24**. You see that -doSomethingStupid goes on to call into Cocoa, and it's spending lots of time just creating the array. While it doesn't tell you why, it certainly draws your attention to it. The reason, for those still wondering, is that you're abusing -[NSMutableArray arrayWithCapacity:] by allocating memory you aren't even using. Of course it'd take just as long to allocate all that space if you were using it, but the point is that the problem wasn't where so many developers would've initially suspected (especially if that allocation were done in another part of the code).

FIGURE 15.24 The call tree with system libraries included

Although this was a contrived example, it neatly demonstrates Instruments' powerfully intuitive way of visualizing trace information—a way that takes only a few clicks to reveal the source of a performance problem. Now that you know what the problem is, it might be easiest to use a saner capacity (especially since you already know you need 100,000 objects). Contrast this approach with using -[NSMutableArray array] to create the array by profiling both scenarios. You'll see that the -arrayWithCapacity: approach is the better way to go, as long as you use it wisely.

OTHER INSTRUMENTS

There are a number of other excellent Instruments templates, and there is nowhere near enough space in this book to detail them. There are templates for analyzing memory management, garbage collection, multi-core processes, Grand Central Dispatch queues, file system access, and Mountain Lion's Autolayout, and there's even a UI recorder that can record and play back user interface events for repeated UI testing. See the Instruments documentation via its Help menu for more details.

UNIT TESTING

Most sources define unit testing as a method of testing the functionality of individual units of code to make certain they behave as expected under any possible condition. A unit is a logical, testable piece of your code. For example, if you have a `MyCalculator` class with methods that perform various calculations (such as additions, subtractions, factorials, or square roots), you might have a matching `MyCalculatorTests` class that tests each of those functions. Each test is typically its own method with a descriptive signature—such as `-testSquareRootOfNumber:`—that does exactly as its name suggests.

Of course, methods can pass objects back and forth, so you may have test cases that involve making sure that a valid object is returned from a method with various types of input under certain conditions, including verifying that no object is returned with certain input or conditions. For example, you may need to test a method that returns an object representing a network connection. The method may not be able to fulfill the request, either because you failed to provide it some valid input (such as a valid host name) or because of networking errors (such as an unplugged network cable or deactivated Wi-Fi connection).

The tests should be designed to cover all the imaginable ways the code could fail, to make sure that it doesn't. No matter what changes you make to the code, the existing tests should still pass, and new tests (to cover new functionality or new scenarios) should pass too.

Developers tend to be an obsessive lot. We like the idea of unit testing. It's neat, predictable, and verifiable. The trouble is, many of us admit we don't unit test. The most often cited reason is the amount of work it takes to create and maintain the tests to maintain "full coverage" of all your code's functions (and all the possible scenarios those functions may face). For independent software developers in particular, the engineering time proper unit testing takes may be unacceptable for a number of reasons.

Adding to the controversy is confusion over what exactly to test and how to test it. More specifically, those new to unit testing have trouble determining how to design the tests for their code. That particular subject is well beyond the scope of this book, so this section will focus on the tools that Xcode provides, leaving the study of unit test design for a better-suited book. Whether or not unit testing is for you (and how best to approach it for your project) is up to you to explore.

UNIT TESTING IN XCODE

As you saw in Chapter 13, Xcode provides a specific Build action called Test (which you can initiate by pressing Command+U or by choosing Product > Test from the main menu). You can see the tests that are to be run for the active scheme in the scheme's Test action (**Figure 15.25**). These tests are automatically detected based on their formatting, which you'll learn later in this chapter.

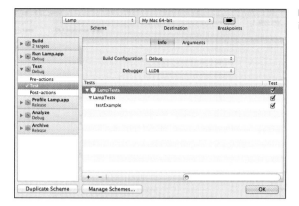

FIGURE 15.25 The default tests in the Scheme editor

To take advantage of Xcode's unit testing support, you need to select the Include Unit Tests check box when creating a new project (**Figure 15.26**); or you can create a new target for your existing project by selecting File > New > Target from the main menu and choosing either the OS X > Other > Cocoa Unit Testing Bundle template or the iOS > Other > Cocoa Touch Unit Testing Bundle template (**Figure 15.27**).

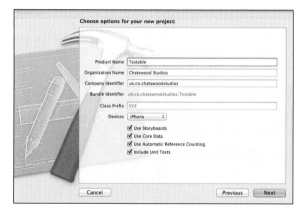

FIGURE 15.26 Including unit tests in a new project

FIGURE 15.27 Adding unit tests to an existing project

In Figure 15.25, the LampTests target is expanded, showing another node named LampTests. This corresponds to the only file that belongs to the LampTests target: LampTests.m. The LampTests class defines the individual tests available (in the form of methods). The class currently has one test method: -testExample, which can be seen when the LampTests class node is expanded. The Test column lets you toggle individual tests on or off.

If we were to run the LampTests suite now, there would be a single failure. This is because Xcode's template for a new test class is to deliberately make the tests fail—giving you a healthy reminder to add some code to make them pass!

POWERED BY OCUNIT

It's important to know that Xcode uses OCUnit, part of the SenTestingKit framework. OCUnit provides the test management and interface code, the Cocoa Unit Testing Bundle target template, and the Objective-C test case class template.

TEST TARGETS AND CLASSES

The unit test target links against `SenTestingKit.framework`. When creating test classes, you should ensure that they are built into the unit test target—building them into the main target serves no purpose but to slow down your compilation phase and bloat your application.

If you selected the Include Unit Tests check box when creating your project, you will notice that the sample test case class is compiled only into the unit test target. It is no longer necessary to compile the classes from your main target into your test target as well, making your test target compile much faster.

When adding a unit test target to an existing project, you will need to perform an additional step to make this work. Select the project in the Project navigator, choose the unit test target, and then open the Build Settings tab. Search for the Bundle Loader setting, and for OS X targets set it to:

```
$(BUILT_PRODUCTS_DIR)/<App>.app/Contents/MacOS/<App>
```

For iOS targets, set Bundle Loader to:

```
$(BUILT_PRODUCTS_DIR)/<App>.app/<App>
```

Replace *App* with the name of the app that contains the classes required by the unit tests. For iOS targets, you also need to ensure that the Test Host build setting is set to `${BUNDLE_LOADER}`. It also helps to set your app target as a dependency for the unit test target in the Target Dependency build phase—see Chapter 13 for more information about build phases.

Test case classes can be created using the Objective-C test case class template (accessed from the Add Files panel or by dragging the template file into the project from the File Template library, as in **Figure 15.28**).

FIGURE 15.28 The test case class file template

The test case classes are subclasses of the `SenTestCase` class provided by `SenTestingKit.framework`. It is up to you to add individual tests in the form of methods. A test method is any method in a test case class that starts with the word `test` and has a return type of `void`. For example:

```
- (void)testValidDataStructure { }
```

Tests are executed in alphabetical order based on the method name. Developers new to unit testing frameworks often use the execution order to perform setup in the tests executed first in an attempt to save having to duplicate setup code in every test. To make your tests most effective, you should be striving to make them self-contained and executable in isolation.

> **NOTE:** If you select the Include Unit Tests check box when you create a project, the test case class template provides the stub methods for setup and tear-down of the testing environment. If you add new test case classes (using File > New > File or the template from the File Template library), you will have to create these methods yourself.

As mentioned earlier, OCUnit helps with this by providing a pair of methods that are run before and after each test case is run. These methods (named -setUp and -tearDown) are a good place to reset or pre-populate data structures between tests to ensure that each test has a clean slate to start with and clears away resources used afterward.

There are similar class methods (+setUp and +tearDown) that are executed at the start and end of each test class. This provides another opportunity to establish resources (for example, a test server) and clear them up after the test class has finished.

ASSERTING YOURSELF

Tests ultimately pass or fail an assertion. Depending on what you're testing, you will assert that a condition must be satisfied. For example, you may assert equality with an expected value, or that an exception must or must not be raised, or that a return value must or must not be nil. **Table 15.2** shows some of the assertions provided by OCUnit, with descriptions of what they are intended to be used for.

TABLE 15.2 OCUnit assertions

ASSERTION	DESCRIPTIONS
STAssertEquals	Generates a failure if the two scalars, structs, or unions passed to it are not equal
STAssertEqualObjects	Generates a failure if the two objects passed to it are not equal according to the objects' isEqual: method
STAssertEqualsWithAccuracy	Generates a failure if two scalars are not equal to within some accuracy
STAssertFail	Generates an unconditional failure
STAssertNil	Generates a failure if the passed object is not nil
STAssertNotNil	Generates a failure if the passed object is nil
STAssertTrue	Generates a failure if the expression evaluates to false/NO
STAssertFalse	Generates a failure if the expression evaluates to true/YES

Each test should contain at least one assertion. Some argue that each test should include only one assertion so that the test's name (the method signature) is precisely descriptive of what is being tested, making the precise failure easier to identify should it arise.

TEST RESULTS

As mentioned previously, the test result output shows up in the Log navigator. When a test run succeeds, you will be presented with a nice green check mark like that in **Figure 15.29**. If tests fail, you will be greeted with a failure warning like that in **Figure 15.30**.

FIGURE 15.29 A successful test suite run

FIGURE 15.30 An unsuccessful test suite run with failures highlighted

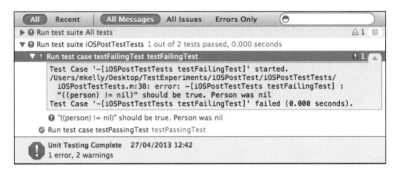

Testing offers more than just logging. Upon encountering a failure, the point of failure is highlighted as an error in the Source editor (**Figure 15.31**). The Issue navigator (**Figure 15.32**) also dutifully displays not only the test failure, but also a description of the nature of the failure (based on the type of assertion you used) and the custom message if you provided one.

FIGURE 15.31 A unit test failure highlighted in the Source editor

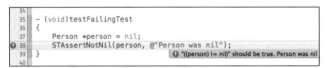

FIGURE 15.32 The same unit test failure displayed in the Issue navigator

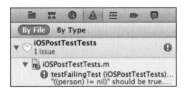

WRITING A UNIT TEST

Having spent enough time talking about unit testing, let's take a practical walk through the process. Create a new iOS project by selecting File > New > Project from the main menu, and select iOS > Application > Single View Application from the template chooser. Give your project a name—we'll call ours Testable—and ensure that the check boxes Use Automatic Reference Counting and Include Unit Tests have been selected. Once the project is created, verify that it has a target named TestableTests, that it has a group in the Project navigator named Testable containing the code for the main app, and that it also has a group named TestableTests containing the code for the tests.

CREATING SOMETHING TESTABLE

You'll start by adding a `Person` class to Testable. To do so, highlight the Testable group in the Project navigator, then add a new Objective-C class to the project by choosing File > New > New File from the main menu. Name the `Person` class and make it a subclass of `NSObject`. Make certain before saving that the new `Person` class is added only to the Testable targets (**Figure 15.33**). Click Create to add the file.

FIGURE 15.33
Adding a Person class

Build a basic Objective-C class using the following code. Make the interface file (Person.h) look as follows:

```
#import <Foundation/Foundation.h>

@interface Person : NSObject
@property (nonatomic, strong) NSString *firstName;
@property (nonatomic, strong) NSString *lastName;
@end
```

The implementation file (Person.m) should remain as it is:

```
#import "Person.h"

@implementation Person
@end
```

This code describes a basic class representing a person with a first and last name. Assuming you're familiar with Objective-C, you'll realize that the two name properties will be nil when the person is first created. Additionally, the synthesized accessors for those properties will allow the names to be set to nil or an NSString (which could be empty). These are scenarios you should avoid—a person should always have a first and last name, even if created without a first and last name. For that, you need to design a test.

NOTE: We've taken advantage of newer Objective-C language features such as automatic synthesis to keep the code to a minimum.

DESIGNING THE TEST

Your goal for the Person test coverage is simple: All Person instances must have a valid first and last name. That is, they cannot have nil or an empty NSString set as their first or last name, nor can the Person instance be initialized in such a state.

For minimal coverage, you need four tests:

- testLastNameCannotBeNil
- testLastNameCannotBeEmptyString
- testFirstNameCannotBeNil
- testFirstNameCannotBeEmptyString

You already know that all four tests will fail with the Person class in its current state. There is no code to check for and enforce these requirements. Time to write the test.

WRITING THE TEST

To write the test, you'll need to add an Objective-C test case class to the project. You can do this by dragging an Objective-C test case class from the File Template library into the Project navigator (under the TestableTests group), as seen in **Figure 15.34**.

FIGURE 15.34 Adding a test case class to the project

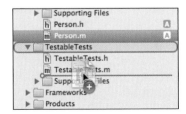

Name the class `PersonTests` so it's clear to which class this test belongs. Also add the test *only* to the TestableTests target (since it does not need to be built for Testable to run). Your settings should resemble **Figure 15.35**. Click Create.

FIGURE 15.35 Naming and configuring the test case class

Replace the contents of `PersonTests.h` with the following code:

```
#import <SenTestingKit/SenTestingKit.h>
@class Person;
@interface PersonTests : SenTestCase
@property (nonatomic, strong) Person *personToTest;
@end
```

Replace the contents of `PersonTests.m` with the following code:

```
#import "PersonTests.h"
#import "Person.h"
@implementation PersonTests
- (void)setUp
{
    [super setUp];
    // Create a person to test
```

(code continues on next page)

```
        Person *newTestPerson = [[Person alloc] init];
        self.personToTest = newTestPerson;
    }
    - (void)tearDown
    {
        // Kill the test person
        self.personToTest = nil;
        [super tearDown];
    }
    - (void)testLastNameCannotBeNil
    {
        self.personToTest.lastName = nil;
        STAssertNotNil(self.personToTest.lastName,
            @"Last name cannot be nil!");
    }
    - (void)testLastNameCannotBeEmptyString
    {
        self.personToTest.lastName = @"";
        STAssertTrue((self.personToTest.lastName.length > 0),
            @"Last name cannot be empty string.");
    }
    - (void)testFirstNameCannotBeNil
    {
        self.personToTest.firstName = nil;
        STAssertNotNil(self.personToTest.firstName,
            @"First name cannot be nil!");
    }
    - (void)testFirstNameCannotBeEmptyString
    {
        self.personToTest.firstName = @"";
        STAssertTrue((self.personToTest.firstName.length > 0),
            @"First name cannot be empty string.");
    }
    @end
```

If you look in the Scheme editor for the Testable scheme, under the Test action, you should now see your four new tests being picked up under the new PersonTests entry there (**Figure 15.36**).

Testable
iPhone 6.1 Simulator
Scheme
Destination
Breakpoints
Build
2 targets
Run Testable.app
Debug
Test
Debug
Profile Testable.app
Release
Analyze
Debug
Archive
Release
Info
Arguments
Build Configuration
Debug
Debugger
LLDB
Tests
Test Application Data
Test Location
Test
TestableTests
None
None
PersonTests
testFirstNameCanno...
testFirstNameCanno...
testLastNameCanno...
testLastNameCanno...
TestableTests
Duplicate Scheme
Manage Schemes...
OK

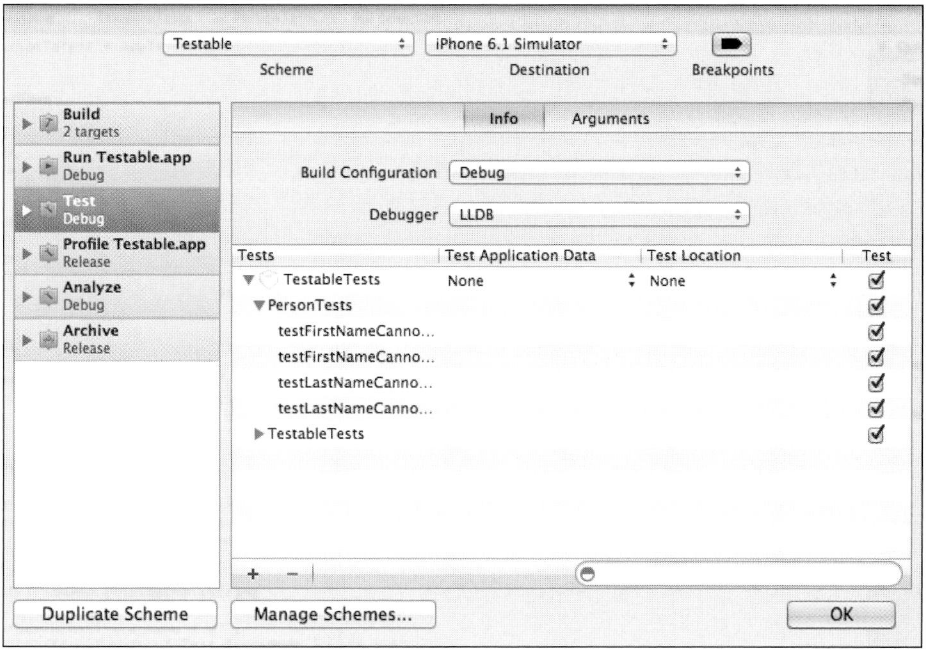

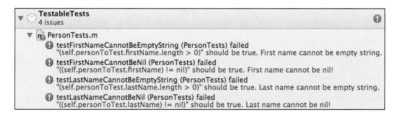

FIGURE 15.36 The Test action populated with the new tests

You probably noticed an additional test class listed in Figure 15.36 named TestableTests. This is the default test class added when creating a unit test target, and it contains a single test (named `testExample`) that is designed to fail. We can ignore it for this exercise by opening the `TestableTests.m` file and commenting out the line that begins `STFail....`

TESTING THE TEST

It's now time to make sure your test works properly. Press Command+U, or choose Product > Test from the main menu. When you do, you'll get four expected failures. They'll be highlighted in the editor as well as listed neatly in the Issue navigator (**Figure 15.37**).

TestableTests
4 issues
PersonTests.m
testFirstNameCannotBeEmptyString (PersonTests) failed
"(self.personToTest.firstName.length > 0)" should be true. First name cannot be empty string.
testFirstNameCannotBeNil (PersonTests) failed
"((self.personToTest.firstName) != nil)" should be true. First name cannot be nil!
testLastNameCannotBeEmptyString (PersonTests) failed
"(self.personToTest.lastName.length > 0)" should be true. Last name cannot be empty string.
testLastNameCannotBeNil (PersonTests) failed
"((self.personToTest.lastName) != nil)" should be true. Last name cannot be nil!

FIGURE 15.37 Expected failures in the Issue navigator

TIP: You might try disabling one of the tests in the Scheme editor's Test action panel by deselecting the Test check box next to the desired test. Run the test again, and you'll see that failure missing from the list because that test was not executed.

PASSING THE TEST

To pass the test, your Person class clearly needs to guard against nil or blank names. It needs not only smarter setter accessors but some default values in an -init method as well. Replace the entire contents of Person.m with the following code:

```objc
#import "Person.h"
@implementation Person
- (id)init
{
    self = [super init];
    if (self) {
        self.firstName = @"John";
        self.lastName = @"Smith";
    }
    return self;
}
- (void)setFirstName:(NSString *)firstName
{
    if (_firstName != firstName && firstName.length > 0) {
        _firstName = firstName;
    }
}
- (void)setLastName:(NSString *)lastName
{
    if (_lastName != lastName && lastName.length > 0) {
        _lastName = lastName;
    }
}
@end
```

The changes to Person.m ensure several things. First, the -init method always makes sure there's a default first and last name. Second, the custom setter methods make sure the newly passed name is neither nil nor an empty NSString.

Now you can check to make sure the code works as desired by repeating the tests. This time, all four tests should pass. Press Command+U to run the unit tests, and notice happily that no errors come up in the Issue navigator. You can further verify the tests passed by finding the test results in the Log navigator (**Figure 15.38**).

FIGURE 15.38
A successful test run
for PersonTests

```
▼ ⊘ Run test suite All tests  5 out of 5 tests passed, 0.003 seconds
    Test Suite 'All tests' started at 2013-05-13 21:15:19 +0000
    Test Suite '/Users/mkelly/Library/Developer/Xcode/DerivedData/Testable-fkbquglcbgsnpseowwedkywbnbum/Build/
       Products/Debug-iphonesimulator/TestableTests.octest(Tests)' started at 2013-05-13 21:15:19 +0000
    Test Suite 'PersonTests' started at 2013-05-13 21:15:19 +0000
    Test Case '-[PersonTests testFirstNameCannotBeEmptyString]' started.
    Test Case '-[PersonTests testFirstNameCannotBeEmptyString]' passed (0.000 seconds).
    Test Case '-[PersonTests testFirstNameCannotBeNil]' started.
    Test Case '-[PersonTests testFirstNameCannotBeNil]' passed (0.000 seconds).
    Test Case '-[PersonTests testLastNameCannotBeEmptyString]' started.
    Test Case '-[PersonTests testLastNameCannotBeEmptyString]' passed (0.000 seconds).
    Test Case '-[PersonTests testLastNameCannotBeNil]' started.
    Test Case '-[PersonTests testLastNameCannotBeNil]' passed (0.000 seconds).
    Test Suite 'PersonTests' finished at 2013-05-13 21:15:19 +0000.
    Executed 4 tests, with 0 failures (0 unexpected) in 0.000 (0.000) seconds
    Test Suite 'TestableTests' started at 2013-05-13 21:15:19 +0000
    Test Case '-[TestableTests testExample]' started.
    Test Case '-[TestableTests testExample]' passed (0.000 seconds).
    Test Suite 'TestableTests' finished at 2013-05-13 21:15:19 +0000.
    Executed 1 test, with 0 failures (0 unexpected) in 0.000 (0.000) seconds
    Test Suite '/Users/mkelly/Library/Developer/Xcode/DerivedData/Testable-fkbquglcbgsnpseowwedkywbnbum/Build/
       Products/Debug-iphonesimulator/TestableTests.octest(Tests)' finished at 2013-05-13 21:15:19 +0000.
    Executed 5 tests, with 0 failures (0 unexpected) in 0.000 (0.001) seconds
    Test Suite 'All tests' finished at 2013-05-13 21:15:19 +0000.
    Executed 5 tests, with 0 failures (0 unexpected) in 0.000 (0.003) seconds
  ▼ ⊘ Run test suite /Users/mkelly/Library/Developer/Xcode/DerivedData/Testable-fkbquglcbgsnpseowwedkywbnbum/Build/Products/...
    ▶ ✓ Run test suite PersonTests  4 out of 4 tests passed, 0.000 seconds
    ▶ ⊘ Run test suite TestableTests  1 out of 1 test passed, 0.000 seconds
  ⊘ Unit Testing Complete   13/05/2013 22:15
    No issues
```

Congratulations! You've just passed your first test-driven development (TDD) cycle. Achievement unlocked!

WRAPPING UP

Poor-quality code should now be a thing of the past. You've seen how to perform advanced debugging techniques using LLDB, and how Instruments provides a simple GUI interface to a powerful tracing and profiling system. And whatever your feelings about unit testing, you cannot argue that Xcode 4 doesn't make it easy to set up and use. You've got the tools at your disposal, so improving code quality comes down to your own discipline.

In the next chapter, you will examine how to make the most of Xcode's command-line tools and how to delve into the application bundle to increase its flexibility.

CHAPTER 16

Scripting and Preprocessing

This chapter is about using scripting as well as the preprocessor to customize the build process. One size most certainly does not fit all coding environments, but large groups as well as independent developers can take advantage of Xcode's scripting and preprocessing capabilities to automate a variety of testing and deployment tasks.

This chapter will not serve as an exhaustive list of everything you can achieve—that would be an entire book unto itself. Instead, the goal is to introduce you to the scripting hooks and to some preprocessor tricks to spark your imagination so you will be better equipped to dream up your ideal automation pipeline.

EXTENDING YOUR WORKFLOW WITH CUSTOM SCRIPTS

In Chapter 13, you explored Xcode's redesigned build system. You learned that there are separate build actions that are run against the active scheme. You also learned that the action you perform will automatically build the specified targets in the way that makes the best sense for that action (a build for running yields a Debug build; a build for archiving yields a Release build). Two important features were mentioned briefly: the ability to run scripts before and after each type of action and the ability to run a script as part of a build phase.

SCRIPTING OPPORTUNITIES

Xcode offers several opportunities to hook in your custom scripts to extend functionality. Xcode has always come with the Run Script build phase (see Chapter 13), which, as its name suggests, runs the specified script when the target to which it belongs is built. The limitations of such a script are the same as its benefits: It runs only when its target is built.

PRE- AND POST-ACTION SCRIPTS

Xcode 4 adds pre- and post-action scripts, which are run before and after each major action. The ability to run a script just before (or after) a Test action, however, would let you reset the application's test data before launch to always run against the same test data (or clean up a mess after the app finishes running). A bit of post-processing for an archive created by the Archive action would be helpful for many developers as well.

NOTE: It is not possible to create pre- and post-action scripts for the Analyze action. When you select either of these options, Xcode tells you that the actual analysis takes place during the Build phase, so you should place your scripts there instead.

To manage pre- and post-action scripts, you edit the scheme into which you want to place them. From there, you select the action and expand it by clicking the disclosure button and selecting Pre-actions or Post-actions. **Figure 16.1** shows the Post-action editor for a Build action.

The nomenclature is a bit messy: A post-action script for the Build action could be called a "post-Build-action action." Whatever you choose to call them, actions (pre- or post-) are added and removed using the Add (+) and Remove (–) buttons. Note that the Remove (–) button will be inactive until you select the action by clicking its title bar. There are currently two types of actions: Run Script and Send Email. We'll ignore the obvious mail-sending feature in favor of the considerably more powerful scripting capabilities.

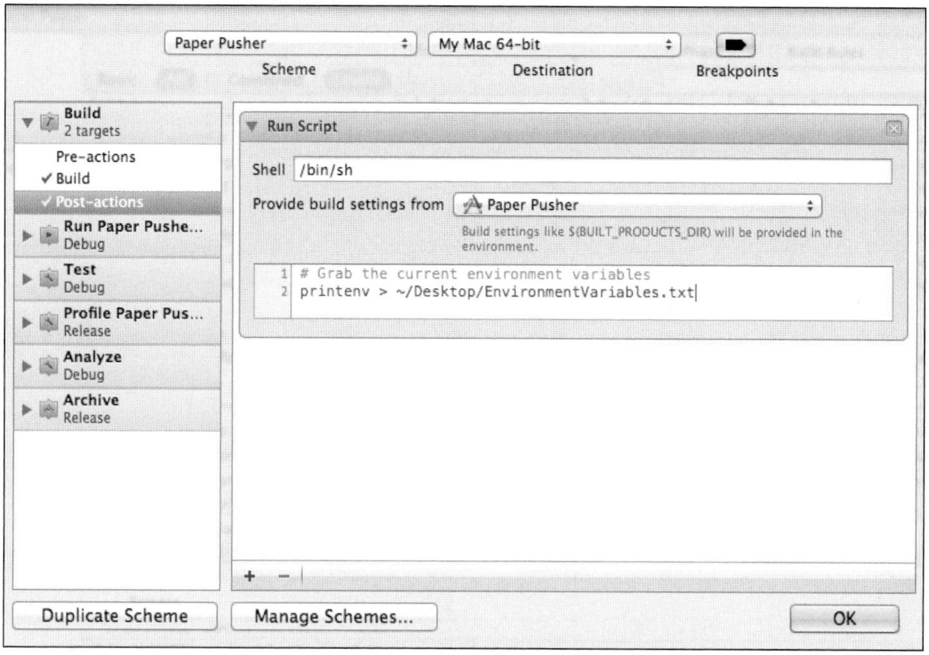

FIGURE 16.1 The Post-action editor

The Run Script action has three controls. The Shell field lets you specify a path to a specific scripting shell; the default is /bin/sh, but you can specify just about any scripting interpreter that you might have installed on your Mac. If you share your projects with other developers, you may want to stick to well-known shells like Bash (/bin/sh or /bin/bash), Zsh (/bin/zsh), and tcsh (/bin/tcsh), or preinstalled scripting languages like Ruby (/usr/bin/ruby), Python (/usr/bin/python), and Perl (/usr/bin/perl).

The second control, a drop-down menu, lets you choose the source of the environment variables supplied to your scripting environment. For example, BUILT_PRODUCTS_DIR always points to the folder into which the target's built products are placed. The drop-down menu lets you choose the target from which these variables are populated. You can also choose to use no target at all, but you might find that most of the useful information is missing to you. The third control is a small script editor.

Figure 16.1 shows that the script does just one thing: It executes the printenv command to capture the environment variables in a file named EnvironmentVariables.txt on the current user's desktop. If you have any shell scripting experience at all, you're likely already imagining many ways to take advantage of these additional scripting hooks.

Notice that the script redirects the output of the `printenv` command to a file rather than allow the output to go to the console. This is a deliberate action because the output of these run scripts cannot be relied upon—in previous versions of Xcode it has sometimes appeared in build logs, sometimes at the system console. In the current version (4.6), it does not appear anywhere, so if you want to see the script output, you need to capture it yourself.

RUN SCRIPT BUILD PHASES

The pre- and post-action run scripts allow you to inject your scripts on specific actions for specific schemes. Sometimes you want to run a script as part of the building of a specific target, regardless of the scheme it is being created for. For this there is the tried-and-true Run Script build phase, which you learned about in Chapter 13. Its output is easily located, and you can add as many as you like to the build phases of a given target.

Figure 16.2 shows an empty Run Script build phase expanded to show its settings. Run scripts are executed in the order in which they appear in the target's build phases list, and you can insert them between the regular build phases if you have an extremely complicated build process to maintain.

FIGURE 16.2 An empty Run Script build phase

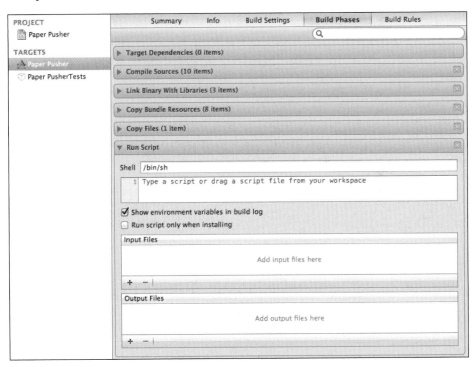

The Shell field lets you specify the shell you want to use to execute the script and supports the same range of shells and scripting languages as the pre- and post-action run scripts—Bash, Zsh, tcsh, Ruby, Python, Perl, and so on.

The editor area directly beneath the Shell field will contain your script. You can type or paste a script directly into the field or drag a script file from your workspace. Since the field grows to match the size of your script, you'll likely find it easier to take the drag-a-script-file-from-your-workspace approach. To do this, add a new shell script file to your workspace from the template (**Figure 16.3**). You can then drag the script into the script editor field. This way, you can edit your script in the Source editor, which causes the build phase to call your script when executed.

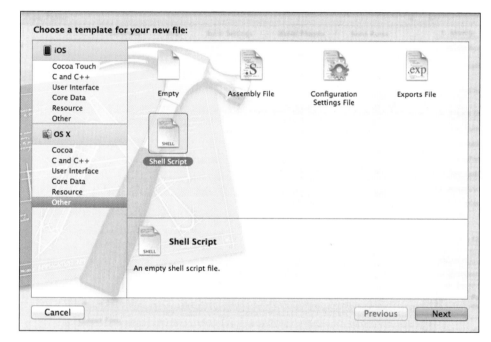

FIGURE 16.3 The shell script file template

NOTE: When you drop a script from your workspace into the script editor, Xcode inserts the full path to your script file. This essentially creates a script whose only purpose is to call the script in your workspace. The inserted path is absolute, however, and will break if you move your project to another folder or disk, so you may want to use a relative path instead. You may also need to ensure that the script is executable.

The "Show environment variables in build log" check box (Figure 16.2) is a handy option for debugging your script to make sure the variables you use have the values you expect. When this check box is selected, the environment variables available to the shell will be included in the build log. Once you are happy that your script is working correctly, you can safely turn off this option without affecting the script's environment and cut down on the build log size.

When the "Run script only when installing" check box is selected, the script will be executed only when both the Installation Directory build setting is set to a valid path and the Deployment Location build setting is set to yes for the current configuration (triggering an install build).

If your run script is intended to process a set of input files producing another set of output files, then you can specify these in the Input Files and Output Files sections. When Xcode is about to run your script, it will check the timestamps of the input files against the output files. If any of your input files are newer than the output files, then the script will be run.

XCODE'S ENVIRONMENT VARIABLES

Xcode provides a number of environment variables that contain information useful to your scripting endeavors. For example, it may be important to know the path to a built product or to some resource that is external to the project but relative to the project's folder. It might also be useful to know what build configuration is being used or what install directory is specified in the build settings.

This build environment information is invaluable when using scripts to extend the build process with your own post-processing. There are a number of ways to get this information:

- Xcode builds can be executed at the command line using the xcodebuild tool. xcodebuild comes with a handy option to show the build settings: xcodebuild -showBuildSettings. You can find more information about this tool in Chapter 17.
- All run scripts feature a "Show environment variables in build log" check box—select this setting to get a dump of the environment in the build log.
- The first run script we created used the printenv command to dump all the known shell variables to a file—this is a handy way to get a record of the environment used during the execution of a specific run script.

If you use the last method in a pre- or post-action run script, you will get the environment variables that correspond to the "Provide build settings from" drop-down. They will vary according to the target, and you'll get a lot less output if you don't specify a target at all.

EXAMINING A SIMPLE SCRIPTING EXAMPLE

A great many words could be spent detailing scripting examples both simple and elaborate. Since this book focuses on Xcode, only a basic practical example is needed to demonstrate some of the power of extending the build system with your custom processing.

In Chapter 10, you learned how to deploy an application using Xcode 4's preferred method: the Archive action. This action builds a target for release and then creates an Xcode archive that is meant to be submitted to Apple's App Store. As mentioned in Chapter 10,

Apple seems to assume that by "deploy," developers of course mean "sell on the App Store." But many independent software vendors with OS X products may not necessarily be ready to abandon their existing distribution channel in favor of Apple's. Some extra effort is necessary, therefore, to customize the deployment process for these heretics.

SETTING UP THE SCENARIO

Consider the following scenario. You want to distribute your app on your own website, flouting Apple's benevolence. You'd like your users to download the application in the form of a simple zip file whose only content is the application itself. The zip file (or some archive) is necessary because application bundles are essentially special folders, which would be cumbersome to download. Upon archiving, you want to produce this zip file and have it pop up in a Finder window so you can conveniently copy the file to a server. Of course this is a very basic solution, but this simple "gateway script" can lead you to more elaborate solutions (see the "Extending the Script" section) to suit your needs.

One way is to hook into the Archive process, because it automatically builds for release and does indeed result in an archive intended for distribution. Xcode will still create its own archive (there's currently no way to prevent it), but the custom script will create your archive as well.

> **NOTE:** Of course you can hook your archive manipulation script into the Archive action's post-action, but the example that follows will serve as a practical example of scripting in general.

CREATING THE SCRIPT

To get started, navigate to your project in the File navigator, select your main app target, and then click the Build Phases tab. Click the Add Build Phase button, and choose Add Run Script from the menu. Double-click the Run Script title, and name it **Run Archive Script** for clarity. Expand the new Run Archive Script phase, and add the following script:

```
# Move to the built products directory - exit if unsuccessful
cd "$BUILT_PRODUCTS_DIR" || exit 1
# Clean up any previous archiving folder and create a new one
rm -rf Archive
mkdir Archive
# Compress the target into a zip file in the Archive folder
zip -r "Archive/$TARGETNAME.zip" "$FULL_PRODUCT_NAME"
# Show the Archive folder in the Finder
open ./Archive
```

Figure 16.4 shows the completed script in the Run Archive Script build phase. If you're familiar with shell scripting, the script should be easy enough to follow. It uses environment variables that Xcode provides for easy access to the built products directory, the target name, and the full product name. A couple of points are worth noting: When changing directories, it is a good idea to test the success of the operation—if for some reason it didn't succeed, subsequent operations could have unexpected consequences. It is also a good idea to surround paths with quotation marks to guard against variables that may contain spaces.

Line 2 changes the working directory to the built products directory. Lines 5 and 6 make sure there's a clean `Archive` folder into which to place the completed archive (this avoids clutter when looking for the archive in the Finder window). Line 9 calls the `zip` command-line program to create a zip file named after the target, using the full product name and placing the file into the `Archive` subfolder created on line 6. Finally, line 12 uses the `open` command-line program to open the `Archive` folder in a Finder window, neatly presenting your new archive.

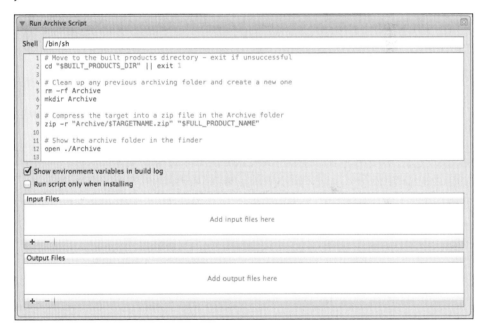

FIGURE 16.4 The completed custom archiving script

To test it, run the Archive action by choosing Product > Archive from the main menu. The Archive action runs as usual, but you should also see the Finder window appear.

TIP: You may prefer to prevent Xcode from opening the Organizer (enabled by default). To do this, edit the scheme and select the Archive action. Deselect the Reveal Archive in Organizer option, and click OK.

ARCHIVING ON RELEASE BUILDS ONLY

You're not quite finished yet. Currently, the script will run every time the target is built. Run the application (which builds for debugging). The archiving script also runs and pops up in a Finder window when the application is running. Since the stated goal was to run this script only when archiving (synonymous with "building for release"), this is less than ideal. There are two ways that we can deal with this—by customizing the current Run Script build phase to detect a Release build, or by using a post-action script on the Archive action.

CREATING THE ARCHIVE CONDITIONALLY

Using a build phase run script is a somewhat blunt tool. Any scheme in your project that includes the target that your run script is attached to will be subject to its effects—the build phases will be blindly executed on build regardless of the scheme action (Run, Test, Analyze, or Archive). We do have an advantage in that by default a Run action will use a Debug build configuration, whereas an Archive action will use a Release configuration.

Luckily for us, one of the build environment variables that Xcode provides us is called CONFIGURATION. You can use an if conditional to check whether the script is run under the Release configuration. Replace the existing script with that shown in **Figure 16.5**. The if condition on line 2 evaluates the CONFIGURATION variable to check for the Release configuration. Line 17 ends the conditional block (fi is if spelled backward).

FIGURE 16.5 The amended archiving script

Test the script. Run your application normally—the script should not run. Now call the Archive action. This time the script runs, and the Finder reveals your archive.

This may be enough for some users, but there are circumstances where it may not suit everyone. Say, for example, that you have a collection of trusted beta testers for whom you want to produce an archive that is built with debugging symbols included. A simple way to do this would be to alter the Archive action to use the Debug build configuration (switching it back when it is time to do a real Release build). Unfortunately, your archiving script is dependent on a Release build configuration, so you will no longer automatically be producing a zip file on Archive.

Alternatively, you may be collaborating on a project with other developers. Any changes made to the build phases will be saved into the main project file and propagated to your collaborators. In some circumstances, this is exactly what you want, but if you have your own customizations that are not intended to be shared, this rules out using build phases.

USING THE POST-ACTION ARCHIVE ACTION

While they are not without their own limitations, the pre- and post-action run scripts can go some way to solving the potential problems detailed in the previous section. Pre- and post-actions are tied to a scheme rather than a target, so this allows more precision with their execution.

If you needed to produce a special build for your beta testers, you could create a custom scheme with its own settings—this would allow you to add the archiving run script to the post-action of the Archive action and configure it to produce a Debug build just for your testers. If you were working on a collaboration, you could attach run scripts to your own schemes that you don't need to share with your colleagues. For detailed information about the sharing (or not) of schemes, see Chapter 13.

FIGURE 16.6 Archive post-action run script

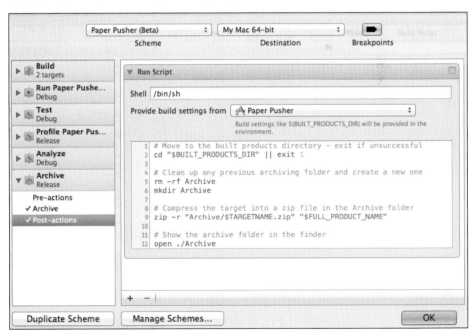

To take advantage of this precision, you should take a copy of the script (without the conditional `if` statement) from the Run Archive Script build phase on your target and then remove the build phase by clicking the title area and pressing the Delete key.

You can create a post-action run script by selecting the Edit Scheme entry from the Scheme menu on the toolbar. An action sheet appears (**Figure 16.6**) in which you can select your scheme from the drop-down menu near the top. In the list of actions on the left side, expand the Archive action and select the Post-actions entry that appears.

Use the Add (+) button to create a new Run Script action. In the newly created action, enter the shell as `/bin/sh`, choose the appropriate target from the "Provide build settings from" menu, and enter your shell script (without the recent conditional addition). Finally, click OK to save the changes and close the Scheme editor. Now that your action is set up, you can test it by ensuring that your scheme is selected and then selecting Product > Archive from the main menu. Your archive should be presented in a Finder window.

While the pre- and post-action scripts can be very useful, their surgical precision can also be their undoing. If you have a very carefully crafted set of scripts operating on a particular scheme, these are not available to your other schemes. Moving or copying them can be a painstaking (and potentially error-prone) process of re-creating the actions on another scheme, so choose wisely before using them or consider whether duplicating schemes might be more effective.

EXTENDING THE SCRIPT

As mentioned, this simple script shows how easy it is to customize the build process. The web reveals a number of creative deployment scripts cobbled together and shared by Xcode users. Some involve uploading to a build server for testing in continuous integration environments. Some involve checking things into and out of repositories and even setting build numbers to revision numbers pulled from those repositories. If you have a product that includes a framework of your own creation (see Chapter 14), you may wish to strip the headers out of the framework bundle to stop them from being shipped. Some scripts use release notes to generate update entries for appcast feeds, such as those used by Andy Matuschak's venerable Sparkle automatic update framework. Others upload the archive (and associated appcast, release notes, and so on) to a staging area for testing prior to deployment on their public web server.

With some scripting knowledge and a list of available command-line programs and Xcode environment variables, you can build quite a complex process. If you're new to a Unix-based platform (of which OS X is one), you owe it to yourself as a professional developer to explore the possibilities shell scripting offers and to leverage the rich tools the OS offers to automate your deployment tasks.

USING THE PREPROCESSOR

In Chapter 12, you saw how you can use the C preprocessor (CPP) to create separators that show in the jump bar and aid code navigation. If you're unfamiliar with the preprocessor, it may surprise you to know that it's far more powerful than that. It has a lot more to offer than the simple pragma mark directive.

TIP: To learn more about what the C preprocessor can do for you, visit http://xcodebook.com/cpp.

MACROS

One of the simplest ways to use the preprocessor is to define macros. Since the preprocessor does as its name suggests—processes the text prior to compilation—macros are automatically expanded for the compiler. This means you can use the #define command to create a kind of "lazy man's constant" or to compress a set of nested method calls down to a simple stand-in symbol.

WHERE TO PUT THEM

It's usually preferable to define macros in a header file so they can be imported elsewhere without needing to repeat them. Many developers use a global header file for this. The default .pch file found under your project's Supporting Files group is included everywhere and is a great place to keep global macros.

HOW TO DEFINE A MACRO

A macro is defined using the #define directive and a macro name (such as PlaceholderString or TRUNCATED_PI), followed by the expanded text for the macro. For example, the following defines a macro:

```
#define TRUNCATED_PI 3.14
```

Any time the preprocessor encounters TRUNCATED_PI in source files, the value will be expanded to (or replaced by) 3.14.

In Cocoa applications, it's commonplace to use Uniform Type Identifiers (such as com.mycompany.TestApp.testappdocument) to identify data types such as documents, pasteboard drag types, and more. As with constants, the benefit of using a macro is to cut down on the number of opportunities you might mistype a string constant (which the compiler cannot verify for you). Since a macro, like a symbol, must be typed properly (and participates in code completion), Xcode will help you spell it correctly, and the compiler will flag it as an error if you miss. A simple string macro can be defined like this:

```
#define TestAppDocType @"com.mycompany.TestApp.testappdocument"
```

This will define the macro `TestAppDocType`, which will be expanded to `@"com.mycompany.TestApp.testappdocument"` anywhere it's used.

Another handy use for macros is to shorten long, deeply nested method calls. Many non-document-based Cocoa applications "hang" top-level controllers from the application delegate to provide an easy means of reaching them from anywhere else in the application's code. A call to such a controller might look like this:

```
[[[NSApp delegate] importantController] doSomethingImportant];
```

You can shorten the call by defining a macro for the controller:

```
#define ImportantController [[NSApp delegate] importantController]
```

The shortened call is now:

```
[ImportantController doSomethingImportant];
```

Macros can be used as functions as well. In fact, many common (but verbose) evaluations have macros predefined in `Foundation.framework` (under `NSObjCRuntime.h`). For example, finding the larger of two values can be evaluated as follows:

```
int largest = (a > b) ? a : b;
```

The `MAX` macro, however, simplifies this (for any type, not just `int`) as:

```
int largest = MAX(a, b);
```

> **TIP:** An easy way to find system-defined symbols and macros is to type them into the Source editor and then Command-click them. The editor will navigate to the definition. Try it by typing **MAX** and Command-clicking the word.

POISON

Although not quite as severe as it sounds, the Clang `pragma poison` directive can turn the use of any symbol or macro into a hard error. This is useful when trying to avoid using a particular function, variable, or predefined macro. For example, if you wanted to make sure all logging calls are made to Cocoa's `NSLog()` rather than to `printf()`, you could "poison" `printf()`. This would cause the compiler to flag all existing calls and ensure any future slip-ups are avoided, should you forget and try to use `printf()` again later. To poison a symbol, use the following (substituting the desired symbol for `printf` in this example):

```
#pragma clang poison printf
```

Now `printf()` is considered poison. This could be useful in a project with multiple developers who agree not to use particular methods. Rather than rely on code review to find where these methods are used, the `pragma poison` can have the compiler do it for you.

If you decide you have made a mistake, the antidote is to simply delete or comment out the pragma directive you just set:

```
// #pragma clang poison printf
```

IGNORE

The `pragma poison` directive is a great way to enlist the compiler's help in finding illicit use of banned symbols, but on the flip side you may sometimes want to ignore the compiler's sagely advice. The Clang compiler is extremely helpful and can output warnings ranging from measly unused symbols to detecting the use of FourCharCode (see http://cocoadev.com/wiki/FourCharCode). Usually you want to take heed of everything that Clang has to say, but there will be times when you want to ignore its advice.

The brute force way to do so is to select your project in the File navigator and in the Project Settings editor select the Build Settings tab. With the filter level set to All, you can see (and adjust) the full range of compiler warnings for your project or target.

Unless you really want to loosen up your whole project, you can selectively disable warnings using the `pragma diagnostic ignored` directive. **Figure 16.7** shows a method from a project where unused method parameters generate a warning—this is not usually on by default, but we've enabled it for the purposes of example. In this case, it is an `IBAction` that takes an `id` parameter called sender, which is not used in the method body.

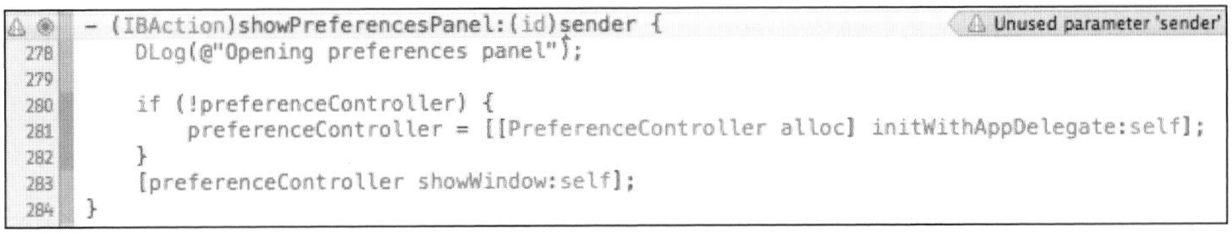

FIGURE 16.7 Unused parameter warning

```
   - (IBAction)showPreferencesPanel:(id)sender {                    ⚠ Unused parameter 'sender'
278      DLog(@"Opening preferences panel");
279
280      if (!preferenceController) {
281          preferenceController = [[PreferenceController alloc] initWithAppDelegate:self];
282      }
283      [preferenceController showWindow:self];
284  }
```

To request that the compiler ignore this warning, we place the following line before the method signature:

```
#pragma clang diagnostic ignored "-Wunused-parameter"
```

This instruction tells the compiler to ignore subsequent warnings. The `"-Wunused-parameter"` is the type of the warning—we were able to determine this value by selecting the warning in the Project editor and selecting the Quick Help inspector (**Figure 16.8**).

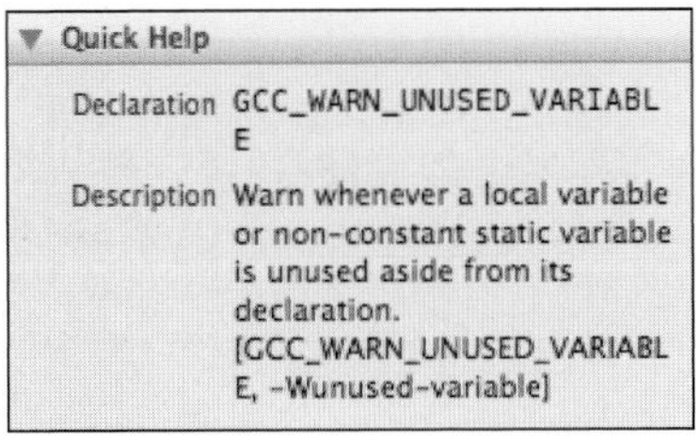

FIGURE 16.8 Quick help showing the warning name

```
▼ Quick Help

  Declaration  GCC_WARN_UNUSED_VARIABL
               E

  Description  Warn whenever a local variable
               or non-constant static variable
               is unused aside from its
               declaration.
               [GCC_WARN_UNUSED_VARIABL
               E, -Wunused-variable]
```

This removes the warning but has a side effect. All subsequent occurrences of the same warning in the file and in all files compiled after this file will now be ignored. This is rarely desirable, so Clang provides a way to counter this using the familiar concept of a stack. Using a push directive before the ignore and a pop directive after the ignore allows us to place a temporary exclusion on the stack and remove it when we don't want to feel its effects any longer. The push can be performed as follows:

```
#pragma clang diagnostic push
```

The pop can be performed as follows:

```
#pragma clang diagnostic pop
```

The complete arrangement can be seen in **Figure 16.9**—it doesn't make for pretty code, but if you prefer not to have genuine compiler warnings drowned in warnings you are prepared to ignore, it can be tolerable in small doses.

```
279   #pragma clang diagnostic push
280   #pragma clang diagnostic ignored "-Wunused-parameter"
281   - (IBAction)showPreferencesPanel:(id)sender {
282   #pragma clang diagnostic pop
283       DLog(@"Opening preferences panel");
284
285       if (!preferenceController) {
286           preferenceController = [[PreferenceController alloc] initWithAppDelegate:self];
287       }
288       [preferenceController showWindow:self];
289   }
```

FIGURE 16.9 A precisely targeted pragma ignore directive

CONDITIONALS

The preprocessor has another handy trick up its sleeve. You can use conditionals to include (or exclude) blocks of text between #ifdef and #endif or to issue errors and warnings that are dependent on the environment. The supported conditionals are #if, #ifdef, #ifndef, #else, #elif, and #endif. The #ifdef and #ifndef (if defined and if not defined, respectively) conditionals are the most commonly used.

You might use conditionals to exclude blocks of code at build time depending on some set of criteria. For example, you might include a message dialog box that appears when an application is launched and that warns the user they're running a beta version. A simple beta flag can be defined in the configuration used by a beta build scheme, while the normal scheme does not define it. Depending on which scheme is used, the beta warning code block may or may not be included at compile time.

You can write a conditional block of code as follows:

```
#ifdef SOMEMACRO
    NSLog(@"This code will only be included if SOMEMACRO is defined... ");
#endif
```

The NSLog() statement will not be included in the compiled code unless SOMEMACRO is defined. The #ifdef directive doesn't care what SOMEMACRO represents, only that it is defined. Recall that you can define SOMEMACRO like this:

```
#define SOMEMACRO 1
```

MACROS IN THE BUILD ENVIRONMENT

Defining a macro and then checking whether it's defined is easy enough. Whether a macro is defined can also be based on the current build settings, as the BETABUILD flag is. To try this out, create a new Cocoa Application in Xcode named BetaApp, and add the following code to the end of the application delegate class's -applicationDidFinishLaunching: method:

```
#ifdef BETABUILD
    [[NSAlert alertWithMessageText:@"Beta Version"
    defaultButton:@"Ok"
    alternateButton:nil
    otherButton:nil
    informativeTextWithFormat:@"Warning: you are using a beta version of this
    → application. Bad stuff might happen."] runModal];
#endif
```

Figure 16.10 shows the completed -applicationDidFinishLaunching: method. The NSAlert code block is wrapped in #ifdef and #endif preprocessor directives and will be included only if a macro named BETABUILD is defined.

```
17   - (void)applicationDidFinishLaunching:(NSNotification *)aNotification
18   {
19   #ifdef BETABUILD
20       // Display beta warning if built using Beta configuration
21       [[NSAlert alertWithMessageText:@"Beta version"
22                       defaultButton:@"OK"
23                     alternateButton:nil
24                         otherButton:nil
25           informativeTextWithFormat:@"Warning: you are using a beta version of
                     this application. Bad stuff might happen."] runModal];
26   #endif
27   }
```

FIGURE 16.10 The completed applicationDidFinishLaunching: method

Next, you'll need to define the BETABUILD macro somewhere. If you were to define it within the file, then it would always be enabled. Instead, you'll need to let the build environment take care of defining it by adding a separate build configuration for the beta build, defining the macro in the target's build settings (specifically, the Preprocessor Macros setting), and then creating a separate scheme that uses the beta build configuration.

To do this, you'll start by creating a beta configuration. Navigate to the BetaApp project, and click the Info tab if it's not already selected (**Figure 16.11**).

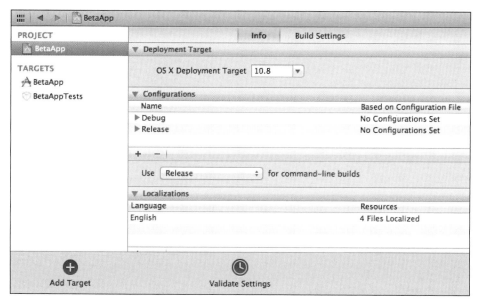

FIGURE 16.11 The Info tab for the BetaApp project

The beta configuration should be based on the Release configuration because you intend to present beta warnings only in released copies of the application. Using the Add (+) button just beneath the configuration list, choose Duplicate "Release" Configuration from the menu (**Figure 16.12**). Change the name from "Release copy" to **Beta Release**, and press Return.

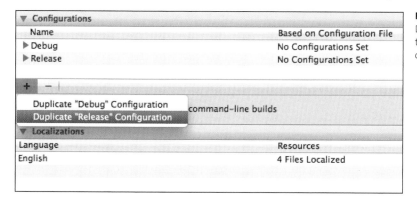

FIGURE 16.12 Duplicating the Release configuration

To use the separate configuration, you'll need a separate scheme. Click the Schemes drop-down menu on the toolbar, and choose Manage Schemes from the menu. In the Scheme Manager sheet (**Figure 16.13**), select the BetaApp scheme, click the gear icon button, and choose Duplicate from the menu. In the Scheme Editor sheet that appears, set the scheme's name to "BetaApp (Beta)" and then select the Archive action. Choose Beta Release from the Build Configuration menu (**Figure 16.14**), and click OK. There are now two schemes that build BetaApp, but the beta scheme (when built for archiving) will use the Beta Release configuration you created.

FIGURE 16.13
Managing the schemes

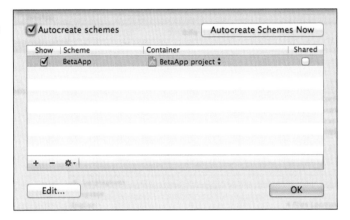

FIGURE 16.14
Editing the beta scheme's Archive configuration

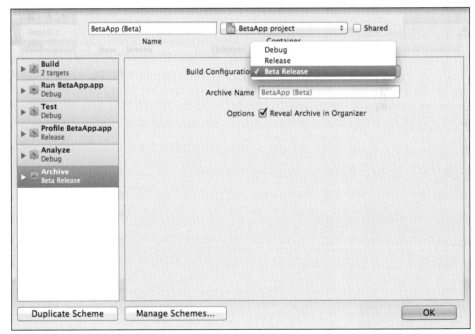

The final step is to define BETABUILD in the BetaApp target's build settings for the Beta Release configuration. Navigate to the BetaApp project, select the BetaApp target, and click the Build Settings tab. Search the settings for the Preprocessor Macros setting. Expand the setting so you can see the three configurations (Debug, Release, and Beta Release), as seen in **Figure 16.15**. Click the value column in the Beta Release row, and add the macro name BETABUILD.

FIGURE 16.15 Adding a preprocessor macro

Now you can test it.

Make sure the original BetaApp scheme is selected. From the main menu, choose Product > Build For > Build For Archiving and wait for the build to finish. In the Project navigator, expand the BetaApp project's Products group. Right-click the BetaApp.app product, and choose Show in Finder from the menu. You should see your normal-release built BetaApp application in the Release folder. Double-click it to launch it, and note the lack of a beta warning. Quit BetaApp.

> **NOTE:** If you are not using column view in the Finder, you may need to navigate up a directory to find the Release and Beta Release versions of BetaApp. The Products folder in the Project navigator usually only references the Debug build of the product.

Now select the BetaApp (Beta) scheme. From the main menu, choose Product > Build For > Build For Archiving, and wait for the build to finish. Again, in the Project navigator, right-click the BetaApp.app product in the Products group and choose Show in Finder from the menu. You should see the beta-release built app in the Beta Release folder. Launch it and be warned—it's a beta (**Figure 16.16**).

FIGURE 16.16 The beta warning

> **TIP:** You might also use the Beta Release configuration to avoid stripping debug symbols. For this configuration, you might disable the Strip Debug Symbols During Copy setting, which will make it easier to debug the problems found by your beta testers.

LIMITATIONS

It's important to understand the distinction between compile (or build) time and runtime. The C preprocessor processes source files prior to compilation. All effects on the source code happen when the code is built, not when it is run. You cannot, for example, use a preprocessor conditional to run one block of code if the application is running on OS X 10.8 and another block of code if running on OS X 10.7.

WRAPPING UP

You've seen how Xcode's scripting hooks can be used to extend and automate various tasks. You've also explored the C preprocessor's ability to provide macros with text replacement and conditionally include text in source. Armed with a basic knowledge of these two tools, Xcode can be extended and integrated into a much larger workflow, automating tasks and making them less prone to human error. In the next chapter, you'll learn how to drive Xcode builds from the command line to take advantage of the powerful build system without needing to run a full UI.

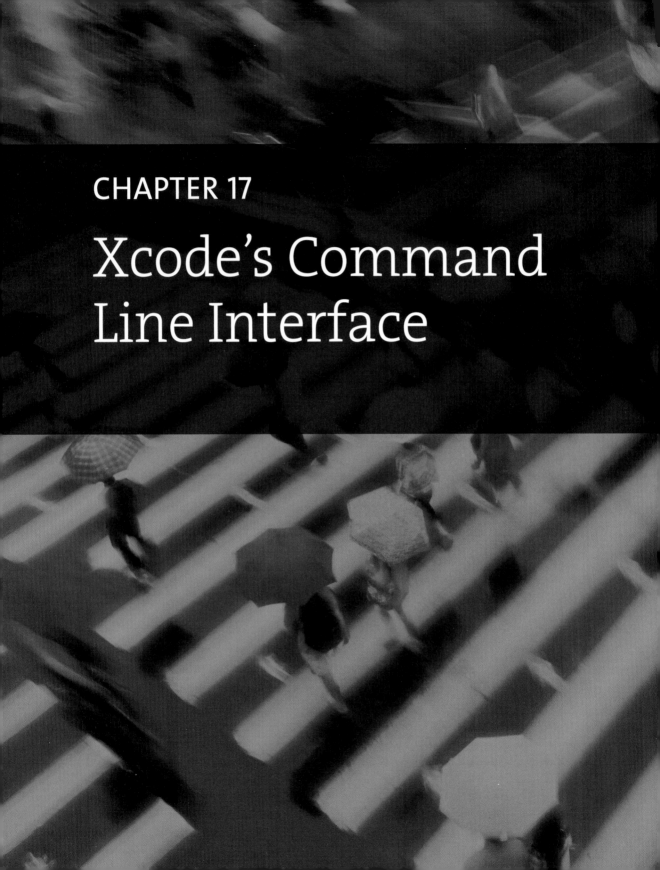

CHAPTER 17

Xcode's Command Line Interface

Underneath the skin of Xcode's GUI lies an astounding collection of developer tools. In this chapter, you will learn how to build your projects without having to run the Xcode GUI. You will also look at how to manage multiple installations of Xcode and how to access some of Xcode's internal tools for your own purposes.

THE COMMAND LINE TOOLS

In the grand scale of software development environments, Xcode is at the complex end of the scale with the likes of Visual Studio and Eclipse. At the simpler end of the scale are the lowly text editor and the compiler/interpreter. Although it may seem that Xcode has evolved beyond such humble tools, Xcode does much of its heavy lifting by executing command line tools in the background.

For the most part the user does not need to worry about how Xcode compiles and links their source code into applications. Then there are times when something goes awry and it can be useful to know exactly what is happening behind the scenes. Thankfully, there is no need to go digging around in the terminal. Select the Log navigator and click the entry that corresponds to your failing build. The editor pane will change to display the log viewer (**Figure 17.1**).

FIGURE 17.1 The log viewer

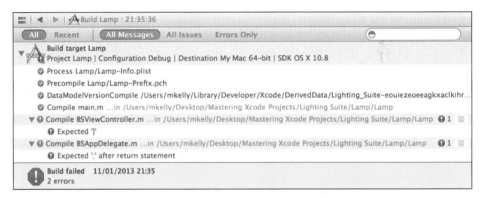

The log viewer will display a top-level entry for each target built as part of your run action, as well as a summary for the build status. If your build failed, the log viewer should display the first failure. If you just want to view the output of a successful run, you can change the filter at the top of the viewer to the All Messages setting.

Look down the list of build steps under a target to get an idea of exactly what Xcode is doing for you every time you click Run. Our simple Flashlight app could generate ten or more individual build steps, such as Compile and Link. Clicking one of these steps (or just hovering over the line at the right edge of the pane) will display a symbol that indicates "more lines." This is a way to expand the step so that you can see all the effort that goes into one of these steps. For example, clicking a Compile step will look something like **Figure 17.2**.

```
▼ ! Compile BSViewController.m ...in /Users/mkelly/Desktop/Mastering Xcode Projects/Lighting Suite/Lamp/Lamp   ! 1

    CompileC /Users/mkelly/Library/Developer/Xcode/DerivedData/Lighting_Suite-
      eouiezeoeeagkxaclkihrxpaaxwy/Build/Intermediates/Lamp.build/Debug/Lamp.build/Objects-normal/
      x86_64/BSViewController.o Lamp/BSViewController.m normal x86_64 objective-c
    com.apple.compilers.llvm.clang.1_0.compiler
        cd "/Users/mkelly/Desktop/Mastering Xcode Projects/Lighting Suite/Lamp"
        setenv LANG en_US.US-ASCII
        /Applications/Xcode46-DP4.app/Contents/Developer/Toolchains/XcodeDefault.xctoolchain/usr/
    bin/clang -x objective-c -arch x86_64 -fmessage-length=0 -std=gnu99 -fobjc-arc -Wno-trigraphs
    -fpascal-strings -O0 -Wno-missing-field-initializers -Wno-missing-prototypes -Wreturn-type -
    Wno-implicit-atomic-properties -Wno-receiver-is-weak -Wduplicate-method-match -Wformat -Wno-
    missing-braces -Wparentheses -Wswitch -Wno-unused-function -Wno-unused-label -Wno-unused-
    parameter -Wunused-variable -Wunused-value -Wno-empty-body -Wuninitialized -Wno-unknown-
    pragmas -Wno-shadow -Wno-four-char-constants -Wno-conversion -Wno-constant-conversion -Wno-
    int-conversion -Wno-enum-conversion -Wshorten-64-to-32 -Wpointer-sign -Wno-newline-eof -Wno-
    selector -Wno-strict-selector-match -Wno-undeclared-selector -Wno-deprecated-implementations -
    DDEBUG=1 -isysroot /Applications/Xcode46-DP4.app/Contents/Developer/Platforms/MacOSX.platform/
    Developer/SDKs/MacOSX10.8.sdk -fasm-blocks -fstrict-aliasing -Wprotocol -Wdeprecated-
    declarations -mmacosx-version-min=10.8 -g -Wno-sign-conversion -iquote /Users/mkelly/Library/
    Developer/Xcode/DerivedData/Lighting_Suite-eouiezeoeeagkxaclkihrxpaaxwy/Build/Intermediates/
    Lamp.build/Debug/Lamp.build/Lamp-generated-files.hmap -I/Users/mkelly/Library/Developer/Xcode/
    DerivedData/Lighting_Suite-eouiezeoeeagkxaclkihrxpaaxwy/Build/Intermediates/Lamp.build/Debug/
    Lamp.build/Lamp-own-target-headers.hmap -I/Users/mkelly/Library/Developer/Xcode/DerivedData/
    Lighting_Suite-eouiezeoeeagkxaclkihrxpaaxwy/Build/Intermediates/Lamp.build/Debug/Lamp.build/
    Lamp-all-target-headers.hmap -iquote /Users/mkelly/Library/Developer/Xcode/DerivedData/
    Lighting_Suite-eouiezeoeeagkxaclkihrxpaaxwy/Build/Intermediates/Lamp.build/Debug/Lamp.build/
    Lamp-project-headers.hmap -I/Users/mkelly/Library/Developer/Xcode/DerivedData/Lighting_Suite-
    eouiezeoeeagkxaclkihrxpaaxwy/Build/Products/Debug/include -I/Applications/Xcode46-DP4.app/
    Contents/Developer/Toolchains/XcodeDefault.xctoolchain/usr/include -I/Applications/Xcode46-
    DP4.app/Contents/Developer/Toolchains/XcodeDefault.xctoolchain/usr/include -I/Applications/
    Xcode46-DP4.app/Contents/Developer/Toolchains/XcodeDefault.xctoolchain/usr/include -I/Users/
    mkelly/Library/Developer/Xcode/DerivedData/Lighting_Suite-eouiezeoeeagkxaclkihrxpaaxwy/Build/
    Intermediates/Lamp.build/Debug/Lamp.build/DerivedSources/x86_64 -I/Users/mkelly/Library/
    Developer/Xcode/DerivedData/Lighting_Suite-eouiezeoeeagkxaclkihrxpaaxwy/Build/Intermediates/
    Lamp.build/Debug/Lamp.build/DerivedSources -F/Users/mkelly/Library/Developer/Xcode/
    DerivedData/Lighting_Suite-eouiezeoeeagkxaclkihrxpaaxwy/Build/Products/Debug -include /Users/
    mkelly/Library/Developer/Xcode/DerivedData/Lighting_Suite-eouiezeoeeagkxaclkihrxpaaxwy/Build/
    Intermediates/PrecompiledHeaders/Lamp-Prefix-cvwkznehmbsltwepwedizjzppvxa/Lamp-Prefix.pch -MMD
    -MT dependencies -MF /Users/mkelly/Library/Developer/Xcode/DerivedData/Lighting_Suite-
    eouiezeoeeagkxaclkihrxpaaxwy/Build/Intermediates/Lamp.build/Debug/Lamp.build/Objects-normal/
    x86_64/BSViewController.d --serialize-diagnostics /Users/mkelly/Library/Developer/Xcode/
    DerivedData/Lighting_Suite-eouiezeoeeagkxaclkihrxpaaxwy/Build/Intermediates/Lamp.build/Debug/
    Lamp.build/Objects-normal/x86_64/BSViewController.dia -c "/Users/mkelly/Desktop/Mastering
    Xcode Projects/Lighting Suite/Lamp/Lamp/BSViewController.m" -o /Users/mkelly/Library/
    Developer/Xcode/DerivedData/Lighting_Suite-eouiezeoeeagkxaclkihrxpaaxwy/Build/Intermediates/
    Lamp.build/Debug/Lamp.build/Objects-normal/x86_64/BSViewController.o

/Users/mkelly/Desktop/Mastering Xcode Projects/Lighting Suite/Lamp/Lamp/BSViewController.m:
19:69: error: expected ']'
    self = [super initWithNibName:nibNameOrNil bundle:nibBundleOrNil;
                                                                    ^

1 error generated.

❶ Expected ']'
```

FIGURE 17.2 Compile step detail

This is where the real Xcode magic happens. It is possible to take the series of commands from each of these steps and execute them in a terminal window to manually reproduce the Xcode build. Of course, this would be exceptionally tedious, which is why we are so grateful that Xcode does this on our behalf.

If you view the output of a failing build step, you see not only the command line invocations used but also the output of the failing step. Although this is generally the same as the output that Xcode displays in the Issue navigator, it can sometimes be helpful to view the error in the context of its build command. Experienced developers can examine the command and may be able to spot problems with parameters being passed to the compiler or other tools.

BUILDING FROM THE COMMAND LINE

Having established that the Xcode build process is mostly the internal execution of a series of command line invocations, the next question is naturally, "Can I somehow replicate this process without having to run the entire Xcode application?" It may seem puzzling, and almost a regression, for a developer with a perfectly good development environment like Xcode to want to eschew the UI in favor of the command line, but there is a good reason to do so.

CONTINUOUS INTEGRATION

The software engineering practice of continuous integration (CI) has been around for many years but has become popular in recent times. The idea behind it is simple: build regularly, build often, and run tests against every build. An automated process can be established whereby changes to an SCM repository can be synced to a build server. The entire project can be built with a unit test run against the output and an email sent to the developer(s) to indicate the success or failure of the build and test process.

This may seem like overkill for a single developer, but it is a valuable practice when a number of developers collaborate on a project, especially if those developers are working in a distributed team. If a developer commits a change that causes a compilation or test failure, the entire team can be informed so someone can fix the problem as soon as possible.

The availability of CI server software (such as Jenkins and CruiseControl) means that the process of monitoring an SCM repository for changes, initiating a build, and checking the results of test output can be quickly automated. But the number of steps required to build an Xcode project can grow rapidly, and it would be a thankless task to continually update the CI server as each developer adds more source files.

XCODEBUILD

Apple provides a command line tool named xcodebuild, which has the specific goal of building an Xcode project or workspace directly from a terminal window or executed by another script or service. xcodebuild should be installed by default on all modern versions of OS X, so open a terminal window and type the following:

```
xcodebuild -usage
```

The output of this command will show you a summary of what xcodebuild can do. Running the command with -help instead of -usage will show more information, and for even more you can use man xcodebuild.

The most straightforward thing we can do with xcodebuild is to compile our project. In your terminal window, navigate to a folder that contains an Xcode project—in these examples we're going to use the Flashlight project, which lives in a subfolder of the Lighting Suite workspace. Once in your chosen folder, type xcodebuild and watch the project compile before your very eyes. You should see a message like the following:

```
** BUILD SUCCEEDED **
```

This convenient shortcut will build the first target it finds in the current project directory and is only really useful for the simplest of projects. As Xcode projects become increasingly complex—and are often collected together inside workspaces—you will need a much finer level of control in the execution of xcodebuild.

DEALING WITH WORKSPACES, PROJECTS, TARGETS, AND SCHEMES

Although we moved to a specific project directory in the previous section, it was purely for the convenience of being able to execute xcodebuild quickly. In practice, you are more likely to specify the full path to the project or workspace you want to work with.

WORKSPACES AND SCHEMES

When building a workspace, you need to specify the path to the workspace file and to a scheme within the workspace. For our Lighting Suite workspace, we can build the Lamp scheme using the following:

```
xcodebuild -workspace <path_to_workspace>/Lighting\ Suite.xcworkspace
→ -scheme Lamp
```

You should be aware that the names of schemes (and targets) are case sensitive, so "lamp" is a different target from "Lamp." If you have trouble remembering the names of the schemes in your workspace, xcodebuild can save you from having to start up Xcode to check them in the Scheme editor. The following invocation will display a list of schemes in the workspace:

```
xcodebuild -workspace <path_to_workspace>/Lighting\ Suite.xcworkspace -list
```

When building a scheme from a workspace, Xcode will use the build configuration for the Run action, so unless you changed it from the default, the build configuration for Run is Debug. This is fine for most purposes, especially because it will give you a better chance of debugging crashes, but if you intend to use the output of this build for performance testing or for release you may wish to use the configuration option to specify an alternative build configuration:

```
xcodebuild -workspace <path_to_workspace>/Lighting\ Suite.xcworkspace \
→ -scheme Lamp -configuration Release
```

For more information on the use and creation of custom build configurations, refer to Chapter 13.

One limitation of specifying a workspace is that you cannot choose to build an individual project, or targets within a project. If you have a target that is not built as part of a scheme, then you can either add a scheme to include the target in Xcode or use xcodebuild with projects instead of with workspaces.

PROJECTS AND TARGETS

To work with a project within a workspace, you need to specify the full project path. For our Lighting Suite project we would use:

```
xcodebuild -project <path_to_workspace>/Lamp/Lamp.xcodeproj
```

This will build the project and the default target within that project. To build a specific target, you can use the target option, as follows:

```
xcodebuild -project <path_to_workspace>/Lamp/Lamp.xcodeproj -target Lamp
```

If you know that you need to build all the targets, use the following option:

```
xcodebuild -project <path_to_workspace>/Lamp/Lamp.xcodeproj -alltargets
```

If want to specify a target but you can't remember the names—or the precise spelling—you can use the list option to get full details:

```
xcodebuild -project <path_to_workspace>/Lamp/Lamp.xcodeproj -list
```

FIGURE 17.3 Default build configuration for a project

Note that the list option gives much more information when run against a project. You will be presented with a list of the valid targets within the project, the build configurations, and the schemes. If you don't specify a build configuration, Xcode will pick up the default build configuration from the project settings page (**Figure 17.3**). To make things slightly more complex, xcodebuild will take the build configuration from the Run action if you specify a scheme using the following:

```
xcodebuild -project <path_to_workspace>/Lamp/Lamp.xcodeproj -scheme Lamp
```

BUILD OPTIONS

If you have ever needed to use the Product > Clean command to empty your build folder for any reason, then you might be wondering how it is possible to achieve the same effect from the command line.

xcodebuild uses the concept of *build actions* to determine what it should do with the project/target/scheme. So far, we have taken advantage of the fact that the default build action is build. There are a number of other actions that roughly correspond to the available actions in the Scheme editor.

- build—This is the default action. This will compile and link your application in full the first time you run it. Subsequent runs will compile only those portions of your project that have changed since the last build action.

- clean—This action will perform selective pruning of the build output files. This will cause the build action to perform a complete build the next time it runs.

- archive—The archive action is valid only when a scheme is specified as part of the command. It is similar to the build action, but at the end it will validate your app bundle, checking for things like appropriately sized icons. This is useful if you plan to use a CI system to produce builds for submission to the Mac or iOS App Stores.

- test—The test action should be selected when a suitable testing scheme is specified. This will cause the scheme's target to be built and the unit tests run.

- install—This option is used to install the output of the build directly to a location on the hard disk defined by the environment variable DSTROOT. Because of the risk of over-writing an existing application, this variable defaults to /tmp/$PROJECT_NAME.dst. If you were to distribute a Mac app as a source archive, you could set DSTROOT to /Applications (or /usr/local/bin for a command line application) and instruct users to install using the xcodebuild install.

- installsrc—This option will copy the source files from your project to an alternative location and cannot be performed when building a scheme. The location must be specified by appending SRCROOT=<path> to the end of the xcodebuild invocation. This may be useful if you are building an open-source project and want to copy the source files to a staging area (a temporary location from which another script can easily locate them) so they can be bundled with the release.

SDKS AND ARCHITECTURES

xcodebuild has quite a number of additional options—too many to cover here—but two more that are worth mentioning are `sdk` and `arch`. These options give a greater level of control over the output of the compile process and are particularly useful if you want to override some of Xcode's default settings.

SDKS

We discussed the differences between the different SDKs in Chapter 13, but as a recap: The SDK you build against defines the selection of APIs you can use in your code and the range of operating systems your application can run on.

You can tell `xcodebuild` to use a specific SDK by executing it with the `sdk` option:

```
xcodebuild -project <path_to_workspace>/Lamp/Lamp.xcodeproj -sdk macosx10.8
```

To get a list of the SDKs that the current version of Xcode supports, run the following command for a helpful list:

```
xcodebuild -showsdks
```

Or if you want even more information, use the following command:

```
xcodebuild -version -sdk
```

Why would you want to build against a specific SDK? Say you produce two versions of an app from a single codebase that run on different versions of OS X. In your code, you can use the pre-processor directive `#ifdef __MAC_10_8` to selectively use features of 10.8, and you can put slower, 10.7-compatible code in the `#else` clause.

So far so good, but if you are building in Xcode all day you might make mistakes in your `#else` clauses that go undetected. Running a CI server with two builds configured to target 10.8 and 10.7 means that you have a safety net.

Alternatively, if you were creating a build of an iOS app for running automated tests against as part of the code check-in process, you might not want to use a default build configuration that produces a build targeted for real devices. Instead you could use the `sdk` option to specify that the iOS Simulator be used instead, resulting in a build that can be run on a Mac:

```
xcode -project <path_to_workspace>/Flashlight/Flashlight.xcodeproj
→ -sdk iphonesimulator6.0
```

ARCHITECTURES

You may recall from Chapter 13 that your targets will specify the range of architectures that they can be built for. A Mac app may be built for the i386 and x86_64 chipsets, and an iOS app for the armv7 and armv7s chipsets. `xcodebuild` has an option called `arch`, which allows you to specify the architecture for which you would like your build to be carried out.

Unfortunately, arch doesn't have a friendly *showarchs* equivalent that lists the valid architectures for your project, so you will need to dip back into Xcode for the list. To build a Mac app for i386 only, use this command:

```
xcodebuild -project <path_to_workspace>/Lamp/Lamp.xcodeproj -arch i386
```

So why would you want to use this option? It isn't a common requirement, but there are still developers out there who need to specify a target architecture. For example, a developer may be working on a legacy project intended to run only on a 32-bit Intel platform. Another developer may have a framework shared between iOS and OS X. A normal build of the library could produce four architectures, which may slow down the build and test cycle of their CI server. The arch option would allow only a single architecture to be targeted in order to reduce build time, though they may have other problems when bugs arise on an architecture they have excluded from being built!

USING MULTIPLE VERSIONS OF XCODE

The rate of change in Xcode means that there are often developer preview versions available to download. There are also many older versions of Xcode available to download from the Apple Developer site. It is possible for a developer to have two or more versions sitting in their Applications folder. They must remember to start the correct one every day—using a developer preview to submit an app for release is a no-no—but it's something they will get into the habit of pretty quickly.

Consider our usage so far of the xcodebuild command. We have spent a lot of time learning how to control the manner in which our code is built, but we have not concerned ourselves with what version of Xcode is being used in the background to compile our code. The version of Xcode that is used determines the SDKs that are available to us and determines the compilers—and other tools—that are used to carry out the builds.

Finding out which version of Xcode that xcodebuild is using is as simple as this:

```
xcodebuild -version
```

Now that we can determine what version we're using currently, how can we change to use a different version of Xcode? Enter the xcode-select tool. This tool can do two things: show you the path to the active Xcode or allow you to set a new active Xcode. Setting a new active Xcode requires knowledge of a path that lies within the Xcode app bundle, so it's worth printing the current version first so you know what format to specify for the new one:

```
xcode-select --print-path
```

This should output a path such as /Applications/Xcode.app/Contents/Developer. You may wonder why it descends into the app bundle—it's because older versions of Xcode were not distributed as apps but instead lived in folders like /Developer (which actually contained the Xcode application). In Xcode 4.3, the app was moved out of the `Developer` folder, and the `Developer` folder was moved inside the app bundle. `xcode-select` has to be able to deal with versions of Xcode prior to this move.

To change your active Xcode, give it a new path with the following command:

```
sudo xcode-select --switch /Applications/Xcode46-DP4.app/Contents/Developer
```

In this code, we have switched to a developer preview version, perhaps to do some testing against a future SDK. Note that we used the `sudo` command to allow us to execute with super-user privileges. Changing the active version of Xcode is a system-wide change, so if you share a machine with other developers, this will affect everyone, including a CI server!

ACCESSING THE COMMAND LINE TOOLS

We've seen previously that Xcode uses a lot of command line tools to carry out its activities—tools like the `clang` or `gcc` compilers, `ld` for linking, and `ibtool` for compiling Interface Builder files. These tools—and many others—are stored within the Xcode app bundle and can accessed and used for external purposes. For example, Xcode contains the `git` and `svn` source code management (SCM) tools, which you might want to use to manage your projects on the command line (see Chapter 18 for more information on SCM).

To access the tools directly, you need to know exactly where within the Xcode app bundle they live. The `git` tool resides at `/Applications/Xcode.app/Contents/Developer/usr/bin/git`, but this is quite a bit to remember and type every time you want to use it. So how can you find this and other tools yourself?

Apple has acknowledged that people may want to take advantage of these tools and has provided a couple of ways to find out. The first way uses `xcodebuild` but is a bit long for typing; the preferred way is to use the `xcrun` tool, as follows:

```
xcrun -f git
```

This will output the full path to the `git` binary but still leaves the problem of how to remember and type it every time. Fortunately, `xcrun` can be used to run any binary stored inside the Xcode app bundle:

```
xcrun git
```

This is handy for infrequent, manual invocations but can cause problems when you want to run existing scripts or when you want to use a third-party package management system (such as Homebrew) that can download and compile software for you. When such a script attempts to use a command line tool (such as `git` or the `clang` compiler), it will be unable to find it and will instead present an error.

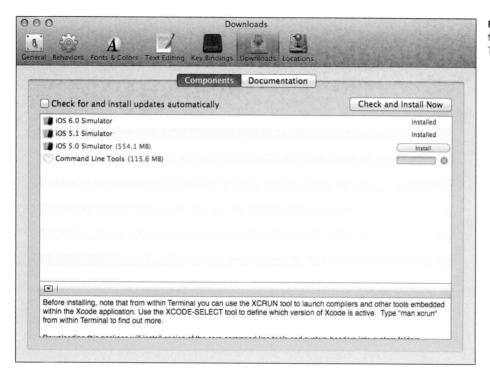

FIGURE 17.4 Installing the Command Line Tools package

Apple has taken care of this and has made many of the bundled command line tools available as a separate package. The package can be installed from within Xcode (**Figure 17.4**) or can be downloaded and installed from Apple's Developer site—this allows you to install the command line tools on a machine without Xcode if you so desire.

WRAPPING UP

This chapter contained a lot of information that you might not find necessary. Many people have no need to go near the command line when working with Xcode—such as lone hobbyists, or developers in a megacorp with a release engineering team to look after things like build and integration testing. But should you have to tackle the challenge of setting up a CI server or just want to know more about what goes on, you should now be fully briefed.

In the next chapter, you will take a tour of Xcode's source code management support and use Git and Subversion to version control your software.

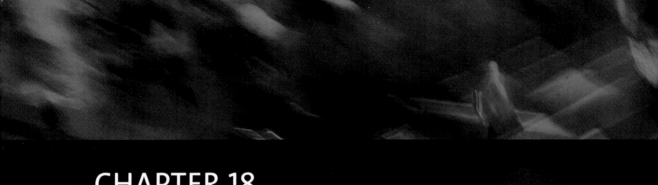

CHAPTER 18

Version Control with an SCM System

In Chapter 6, you looked at using Xcode's snapshots feature to perform basic version control on your projects. For more advanced requirements, Xcode provides integration with two popular source code management (SCM) systems. This chapter explores the facilities for working with Git and Subversion repositories directly from within Xcode.

WORKING WITH GIT AND SUBVERSION

Xcode currently supports and integrates with two well-known SCM systems: Git and Subversion (SVN). Whereas Subversion is primarily server-based (with the server usually but not always being a remote location), Git is what is known as a "distributed SCM" and does not require a server (remote or otherwise) to operate. There are many benefits to distributed SCMs, and this and other reasons make it likely that Git (or some other distributed SCM) will usurp Subversion in the coming years. Apple seems to agree. Xcode's Git support is slightly more pervasive and noticeably more polished than its Subversion support. All that said, Xcode installs the necessary tools for both Git and Subversion support. Type man git or man svn in the terminal for details.

NOTE: To learn more about Git, see http://xcodebook/gitimmersion; for SVN, see http://xcodebook.com/svnprimer.

GIT AND SVN DIFFERENCES

In most cases, the biggest differences are in the terminology. For example, where a Git user *clones*, a Subversion user *checks out a working copy*. Where a Git user *pulls*, a Subversion user *updates* (and possibly merges). Git users *stage* their changes and commit them to their local repository with the option of then pushing them to a remote repository (often called the *origin*); Subversion users *commit* their changes to the server.

One difference between the two systems is that a Subversion user's commit means the change becomes part of the repository (usually on the remote server from which it was checked out), whereas a Git user's commit is a purely local operation. The Git user has a copy of the entire repository (and its full history) and can choose whether or not to push those changes to the origin (usually a central repository hosted on a server). Git commits can happen whether or not the remote server (the clone's origin) is reachable—it is only the subsequent push that may need access to the server.

This chapter will focus on Xcode's Git support only partly because Apple seems to have chosen sides. Mainly, Git gets the spotlight because Xcode provides, where possible, a homogenized user interface that works nearly the same way whether you're using Git or Subversion. The differences, where there are any, are mild.

MANAGING REPOSITORIES

More than likely, you have existing Xcode projects that are tied to existing repositories. You may already have a local clone (in Git) or checked-out working copy (in Subversion). The quickest way to make Xcode aware of an SCM-attached status is to open the project. Xcode will try to set up any connections to the repository's origin or to the Subversion remote server. If authentication is required and Xcode does not have the credentials, it will prompt you for them upon opening the project.

You can manage repositories with the Organizer window. To view them, choose Window > Organizer from the main menu, then choose the Repositories tab. The Repositories tab of the Organizer (**Figure 18.1**) maintains a list, on the left side of the panel, of all repositories it has encountered. This list can get a bit cluttered, especially if you have been checking out a lot of open-source projects. You can remove surplus repositories, by clicking the Remove (–) button, without causing a destructive action to the project itself—they will return if you open the project again.

FIGURE 18.1 The Repositories tab of the Organizer

The repositories feature disclosure triangles (**Figure 18.2**) that display (or hide) extra information about each repository type. A Subversion repository contains a purple Root folder that lets you view the state of the repository on the server—useful for viewing commits that you have yet to pull down. The Trunk, Branches, and Tags folders let you manage the corresponding special directories in your repository, and any blue folders represent working copies you may have.

For Git repositories, things are slightly different. The Branches folder allows you to manage local branches, and the Remotes folder allows you to manage any remote repositories you may have (such as a central server or a colleague's repository). The blue folder (or folders) represents your local clones—normally you will have only one, but if your project contains submodules you will see a blue folder for each submodule.

FIGURE 18.2 Expanded repository information

The repository's details as well as its history are displayed on the right (Figure 18.1) when a repository is selected in the list; when a working copy or clone is selected, the file and folder structure, the working copy's history, and an SCM-specific toolbar are shown. You'll explore this UI in detail throughout the rest of the chapter.

If you've been following along with the examples in the previous chapters, then Xcode has already been tracking the Git repositories for each of the projects you've created. Because you chose to let Xcode create a Git repository for each project, you will have multiple separate repositories. Some may choose to have one repository for a suite of related applications and libraries, but with Xcode's new workspaces concept, the borders between these repositories are barely noticeable and don't get in the way of typical day-to-day tasks.

CREATING REPOSITORIES

As you learned in previous chapters, Xcode will let you create new Git repositories when you create new projects. When you're prompted for a location into which to save a new project, the Save dialog contains a Source Control option at the bottom; **Figure 18.3** shows this option selected.

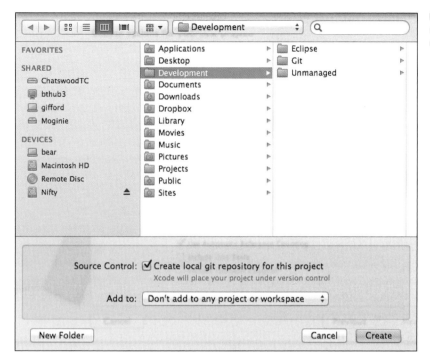

FIGURE 18.3 Creating a Git repository when saving a new project

Unfortunately, this is the extent of Xcode's repository-creating powers. That is, it's limited to creating local Git repositories *at the time a project is created*. It cannot initialize a new repository for existing projects. But all is not lost—you can still take full advantage of Git by using the command line to turn an existing project into a Git repository. In the terminal, type the following (where *your_project_folder* is the full path to your project's main folder):

```
cd your_project_folder
git init
git add .
git commit -m "Initial commit"
```

That's it. The folder is now the home of a Git repository that should appear in the repositories browser—sometimes it can take a while (or even a restart) for Xcode to acknowledge that it really is a repository, but it'll get there eventually.

To create a *locally hosted* Subversion repository, you can't use Xcode, but you can use the terminal. There are two things you need to do: create a repository, then import your existing project into that repository. Subversion repositories have three root directories by default—named trunk, branches, and tags—so we need to create that layout first:

```
mkdir -p /tmp/svn/trunk
mkdir -p /tmp/svn/branches
mkdir -p /tmp/svn/tags
```

We then copy the existing project into the trunk of our new layout:

```
cp -R ../your_project_folder /tmp/svn/trunk
```

We then create the repository itself:

```
svnadmin create /Users/mkelly/subversion_repo
```

Finally, we import the temporary file structure we initially set up into the newly created repository:

```
svn import /tmp/svn file:///Users/mkelly/subversion_repo -m "Initial commit"
```

Not as elegant as Git, but it gets the job done. If you do plan to use Subversion in earnest, it would be worthwhile to read more about it and put a bit more thought into repository planning than we've just done.

ADDING REPOSITORIES MANUALLY

You can add repositories and working copies with the Organizer. Whether you removed them yourself or Xcode could not for some reason add them automatically when opening a project under version control, you can add and remove them manually.

To add a repository, click the Add (+) button and choose Add Repository from the menu. The Add a Repository sheet (**Figure 18.4**) will appear, asking you for a name, location, and type. The name is just a convenient identifier and can be anything you like (for example, *My Company Repository* or just *Fred*). The location, however, must be a valid URL to a repository.

FIGURE 18.4 Adding a remote Git repository

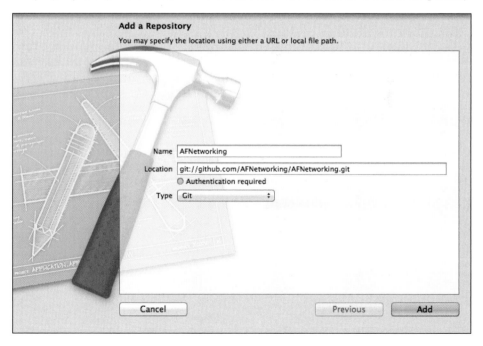

Add a Repository
You may specify the location using either a URL or local file path.

Name AFNetworking
Location git://github.com/AFNetworking/AFNetworking.git
○ Authentication required
Type Git

Cancel   Previous   Add

The type will be automatically detected when using URLs with schemes like svn:// and git://, but those starting with ssh://, http://, https://, or file:/// will require you to choose the correct SCM system type in the Type field. The indicator light beneath the Location field will glow red when there is a problem connecting to the repository and will glow green when the supplied URL points to a valid repository. In practice, though, it will often glow amber (see Figure 18.4), indicating that it can connect to a repository but requires authentication.

> **TIP:** The Add a Repository sheet is probably more useful for Subversion repositories, since a cloned Git repository is a copy of the entire repository. For Git, it's actually more user friendly to add a repository by opening the project in which it's contained—Xcode will set up everything (including the origin, if one exists) for you.

To add a Git clone (or a Subversion working copy), you can either drag it into the source list in the Repositories tab of the Organizer or again use the Add (+) button, selecting Add Working Copy from the menu instead. This time you'll be faced with a standard Open dialog box that allows you to choose the folder containing the working copy or clone. Once you choose the folder, the working copy (and its associated repository entry) should be added to the Organizer.

Older versions of Xcode had limited support for alternative Subversion repository layouts, but you can now use alternative nomenclatures for your Trunk, Branches, and Tags folders. If you import a working copy that has a different layout, Xcode will not list these folders, but you can click the repository name in the list to view a "mapping" panel in the main view (**Figure 18.5**). Once you add the mappings, the Trunk, Branches, and Tags folders will appear underneath the repository entry in the left pane.

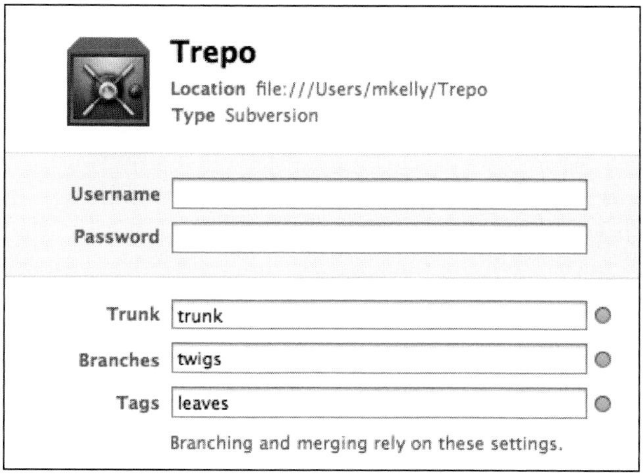

FIGURE 18.5 Mapping a Subversion repository layout

Trepo
Location file:///Users/mkelly/Trepo
Type Subversion

Username	
Password	

Trunk	trunk	○
Branches	twigs	○
Tags	leaves	○

Branching and merging rely on these settings.

CLONING AND CHECKING OUT

If you don't already have a local clone, Xcode offers several ways to create one from within its UI. One way is to use the Organizer's Add (+) button. Another way is to use the Welcome to Xcode window (Command+Shift+1) and select the Connect to a Repository option. **Figure 18.6** shows a Git repository named *dotfiles* that is hosted on a remote server via SSH. The indicator beneath the Location field shows that the host is reachable and that the location is a valid repository, but that it needs to perform authentication to be completely sure.

FIGURE 18.6 Specifying a remote repository location

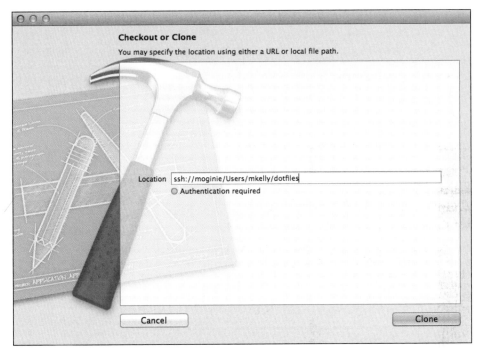

If it is a Git repository, you can click the Clone button to specify where on your local drive you want to save your clone. If it is a Subversion repository, the button will be named Checkout. Whichever button you click, Xcode will connect to the repository (and may prompt you for authentication) before indicating success or failure of the clone/checkout operation. Depending on the size of your repository, the actual checkout or clone may take a while. If it was successful, you will be presented with a reassuring green check mark and a Show In Finder button to open the new clone/working copy. If you decide not to go straight there, you can always find it again through the Repositories section of the Organizer.

NOTE: It's common to set up an SSH key for "passwordless" authentication to an SCM server. If you have a key set up for the server already and Xcode prompts you for a username and password, it's best to leave the username field as it is and supply no password. For a Git-themed example of setting up an SSH key, see http://xcodebook.com/gitkey.

PERFORMING ROUTINE SCM TASKS

You've seen how to clone and generally manage your Git repositories. Now you'll explore how to perform the more typical day-to-day SCM management tasks in Xcode and manage changes to your projects.

MANAGING FOLDERS IN SUBVERSION

Subversion works with files and folders; Git works with files or chunks (changed parts of files). For this reason, Subversion users need to make directory structure changes through Subversion, whereas Git users are able to freely move files and folders around.

In Xcode, you manage Subversion folders using the Repositories tab of the Organizer. You'll need to first select the repository. To add a folder, use the list in the right pane (the one showing your working copy's directory structure) to select a folder in which you want to create the subfolder, then click the New Directory button. To delete a folder, select it in the Organizer and click the Delete button. Rename folders by clicking them in the Organizer and editing them as you would any other filename. Each of these changes will require an immediate commit. Xcode will prompt you to enter a commit message.

CHECKING STATUS

Throughout the book, you've been avoiding the elephant in the room (or rather the symbols in the Project navigator). **Figure 18.7** shows a project in the Project navigator, with "badges" indicating SCM status along the right edge of the list.

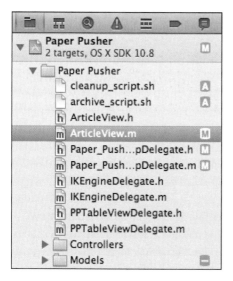

FIGURE 18.7 SCM status in the Project navigator

Here's the meaning of the status badges:

M   Locally modified

U   Updated in repository

A   Locally added

D   Locally deleted

I   Ignored

R   Replaced in the repository

–   Mixed status (for groups and folders)

?   Not under source control (hence, status unknown)

The status messages can have different meanings depending on the SCM system you're using, but these generic symbols represent the least common denominator for the two SCM systems. See the SCM system's documentation for more details if necessary.

You can also filter the Project navigator list so that it shows only those project members that have a pending SCM status. This is accomplished by pressing the middle of the group of three buttons on the left of the Project navigator filter bar, highlighted in red in **Figure 18.8**. Turn off the filter button to go back to showing all project members.

FIGURE 18.8 Project navigator filtered by SCM status

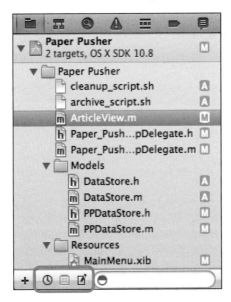

The status of individual files can be examined in slightly more detail by using the File inspector of the Utility area. The Source Control section (**Figure 18.9**) shows the version, status, and location of the source-controlled file. For Subversion repositories, the location is usually the remote location, whereas for a local Git repository, it will just indicate the location of the file locally, even if you have a remote setup.

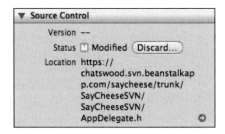

FIGURE 18.9 The Source Control section in the Utility area

COMMITTING CHANGES

Committing your changes to a repository is straightforward, and there are several ways to do it. You can commit all outstanding changes by selecting File > Source Control > Commit, or only selected files by right-clicking one of the files and selecting Source Control > Commit Selected Files.

A commit review sheet similar to **Figure 18.10** will appear. Like the Find and Replace preview sheet you learned about in Chapter 12, this sheet displays a list of files on the left and a preview area on the right. Select any file in the list to preview the differences between the repository and the working copy of the file. To include a file in the commit, ensure that the check box to the left of its name has been selected.

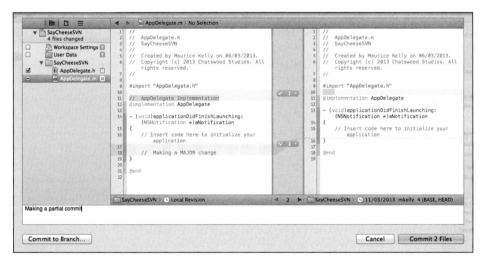

FIGURE 18.10
The commit review sheet

To view a specific file in the commit, select the name in the file list. This will cause the editor area on the right to be populated—the left pane will contain the updated version of the file that you are proposing to commit, and the right pane will contain the last version of the file in the repository. The left pane is editable should you wish to make some more last-minute changes.

Where the file has differences, you will see a numbered control for each change (**Figure 18.11**). This control is a means to include or exclude specific changes from the commit. Clicking the left portion of the control will toggle it between the Commit (check mark) and Don't Commit states. Clicking the right portion of the control will display a menu allowing the same selection as the left-hand portion, as well as the opportunity to completely discard this change from your project. If you are familiar with Git, you will realize that this is how Xcode allows you to perform partial commits; if you use Subversion, this actually gives you some of the flexibility of Git.

FIGURE 18.11 The change inclusion control

Once you have reviewed the files in your change set, you can enter your commit message in the text editor at the bottom of the sheet. If you want to commit the changes to the current branch, click the Commit button on the lower right of the sheet. If you decide that the current branch is not the right home for this change, Xcode now allows you to click Commit to Branch on the lower left of the sheet. Xcode will examine your repository for available branches and allow you to choose one to commit to—if you're using Git, you'll even have the opportunity to create a new branch just for your commit (**Figure 18.12**).

FIGURE 18.12
Committing to a different branch

Once you click Commit, Xcode will either apply the changes to the local Git repository or send the changes to the Subversion repository. Assuming there were no errors, the SCM status flags for the included files will then disappear—any modified files that were not included will retain their flags.

If there were any problems during the commit, Xcode will display some information. For example, if you attempted to commit a file to a Subversion repository that has been updated since you last synced, Xcode will be unable to commit your change. Instead, it will give you the option to not commit those files, or to update your working copy to match the repository and re-attempt your commit (**Figure 18.13**).

FIGURE
18.13 Attempting to commit changes to files already updated in Subversion

NOTE: When you use the main file menu to commit changes to projects across multiple repositories, Xcode treats this as if you'd performed individual commits for each working copy or clone using the same commit message.

PUSHING CHANGES

When using a Git repository cloned from a remote repository, you can also use the Source Control menu to push your local commits to the remote from within Xcode. Choose File > Source Control > Push from the main menu. If your project or workspace contains multiple Git repositories—you may have multiple projects, or your repositories may contain submodules—then Xcode will first prompt you to specify which local repository you wish to push.

A sheet will appear (**Figure 18.14**), asking you to choose the remote (and branch within that remote) to which to push. Once you choose the branch, click Push. Xcode will then push the changes.

FIGURE 18.14 The remote repository and branch selection sheet

NOTE: If your workspace contains uncommitted changes, Xcode will not allow you to push to a remote. This is a valid Git operation, though, so if you do want to perform a push while you have uncommitted changes, you will need to drop to the command line to perform it.

PULLING (OR UPDATING) AND MERGING CHANGES

Pull changes into your clone by choosing File > Source Control > Pull from the main menu. A remote and branch sheet (similar to that displayed when pushing) will appear, asking you to choose the remote from which to pull. Make your selection and click Choose. If there are any differences, Xcode will update your local repository automatically. If one or more of the differences results in a conflict, then a pull review sheet (**Figure 18.15**) will appear, giving you the opportunity to review each difference. This allows you to select the changes you want to pull into your clone, discarding redundant changes or even manually editing the resultant file.

FIGURE 18.15 The pull review sheet

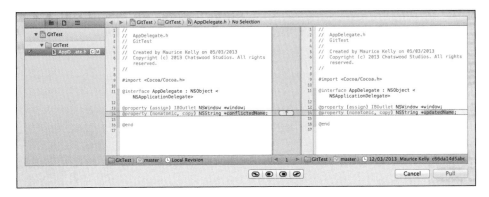

FIGURE 18.16 The merge control buttons

Figure 18.15 indicates a single conflict outlined in red. The question mark icon between the two panes indicates that the conflict has not yet been resolved. You can use the buttons on the bottom of the sheet (**Figure 18.16**) to decide which of the changes to include—yours or the changes from the remote. From left to right, the choices are:

- Left then Right—Keep your changes and insert the remote changes below them.
- Left—Keep your changes and discard the remote changes.
- Right—Discard your changes and accept the remote changes.
- Right then Left—Keep your changes and insert the remote changes above them.

Xcode will not allow you to continue until all conflicts are resolved—the Pull button will remain inactive until you have made a choice to resolve each one. Resolving can be as simple as choosing a side or as complicated as pulling in both changes and performing selective edits in the left pane.

Once all conflicts have been resolved, you can click Pull to proceed. Bear in mind that the resolution has taken place only locally; the changes you made to resolve the conflict will need to be committed and pushed to the remote so that other users can receive your changes.

CREATING AND SWITCHING BRANCHES

Git branches can be created in the Repositories tab of the Organizer. Select the repository's Branches folder in the repositories list, and click Add Branch on the bottom toolbar. A sheet will appear (**Figure 18.17**), prompting you for a name for the new branch and for the "starting point" (the branch from which to create the new branch).

FIGURE 18.17
The Create a Branch
sheet

You can also select the "Automatically switch to this branch" check box to have Xcode immediately switch branches after creating the new one. Subversion users will additionally be asked to type a commit message, and if you opt to check out the new branch, you will be asked to specify a location to place a new working copy. Click Create, and the new branch will be created and will show in the Branches folder.

Switching branches is done similarly in the Repositories tab of the Organizer. For Git, select the clone itself (the blue folder) in the repositories list, then click Switch Branch in the bottom toolbar. A sheet (**Figure 18.18**) will appear, letting you choose the branch you want to switch to. Click OK to switch to the selected branch. Be aware that if you have uncommitted changes in your current clone, Xcode will not let you switch branches—this is a common thing to want to do; you will have to open Terminal.app and perform the change at the command line instead.

FIGURE 18.18 The switch branch sheet

Changing branches in Subversion is a more labored affair—start in the Organizer and click the Branches folder under the repository. The list of branches will appear on the right pane. Choose the branch you want to work with, and click Checkout in the toolbar at the bottom. You will be prompted to specify a location to which you will perform your checkout.

COMPARING AND BROWSING HISTORY

It's often necessary to browse previous versions of files in your repository or to compare versions. Xcode's support for this is hidden in plain sight. You're already familiar with the first two buttons in the editor mode button bar in the main toolbar. The first button is the plain editor mode. The second reveals the Assistant editor. The third button reveals the Version editor (**Figure 18.19**).

FIGURE 18.19
The Version editor

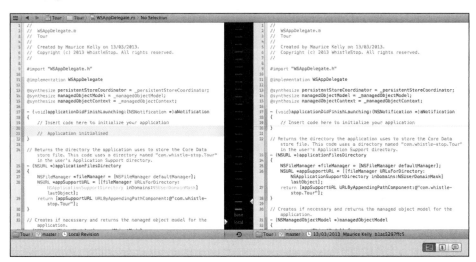

At the bottom of the channel between the two source editors, you can click the clock icon to reveal a timeline. Scrubbing the mouse over the timeline reveals past versions (**Figure 18.20**), much like the user interface of the Mac's Time Machine backup feature. Click a version on the left side of the "dash" to display it in the left editor, and click another version on the right side of the "dash" to display it in the right editor for comparison. Differences are highlighted, as in the pull review sheet (Figure 18.15), and if you hide the timeline, you can go through the changes one by one, discarding them if necessary (though only for your local revision—you can't rewrite history!).

Just beneath each editor is a jump bar that allows you to select revisions directly from any branch in which the file exists (**Figure 18.21**).

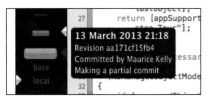

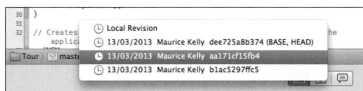

FIGURE 18.20 Scrubbing the revision timeline   **FIGURE 18.21** The revisions jump bar

There are two other handy view modes in the Version editor: Blame and Log. Select a view mode by using the button bar in the lower-right corner of the Version editor (**Figure 18.22**).

Comparison view   Blame view   Log view

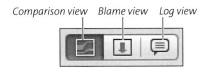

FIGURE 18.22 The view mode button bar

Blame mode (**Figure 18.23**) shows "who is to blame" for each revised section of the file. If the entire file is from the same revision, there will be only one person to blame. If, however, different sections have been revised (changed and committed) at different times, each section might have different people to blame at different times. Each revised section is labeled along the right with the name of the person who made the change, the date they did it, their commit message, and other details. Uncommitted changes in the local revision are also shown, and you can click the Info icon on the right side of each blame section to view complete details of the entire commit it originated from.

FIGURE 18.23
Blame mode

Log mode (**Figure 18.24**) is a history of revisions of the file. It's mainly useful for seeing the history of commits involving that file. For an unfiltered view of history, use the Repositories tab of the Organizer window.

FIGURE 18.24
Log mode

REVERTING AND DISCARDING LOCAL CHANGES

Perfect people don't make mistakes and therefore likely don't need a source code management system. Unfortunately, none of them are employed at software companies, so the rest of us need a way of undoing our mistakes. There are two levels of severity: discarding your local changes (replacing them with the most recently committed version) and reverting to earlier committed versions.

To discard changes in a single file, navigate to it and choose File > Source Control > Discard Changes from the main menu. Confirm the decision by clicking Discard Changes when prompted. To discard changes for multiple files, select each one in the navigator and choose the same menu option. All changes in all selected files will be discarded.

Reverting to earlier committed versions is unfortunately one area where Xcode is not up to par with the majority of SCM tools. For this reason, it is advisable to get used to working with branches (especially if you use Git). Creating a new branch for experimental changes is a good practice, because it allows you to modify your code without fear of consequences. If all your build-breaking changes are in a branch, you can easily discard the branch and resort to your master or trunk.

> **TIP:** If you really do find yourself in need of a way to revert, you should consult the manual for your SCM tool of choice and consider trying it from the command line. For Git, try `git help reset`; for Subversion, you can carry out a reverse merge (`svn help merge`). Proceed with caution!

WORKING WITH HOSTED GIT SERVICES

The use of hosted platforms for managing source code has exploded in recent years. Services such as GitHub, Bitbucket, and Beanstalk (to name but a few) have become essential tools for many developers who want the security and convenience of SCM but who want to let someone else worry about running the service. Features like forking, pull requests, and issue tracking have increased the value of using such a service.

While Xcode's Git feature set has increased since it was introduced, it isn't always apparent how to best use it with a service like GitHub. This section covers some of the interactions common to hosted services.

ADDING A PROJECT TO A HOSTED SERVICE

If you work in a team with other developers, it is often the case that someone has done the "hard" work of creating your remote repository. If you're working solo, or you have been tasked with the responsibility of creating a remote, then you'll need to know how best to achieve this with Xcode.

Start off by creating a project as normal, making sure you select the "Create local git repository for this project" check box when prompted. It's still possible to convert a project (or workspace) after the fact, but you might as well do it up front.

Now get to work and do your job. At some point you'll probably notice that you've got a bunch of SCM statuses on your files and remember that you need to do something with them. Then you'll remember that you need to create that remote repository, so make a few commits as detailed earlier in this chapter.

CREATING A REPOSITORY

Go to your hosted service of choice—we're going to use Bitbucket because, at the time of this writing, they offer private repositories for free—and use their Create Repository function to create a new Git repository (**Figure 18.25**). When you create a new repository, it will initially be empty, and you will usually be prompted to either initialize it or to import an existing project to it. We will do the latter, so follow any links you are presented with for importing a project.

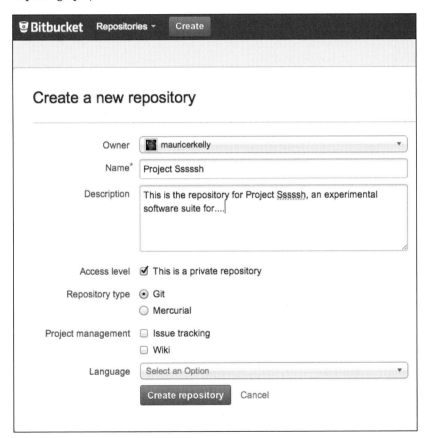

FIGURE 18.25
Creating a repository with a hosted service

Most of the services will then present you with some command-line invocations they need you to perform in order to import your project (**Figure 18.26**). Since we're trying to use Xcode, these instructions are not as useful for us. They can still be carried out and Xcode can live with the resulting changes to the local repository, but we want to know how to do the Xcode equivalent.

FIGURE 18.26
Command-line spells for importing a project

Import an existing repository

You already have a Git repository on your computer. Let's publish it to Bitbucket.

```
$ cd /path/to/my/repo
$ git remote add origin ssh://git@bitbucket.org/mauricerkelly/project-sssssh.git
$ git push -u origin --all    # to push changes for the first time
```

Do you want to grab a repo from another site? Try our Importer!

Next

Grab the repository URL—ours is ssh://git@bitbucket.org/mauricerkelly/project-sssssh.git (Figure 18.26)—and open the Organizer and click the Repositories tab (Figure 18.1). Under your local repository, select the Remotes folder. In the bottom toolbar on the right, click Add Remote. The Add a Remote sheet will appear (**Figure 18.27**). Enter origin in the Remote Name field (this is a naming convention in the Git world for the only, or primary, remote), and paste your repository URL in the Location field. Click Create, and origin now appears in your list of remotes.

FIGURE 18.27 The Add a Remote sheet

Add a Remote
Enter a name and location for the new remote.

Remote Name origin
Location ssh://git@bitbucket.org/mauricerkelly/project-sssss

Cancel   Create

SYNCHRONIZING YOUR LOCAL REPOSITORIES

To synchronize your local repository with the remote, go back to your project and select File > Source Control > Push from the main menu. The remote repository and branch selection sheet will appear, but this time it will give you the option to create the master branch in the origin remote (**Figure 18.28**). Click Push to send your local repository to the remotely hosted service. You should now be able to view your project source and commit history on the service's website (**Figure 18.29**).

FIGURE 18.28 Remote branch selection with create option

FIGURE 18.29 A freshly imported project

WORKING WITH FEATURE BRANCHES

One of the oft-cited advantages of working with Git is that it has a "lightweight branching model." When someone says this, they are trying to simultaneously impress you and point out that Git allows you to create and switch between local branches with a minimum of effort and overhead. This makes working in so-called "feature branches" a particularly effective way to break work down into small chunks.

We covered how to create a branch earlier in this chapter, but as a quick recap you can create a branch by opening the Repositories section of the Organizer, selecting the Branches folder of your repository, and clicking Add Branch in the bottom toolbar. When working with feature branches, it makes sense to give your new branch a meaningful name related to the feature; for example, auth_module.

Once you have switched to a feature branch, you can start developing your code, making plenty of commits along the way. When you are finished with your feature, there are two common workflows for bringing your feature back into the master branch—which one you choose generally depends on whether you work alone or as part of a team.

MERGING BRANCHES LOCALLY

If you are working on your own, then the easiest route for you is to perform a local merge between branches. If you have finished working on your auth_module branch and have made all your commits, then you can go to the Branches folder of your repository in the Organizer and perform a Switch Branch back to the master branch.

NOTE: There are many strategies for developing features, ranging from performing all changes in the master branch to the intimidating but powerful git-flow strategy: http://jeffkreeftmeijer.com/2010/why-arent-you-using-git-flow/. How you do it is up to you.

Once back on the master branch, what you want is to bring the changes from your feature branch in. You can achieve this by selecting File > Source Control > Merge from the main menu. You will be presented with a sheet showing the branches that you can merge into the current branch (**Figure 18.30**). Select a branch from the menu and click Choose.

FIGURE 18.30
The merge branch selection sheet

Xcode will perform the merge, looking for any conflicts, and present a merge review sheet, very similar to the pull review sheet in Figure 18.15. As with the pull review sheet, you can step through the proposed changes, making any modifications needed to resolve conflicts. Once you are satisfied, click Merge to complete the process. If you are satisfied that the feature is complete, you may even want to delete the feature branch by clicking Remove Branch in the Branches view of the Organizer.

PERFORMING PULL REQUESTS ON A HOSTED SERVICE

A common workflow for teams using a hosted service is to perform a pull request. To do so, just make your final commits to your feature branch and select File > Source Control > Push from the main menu. This will give you the option to create a new branch for your feature on the remote repository (**Figure 18.31**).

FIGURE 18.31 Creating a new remote feature branch

Once you have pushed the feature branch to the remote repository, you can switch to your web browser and access the pull request feature provided by the hosted service. The precise details vary according to the service, but the general principle is the same: You create a request that the feature branch be merged into the master branch (**Figure 18.32**).

FIGURE 18.32 Creating a pull request

At this point, someone in your team will diligently review the code you propose to merge into the master branch and, if it's up to scratch, will perform the merge on the remote repository. You can then open the clone (the blue folder) in the Repositories tab in the Organizer, click the Switch Branch button on the bottom toolbar, and choose the master branch. Return to the Xcode project window, and select File > Source Control > Pull from the main menu to get the merged feature back in your project.

Compared to staying within the confines of local branches, it is a slightly more convoluted way of working, but it provides an effective way to control, or simply track, what goes into a shared code base.

WRAPPING UP

Over the last few releases, Xcode has improved its SCM support greatly, but there are still areas (which we've tried to point out) where it is deficient. The great thing about working with Git or Subversion in Xcode is that you always have the option to turn to your favorite GUI front end or to the command line to fill in the feature gaps. If you haven't begun using version control yet, you should start now. Xcode makes it easy.

APPENDIX A

Managing Your iOS Devices

If you're developing for iOS, sooner or later you'll want to test your apps on physical devices to make sure they work properly before submitting them to the App Store. To do this, you must provision your devices for use in development. Provisioning requires a current iOS developer account and enables you to install and debug your own applications as well as access the device's console logs, screenshots, and more. In this appendix, you'll learn how to link Xcode to your developer account, provision your devices for development, and generally manage the device.

USING THE ORGANIZER'S DEVICES TAB

The Organizer's Devices section (**Figure A.1**) lets you manage the iOS devices you use for development, as well as your provisioning profiles, software images, application data, console logs, and screenshots. In this section of the Organizer, you can automatically provision devices for development, letting you run and test applications on the device rather than only in the Simulator. To open the Organizer, choose Window > Organizer from the main menu, and then click the Devices tab in the Organizer toolbar.

FIGURE A.1 The
Organizer's Devices tab

Figure A.1 shows a number of devices registered for development—and the Mac that Xcode is running on—as well as the development and distribution certificates for the selected development team (a personal account). The green indicator next to "Mo's Phone" shows that the device is provisioned and ready for use in development and is plugged into the Mac.

PROVISIONING A DEVICE

In Chapter 10, we discussed provisioning profiles and code signing with respect to deploying your application via the App Store or ad-hoc distribution. Installing and testing your app on a physical device also requires provisioning. If you have a current Apple iOS Developer Program membership, provisioning can be simple in Xcode 4 and is a two-stage affair.

DEVELOPMENT CERTIFICATES

To run your app on a physical device, you will need a development certificate. You can create and download a development certificate from the Certificates, Identifiers & Profiles section of the iOS Dev Center portal, but an easier way is to do it through Xcode itself.

Open the Devices tab of the Organizer, and select the Provisioning Profiles section from the sidebar. Click the Refresh button on the bottom toolbar. Xcode will prompt you to enter the Apple ID and password for your iOS developer account, and then try to retrieve any development and distribution certificates associated with your account. If you do not have a development certificate, Xcode will ask if you would like to request one—click Submit Request to let it do the hard work. After generating a certificate, Xcode will offer to export your developer profile so that you can back it up. This is a good idea—you can copy the exported profile to another machine if you upgrade your Mac in the future.

ADDING DEVICES TO THE PORTAL

To use a device for testing your application, it will need to be registered with your iOS developer account. Registering the device allows Apple to include it in a special provisioning profile associated with your developer account.

To register a device, plug it in to your Mac and open the Devices tab of the Organizer. When the device appears in the list, select it in the sidebar and then click the Use for Development button (**Figure A.2**). Xcode will create two things in the provisioning portal on your behalf: a wildcard app ID called "Xcode iOS Wildcard App ID," and a corresponding provisioning profile called "iOS Team Provisioning Profile: *" (where * represents the wildcard app ID).

FIGURE A.2 A device in the Devices tab of the Organizer

You may be asked again for your iOS Developer Program credentials. Provide your information, and click Log In. When Xcode has performed its background tasks, it will download the new provisioning profile for your development team.

> **NOTE:** Apple uses the concept of development teams to represent lone developers and actual teams of developers. A full list of all teams associated with the Apple ID you entered into the Xcode login sheet is shown in the sidebar of the Devices tab of the Organizer.

Once you've made it over the various hurdles, the team provisioning profile will be installed on the device. The indicator dot to the right of the device in the list will turn green, informing you that it is ready for development use. You should now be able to run your iOS applications on the device by choosing the device in the Schemes pop-up in the workspace window's toolbar and clicking the Run button.

PROVISIONING PROFILES

In addition to automatic provisioning, you can import and export developer and provisioning profiles by using the Import and Export buttons at the bottom of the window when either the Provisioning Profiles section or a team name is selected in the sidebar. This is useful for manually provisioning or for moving your profile to a different computer. You will be required to set a password upon export and use the same password on import to protect the profile from being used by anyone else.

Xcode now also offers the facility to directly create provisioning profiles from within the Provisioning Profiles section. This is a handy way to perform a task that used to require a trip to the provisioning portal online, although it does not represent a complete solution—you still need to create and manage app IDs through the online portal.

To create a profile, click the New button on the bottom toolbar, and enter your developer credentials when prompted. The Create Provisioning Profile sheet will appear (**Figure A.3**), ready for you to create a new profile. Select your team, and give the new profile a meaningful name. Select iOS as the platform, and choose an appropriate app ID. Finally, choose the devices you wish to include in the profile, and the certificate you wish to use for signing. When all the information has been entered, click Finish to create the provisioning profile. Xcode will do its work, and the new profile will be downloaded and visible in the Provisioning Profiles section.

FIGURE A.3 Creating a new provisioning profile through Xcode

NOTE: Apple has done an excellent job automating this cumbersome process in Xcode 4. Nevertheless, it does not always work correctly. Read the guidelines supplied in the provisioning portal site found under your iOS developer account to help you figure out what went wrong and how to complete the process manually.

INSTALLING iOS ON A DEVICE

During development, it is sometimes necessary to install different versions of iOS on your device for compatibility testing. This includes beta versions of iOS itself, to which you have access via the iOS Developer Program. iOS versions are downloaded from the Apple Developer site (http://developer.apple.com).

To install a different version of iOS on a device, make sure the device is plugged in and selected in the list that appears in the Devices tab of the Organizer. You can then select a version from the Software Version pop-up just below the device information. If your version does not appear in the list, choose Other Version from the pop-up and locate the iOS package you downloaded. Click the Restore button and confirm the action in the confirmation sheet, then wait for the iOS version to be installed (restored). When the installation is complete, reactivate the device and restore its contents using iTunes or an iCloud backup (just as you'd do as an end user).

Installing iOS on a device in this way is subject to similar limitations as upgrading a device through iTunes—it tends to be a one-way process. Although it is possible in some circumstances to downgrade an iOS device, it is not guaranteed that it will work.

MANAGING DEVICE SCREENSHOTS

The Devices section of the Organizer also lets you manage the screenshots you take with your device. Screenshots can be located by selecting the Screenshots entry under the desired device in the Organizer list (**Figure A.4**). Screenshots are useful for two reasons: as

FIGURE A.4 The device screenshots list

marketing material for the App Store or your own website, and as a "default launch image," which users see as the application is launching on their device.

TAKING SCREENSHOTS

You can take new screenshots by clicking the New Screenshot button in the lower-right corner of the window. All screenshots are listed as time-stamped thumbnails. Selecting a thumbnail will display the full-size image to the right of the thumbnails list. This image may be scaled down to fit the window (this is especially useful if you have a small display and are viewing screenshots taken from a device with a much higher-resolution Retina display).

To export a screenshot, drag it to the Finder or press the Export button at the bottom of the window.

COMPARING SCREENSHOTS

You can compare screenshots by selecting two or more images and selecting the Compare check box at the bottom of the window (**Figure A.5**), adjusting the tolerance by using the slider to the right of the check box. Figure A.5 shows the difference between two screen-shots. Differences are shown as white areas—in this example there are differences in the status bar and speaker icons—and areas that are the same are shown in black.

FIGURE A.5 Comparing screenshots

USING A SCREENSHOT AS THE DEFAULT IMAGE

To use a screenshot as the default launch image for an iOS application, select it from the thumbnails list and click Save as Launch Image at the bottom of the window. You'll be prompted to give the launch image a name and to select a workspace to which to add the image (**Figure A.6**).

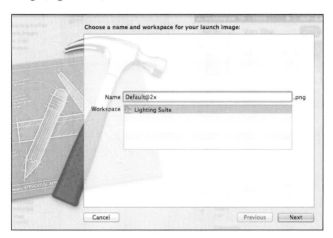

FIGURE A.6 Naming the image and selecting a workspace

If there is more than one target in the workspace, you'll need to click Next to choose the target for which you want to set the default image (**Figure A.7**). Xcode will guess the target or targets to which you intend to add the image; you may need to change the selection using the check boxes. Make your selection, then click Finish. The screenshot will be added as the default launch image for the selected target.

FIGURE A.7 Choosing a target for the default image

NOTE: A workspace containing an iOS application must be open in order to select it in the sheet shown in Figure A.6.

MANAGING APPS AND DATA

The Devices tab of the Organizer gives you a simple interface for adding and removing applications you're developing as well as for downloading the applications' data. To manage the applications, select the Applications entry under the desired device in the Organizer list (**Figure A.8**).

FIGURE A.8 The device applications list

INSTALLING AND REMOVING APPS

You can install applications by clicking the Add (+) button in the bottom toolbar and selecting the application bundle to add. You'll need to have a provisioning profile for the application (which is usually only an issue if a friend is letting you test one of their applications). To uninstall, select the desired applications in the list and click the Delete (−) button in the bottom toolbar. The applications and their associated data will be removed from the device.

DOWNLOADING AND UPLOADING APPLICATION DATA

You can download an application's data for safekeeping (or analysis) by locating it in the list and clicking the Download button in the bottom toolbar. Choose a location to which to save the data, and a package will be created at that location (with the extension .xcappdata) containing the application's data and settings. Only applications for which you have a provisioning profile will allow you to download their data.

If you have previously downloaded app data through the Organizer, you can restore it by selecting the application and then pressing the Upload button. An Open dialog box will appear, allowing you to select any package with the .xcappdata extension. This is useful if you wish to prepopulate some test data into an application, but be careful that you choose the right data. It is possible to upload the data from one app to any other app, which could render an application useless.

REVIEWING LOGS

When running an application on the device without the benefit of an attached debugger, application crashes are a mystery. The logs of all connected devices can be accessed through the Device Logs section in the Devices tab of the Organizer. You can get the logs of individual devices by choosing the Device Logs entry under the desired device (**Figure A.9**).

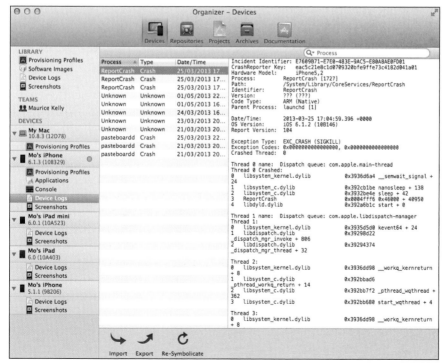

FIGURE A.9 The device logs

To retrieve the log to your Mac, click the Export button in the bottom toolbar to download it as a `.crash` file. If you have been provided with `.crash` files from another source (from iTunes Connect or from a tester's device), you can use the Import button to place a `.crash` file back onto a device.

If your app has been stripped of debugging symbols, it will produce a crash log that does not seem to contain much human-readable information. The process of re-symbolicating a crash log takes the debugging symbols from another source (for example, the dSYM file archived with a build) and updates the crash log to make a bit more sense. The Re-Symbolicate button on the bottom toolbar will attempt this for you.

To remove device logs that you no longer need, either select the log file and click Delete, or right-click the log file and select Delete Log from the context menu.

A device's console log is available under the Console entry under the desired device (**Figure A.10**). The console log can reveal useful information about an application that was running on its own, outside of a debugging session. While this is useful during a debugging phase of development, try not to write too much to the console with NSLog() in a release build—it will add unnecessary bulk to your devices' log files.

FIGURE A.10 The device console log

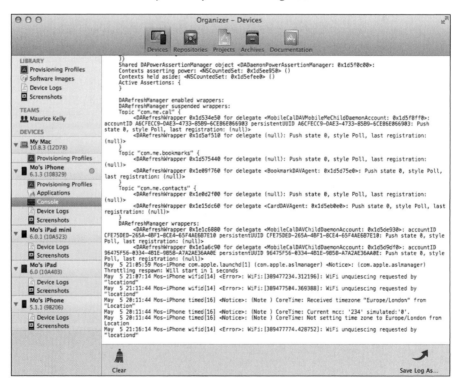

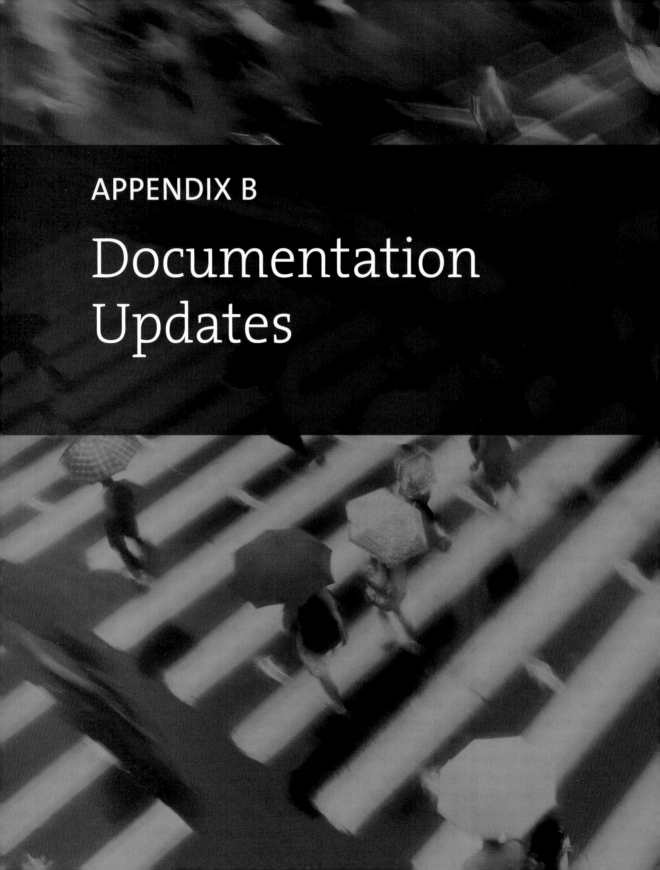

APPENDIX B

Documentation Updates

Xcode automatically downloads and installs documentation updates in the background. In addition, you can control the installed documentation sets and check for updates manually. This is controlled through the Documentation preferences panel.

SETTING DOCUMENTATION PREFERENCES

To open the Documentation preferences panel, choose Xcode > Preferences from the main menu, select the Downloads section, and then select the Documentation tab. **Figure B.1** shows the preferences. Xcode downloads only what it considers "necessary" documentation sets at first.

FIGURE B.1 The Documentation preferences tab

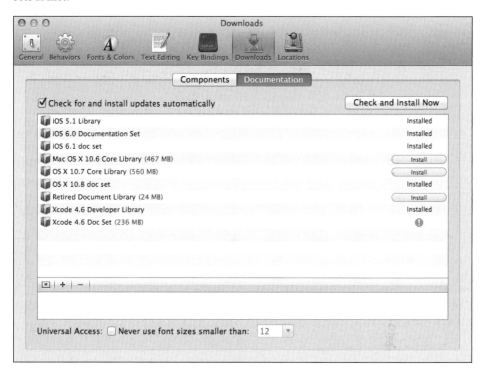

If you want missing documentation sets, you will need to click the Install button beside them. Xcode will download and install the documentation set and from that point forward will include those sets in its automatic update checks. If you see an exclamation point instead of the Install button or the Installed label, then Xcode has encountered a problem with the installation of the documentation set. Click the exclamation point for more information.

You can add third-party documentation sets using the Add (+) button at the bottom of the list. The documentation must come from a URL that starts with http://, https://, or feed://. You can uninstall an Apple-supplied documentation set by clicking the Remove (–) button at the bottom of the list—the Installed label will convert to an Install button.

You can view information about the selected documentation set by clicking the disclosure button to the left of the Add button, as in **Figure B.2**. Finally, you can disable automatic updating and force update checks by using the controls just beneath the toolbar. The check box toggles the automatic updates, and the button forces a check and install immediately.

FIGURE B.2 The documentation set information panel

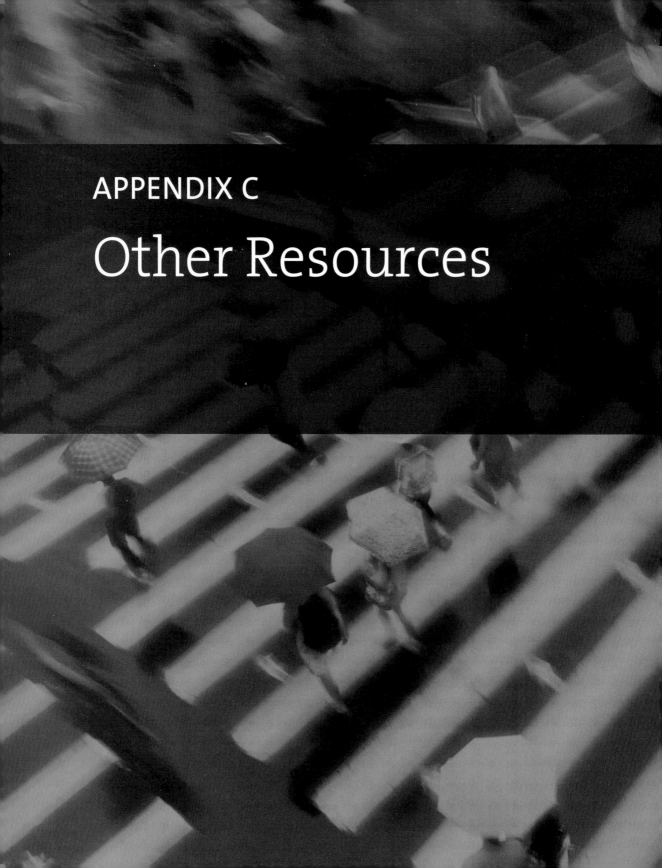

APPENDIX C
Other Resources

There are a number of helpful online resources for learning to use Xcode and for Cocoa development in general. A few author favorites are listed here.

THE BOOK SITE

- This book's companion site (http://xcodebook.com) contains Xcode 4 news, tips and tricks, and errata for the book.

APPLE RESOURCES

- **Developer Forums** (http://devforums.apple.com)
  Apple's developer forums site has an Xcode-specific forum with a number of active members. A current Apple Developer account is required.
- **Xcode-Users Mailing List** (http://lists.apple.com/mailman/listinfo/xcode-users)
  The Xcode-Users mailing list doesn't require an Apple Developer account to use and is an active list full of helpful people.

THIRD-PARTY RESOURCES

- **Stack Overflow** (http://stackoverflow.com/questions/tagged/xcode)
  Stack Overflow is a great developer resource with questions tagged by topic. Questions and answers are voted up or down depending on their clarity and usefulness, encouraging thoughtful questions and answers by community members.
- **CocoaDev Wiki** (http://cocoadev.com)
  Although somewhat dated, this community-built wiki has been pumped full of useful Cocoa developer information over the course of the last decade and still contains many valuable lessons for beginner, intermediate, and expert developers.
- **Cocoa Dev Central** (http://cocoadevcentral.com)
  This celebrated collection of informative how-to articles contains many Cocoa developer favorites. It's worth browsing.
- **Getting Started with Mogenerator**
  (http://raptureinvenice.com/getting-started-with-mogenerator/)
  Mogenerator is a very useful tool to use if you plan to create custom subclasses when working with Core Data. This tutorial is a great introduction to an invaluable tool.

INDEX

A

action connections, explained   68
Activity viewer, features   23–24
Add Files sheet
   Add to Targets option   45
   Destination check box   44–45
   Folders option   45
   using   44–45
Analyze action, invoking   110
API Reference, accessing   28
APIs vs. SDKs   278
   See also build settings
App Store
   code signing apps   123
   distributing iOS apps in   122–123
   ecosystem   5
Apple's developer forums   32
application data
   downloading   315
   uploading   315
application sandboxing
   activating   197
   explained   196
apps. *See also* iOS apps; Mac apps
   installing   314
   managing   314–315
   uninstalling   314
ARC (Automatic Reference Counting)
   converting targets to   144
   previewing conversions   145
architectures   278–279
archive action, described   277
Archive configuration, editing for beta
   scheme   266
archive files
   dSYM folder   117
   as packages   117
archives
   action of Validate button   118–119
   annotating in Organizer   116
   creating   115
   displaying with action buttons   118
   dSYM files   116
   finding   116–117
   finding Lamp.app   118
   storing   117
archiving
   alternatives to   129–130
   build environment   130
   on release builds   257–259

arrays, subscript notation for   142–143
Assistant panes
   adding   19–20
   removing   19–20
Assistant tool
   changing behavior modes   21
   controls   21
   dragging connections into   79
   features   19
   layout options   20
   Manual mode   21
   opening files in   19
attributes, adding to data model   93–94
automatic snapshot, creating   137

B

Beta Release configuration, using   267
BETABUILD macro, defining   264–267
BetaBuilder app, using with iOS apps   124
blocks of code   263
bookmarks, storing in framework project   212
Bookmarks framework
   downloading   208
   embedding   209
   linking against   209
   using in code   209–210
Bookmarks mode, using in Organizer   30
Bookmarks project, creating   210–211
branches
   creating   296–297, 303–304
   merging locally   304
   switching   296–297
breakpoint editor
   Action tool   220
   Condition field   219
   Enable/Disable check box   219
   Ignore directive   220
   Options   220
Breakpoint navigator
   Edit Breakpoint option   105
   features   15
   setting exceptions   105
   setting symbolic   105
   Share Breakpoint option   105
   using   105
breakpoints. *See also* debugging
   customizing   219–220
   enabling   105
   managing in Source editor   105